THE LEADER ON

THE COUCH

THE LEADER ON

THE COUCH

A Clinical Approach to Changing People and Organizations

Manfred F. R. Kets de Vries

JOSSEY-BASS
A Wiley Imprint
www.josseybass.com

Copyright © 2006   John Wiley & Sons Ltd, The Atrium, Southern Gate, Chichester,
West Sussex PO19 8SQ, England
Telephone (+44) 1243 779777

Under the Jossey-Bass imprint, Jossey-Bass 989, Market Street, San Francisco CA 94103-1741 USA
www.jossey-bass.com

Email (for orders and customer service enquiries): cs-books@wiley.co.uk
Visit our Home Page on www.wiley.com

Other Wiley Editorial Offices

John Wiley & Sons Inc., 111 River Street, Hoboken, NJ 07030, USA

Jossey-Bass, 989 Market Street, San Francisco, CA 94103-1741, USA

Wiley-VCH Verlag GmbH, Boschstr. 12, D-69469 Weinheim, Germany

John Wiley & Sons Australia Ltd, 42 McDougall Street, Milton, Queensland 4064, Australia

John Wiley & Sons (Asia) Pte Ltd, 2 Clementi Loop #02-01, Jin Xing Distripark, Singapore 129809

John Wiley & Sons Canada Ltd, 22 Worcester Road, Etobicoke, Ontario, Canada M9W 1L1

Wiley also publishes its books in a variety of electronic formats. Some content that appears in print may not be available in electronic books.

British Library Cataloguing in Publication Data
A catalogue record for this book is available from the British Library

ISBN 13 978-0-470-03079-0 (HB)
ISBN 10 0-470-03079-8 (HB)

Typeset in 11.5/15pt Bembo by SNP Best-set Typesetter Ltd., Hong Kong
Printed and bound in Great Britain by TJ International Ltd, Padstow, Cornwall, UK

This book is printed on acid-free paper responsibly manufactured from sustainable forestry in which at least two trees are planted for each one used for paper production.

To Alicia,
A great bearer of transitional space

CONTENTS

PREFACE

There are . . . things which a man is afraid to tell even to himself, and every decent man has a number of such things stored away in his mind.

—Fyodor Dostoyevsky, Notes from the Underground

Becoming conscious is of course a sacrilege against nature; it is as though you had robbed the unconscious of something.

—Carl G. Jung

"Know thyself?" If I knew myself, I'd run away.

—Johann Wolfgang von Goethe

Man stands in his own shadow and wonders why it's dark.

—Zen proverb

There's a Zen story about a martial arts student who went to his teacher and said, "I have committed myself to master your martial system. How long will it take me to succeed?" The teacher's response was, "Ten years." Impatiently, the student countered, "But that's far too slow. I want to succeed much sooner. I'll work very hard. I'll dedicate myself to practicing however many hours it takes each day. How long will mastery take when I make that kind of effort?" The teacher thought for a moment, and then replied, "Twenty years."

Obviously, the teacher is trying to tell the student that he needs to learn patience before proceeding any further. He's saying, Go slowly to go fast! Certain kinds of learning can't be rushed; they have to be approached one step at a time. This is particularly true of becoming more emotionally attuned. To acquire this kind of knowledge, there are two secrets. The first is to have patience; the second is to be patient! Acquiring higher emotional intelligence—that is, gaining a better understanding of the psychodynamics of human behavior—is never instantaneous. Becoming more psychologically minded requires not only time, but also persistence. Patience and persistence can move mountains. They are the keys to becoming more emotionally astute.

What differentiates the great companies of this world from the merely average ones is the level of emotional intelligence (EQ) among their employees. In our post-industrial knowledge-based society, companies populated with high-EQ personnel have the best shot at creativity and innovation. In such companies, statements like "People are our greatest asset" and "Our capital leaves the workplace every evening" are more than empty slogans; they are credos with real meaning. Executives who run such companies value their people and see them as much more than interchangeable commodities. Realizing that considerable corporate knowledge and wisdom reside in the gray matter of their employees, they view the selection, development, and retention of talent as a source of competitive advantage, they consider leadership development a core competence, and they make a valiant effort to keep their employees motivated.

I have devoted my working life to helping people create emotionally intelligent organizations. I have taken many different routes to make this dream a reality. As a management professor, consultant, leadership coach, psychotherapist, and psychoanalyst, I have had many corporate leaders "on the couch," literally and figuratively. My in-depth interactions with these executives have given me a rare glimpse into the inner world of leaders, revealing the interplay of personality and environment and unveiling the process of personal and organizational change.

In taking this road less traveled, I have noted a clear and compelling connection between the personal objectives of the organization's power holders and the objectives of the organization itself. The intrapsychic themes of the CEO often dictate the structure or priorities of the organization. This linkage comes about because we are what we think. In other words, all that we are arises with our thoughts; with our thoughts, we make our world. Perception carries so much weight that objectivity is nothing more than masked subjectivity. Thus many management theories that explain how people make decisions in organizations are inadequate oversimplifications. In fact, the apparently rational explanations for certain decisions often turn out to be fiction, rationalizations made after the fact to explain how intrapsychic themes were translated into external reality.

In my role as a management consultant to executive boards, I have often been quite successful at creating high-performance teams and high-performance organizations. When I began to work with executive boards, however, I discovered that many executive teams are what I call "unnatural acts." Though they come together to make serious decisions affecting the future of the organization and its people, they engage in ritualistic activities that center on political gamesmanship and posturing rather than substance. The "barons" of the various business entities—the heads of marketing and new-product development, for example—are so busy defending their respective fiefdoms that true conflict resolution doesn't occur. Other, more intangible factors seem to take over as executives circle around "undiscussables." While a six hundred pound gorilla sits on the table, smelling up the place, the senior executive group squanders an incredible amount of energy ignoring its presence. Far too often, it has to be "high noon" (or beyond) before ders are prepared to deal with the real issues. In many an outside consultant, I have taken it upon myself to xecutive team to grapple with their own particular undiscussables. In taking on that role, I have come to understand the meaning of the saying, "Fish start to smell from the head."

As in my consultant work, in my role as an educator I have gone to great lengths to create more emotionally intelligent students. I have made this effort not only in working with MBAs but also in working with executives. The two transformational programs that I run at INSEAD, "The Challenge of Leadership: Creating Reflective Leaders" and "Consulting and Coaching for Change," have been instrumental in accomplishing these goals. In particular, the top management program "The Challenge of Leadership" has been a great human "laboratory," encouraging and promoting mindset change among participants.

I have a dream as an educator dedicated to helping people engage in transformational journeys. This dream goes as follows: If I can increase the EQ level of the approximately twenty people who usually are enrolled in this program at any one time, perhaps I can have a positive effect on the 100,000 or more people for whom they are responsible. I would like to think that I can help make their organizations more effective and more humane. Too many organizations possess "gulag" qualities that prevent the human spirit from self-actualizing.

This book is a manifesto espousing my belief, and that of my colleagues at the INSEAD Global Leadership Center, in high-EQ organizations. It is a natural sequence to a previous book of mine: *The Leadership Mystique*. The difference is that this new book, in introducing the clinical approach to individual and organizational intervention, is more conceptual. It takes a much deeper look at personality prototypes; it introduces a well-tried methodology to help executives change behavior patterns; it deals with leadership coaching; it concerns team building; and it explores system-wide change strategies in organizations.

Like *The Leadership Mystique*, *Leaders on the Couch* is a manifesto in favor of organizations where people are authentic and feel truly alive, where they understand what they're doing and why, and what the consequences will be. It's a manifesto arguing for more reflective, emotionally intelligent executives, and it offers valuable tools toward that end: for example, it gives executives a new lens through which to look at people and concepts—a lens that makes unusual behavior (in self and others) more understandable. Far too many executives engage in "manic" behavior, running and doing all the time, forgetting why they go to work each day. Uncertain what they want, they're nonetheless willing to kill themselves to get it. While it may be true that the really idle person doesn't get anywhere, the perpetually busy person has the same problem. My hope is that this book will be helpful to executives, consultants, and leadership coaches, teaching them to peel back the layers of self-deception to reveal how inner personality—largely hard-wired since early childhood—affects the way we lead and manage others.

For many years I have been intrigued by Zen stories. Actually, acquiring emotional intelligence and becoming a Zen master are learning processes that have many aspects in common. Both Zen and psychoanalysis are disciplines of attention, conferring on successful adherents a profound change in mindset. Both disciplines aim for self-discovery, self-understanding, and the possession of peace with oneself. Psychoanalysis explores the unconscious meanings, desires, and feelings of individuals with the goal of making them feel more creative and alive. The purpose of Zen is to make people fully aware of life as it's actually lived. Zen deals with the capacity to awaken the mind and clarify consciousness. Just as psychological insights can be attained by everyone who makes the effort, Zen teaches that everyone can acquire the Buddha-nature; in other words, everyone has the potential to achieve spiritual enlightenment. Because of ignorance, however, most of us make too little use of this potential.

Disciples of Zen argue that people's innate capacity to become more insightful about themselves and the world around them is best awakened not just by the study of scriptures, the doing of good deeds, the practice of rites and ceremonies, and the worship of images, but also by a sudden breaking through of the boundaries of common, everyday, logical thought. People have to learn how to cope with paradoxical situations to arrive at a new understanding. To quote Pablo Picasso, "Every act of creation is first of all an act of destruction." Thus the paradoxical statements—the riddles, if you will—embedded in koans (Zen stories inaccessible to rational understanding) help Zen disciples progress on the spiritual journey toward enlightenment. Many disciples find the journey more rewarding when undertaken with the help of a master. This method of assisted self-discovery is very similar to the dynamics of leadership coaching, psychoanalysis, or psychotherapy. In these methodologies, the psychoanalyst, psychotherapist, or leadership coach takes on the role of "master," offering spiritual guidance. Like the quest for greater EQ, the Zen form of enlightenment can't be forced; rather, it's a form of slow and silent illumination. And practitioners of Zen and psychoanalysis are never completely satisfied with the results of their approach. The journey is always indeterminate.

Tapping into the parallels between the process of acquiring emotional intelligence and the journey toward spiritual enlightenment, I have chosen to begin each of the chapters of this book with a Zen story. Allow the paradox of each koan to help you discern the leadership message presented in each chapter. As you attempt to move toward increased self-awareness and emotional intelligence, this book will serve as your "master."

Many of these chapters started as articles and working papers in which I explored the clinical orientation to organizational analysis. Many of the papers were first presented to executives taking the "Challenge of Leadership" seminar. This intensive executive program has been a good testing ground for my ideas. Many of the papers had their origin in knotty, paradoxical questions from executives to which I couldn't give an immediate answer—questions that haunted me until I arrived at what seemed like plausible answers. These original papers have been reworked and integrated to help the reader better understand the advantages of using the clinical perspective for the purpose of organizational sense-making.

The main theme of this book, weaving through all the pages, is changing people and organizations. The text starts with an introduction describing the clinical approach to organizational analysis. The body of the book then follows, divided into three parts.

Part One ("Entering the Inner Theater of Leaders") describes various personality prototypes that can be found in the workplace and focuses on personality functioning and its consequences in organizational life. To the extent that executives understand why people do what they do, how the shadow side of human behavior manifests itself at work, and how people with different personality styles relate to each other, they can foster creativity and cooperation among their colleagues and subordinates. The personality prototypes presented in Chapters 2 through 5—useful despite the generalizations that labeling relies on—are tools to help readers become more astute in understanding and helping people. Chapter 6 looks at the contagiousness of emotion in the organizational setting, focusing on the issue of charismatic leadership in the context of the psychology of elation. Chapter 7 addresses the question of neurotic imposture—that is, feeling like a fake in the face of proven competence—a common response among executives.

Part Two ("Changing Mindsets") focuses on the educational "technology" needed to change the mindset of executives. This section discusses methods of intervention that can lead to transformational change. Chapters 8 and 9 explore a highly effective leadership intervention technique that involves creating a safe, transitional space to foster new learning—creating what we might call a "learning community"—with a detailed example showing how such a change process can be successful. Chapter 10 deals with leadership coaching in general and discusses various leadership coaching techniques. Chapter 11 addresses group leadership coaching, a technique that has proved to be highly effective in making true change a reality in "natural" working groups or executive teams.

Part Three ("Understanding the Psychodynamics of Groups and Organizations") deals with the question of system-wide clinical intervention in organizations. Chapter 12 places the psychology of small and large groups under the microscope, looking at group behavior, social defenses, the concept of the organizational ideal, and the "neurotic" (or dysfunctional) organization. The purpose of this chapter is to help the reader better understand the role of systemic organizational dysfunctionality. Chapter 13 presents a leadership/organizational "audit" and explores the possibility of clinical organizational interventions via a change agent or clinically informed organizational consultant. The final chapter (Chapter 14) explores the question of human authenticity, weighing the implications of presenting a true versus a false self, and discusses the creation of authentizotic organizations, places of work where people feel alive and are called to give their best.

Why is it worth an executive's time to read about all these issues? Because people around the world complain that there's a great discrepancy between what their leaders say and what their leaders do, and that discrepancy is grounded in leaders' lack of awareness of their own psychological drivers and mood states— their "inner theater" (a subject that will be addressed in greater detail in the next chapter). That unawareness makes them prisoners of hidden forces that dictate their decisions and their behavior. Leaders and followers alike will continue to send mixed and confusing messages as long as they are unaware of the content of their inner theater.

Readers should be forewarned that uncovering these unconscious patterns can be uncomfortable, anxiety-provoking, and even disorienting. Going one step further and changing the script in one's inner theater is even more formidable. Those who are in situations of personal trauma are typically more willing than the complacent to unlock their inner theater, because the pain of not doing so appears to be worse than the pain of facing their inner truth. Thus preparedness for change differs by individual, with power often being the determining factor. People in positions of power are much more likely than their subordinates to find excuses not to engage in personal work that's emotionally painful. The fact that leaders can easily inflict their inadequacies on others, blaming them for lack of performance and poor communication, makes such an avoidance strategy even more likely. People lower in the power firmament have fewer opportunities to bestow blame; for them, scapegoating isn't an easy option.

The reluctance of leaders to take a hard look at themselves is supported by the societal myth that leadership is a rational endeavor. Unfortunately, this denial of psychological reality encourages leaders to go on sending mixed messages, practicing inappropriate behavior, and blaming external factors for their mistakes rather than taking personal responsibility. To be truly effective, leaders need to preserve a hold on reality; they need to see things as they really are, avoiding the intense pressure from subordinates to reside in a hall of mirrors. In some cases this means being willing to rely on professional support and expertise in uncovering psychological drivers and making the personal shifts necessary for leadership excellence. In all cases it means accepting that such a process takes time. But that time is well spent: raising one's personal awareness and learning how to make the most of strengths and minimize weaknesses is in fact an act of self-sacrifice, done not just for personal gratification but also for the good of one's co-workers and of the organization.

Despite the well-documented benefits to the organization of emotional intelligence, organizational life has typically been hostile to the inner world of feeling. So-called rational, objective thinking is supposed to be superior to mere feeling, which can "contaminate" our judgment so that we fail to act in a "rational" manner. But that's a very tenuous position. In point of fact, without feelings there are no actions. Without feelings there is no passion. Everything important to human beings is affect-ridden. The things important to us have emotional meaning to make us think about them. And that's the case in organizations as much as it is in our personal lives. Feelings stand central in organizational life and are expressed in many different forms.

What I'm doing here—exploring the role of emotion in personality, in decision-making, in the process of change, and in group processes—isn't new. Many poets, novelists, and playwrights have done it before me. They were the early psychologists. Among the best was Shakespeare, who still today is a great teacher regarding the ways of the world and the foibles of leaders. In showing the shadow side of leaders' behavior, he's second to none: Macbeth, Richard III, and King Lear are great examples. On the heath King Lear asks Gloucester: "How do you see the world?" Gloucester, who is blind, answers: "I see it feelingly." My hope is that the men and women who run the world's organizations will do the same.

ACKNOWLEDGMENTS

As people grow older, they sometimes discover that while they can enjoy life on their own, true appreciation of life requires companionship. Voltaire's comment, "By appreciation, we make excellence in others our own property," still has a ring of truth. Books aren't written in isolation. As has been said by many others before, authors stand on the shoulders of others. As the years go by, my memory of which people influenced my way of thinking in various areas has become hazier. I have so deeply internalized many ideas that the original contributors have been lost. Certain memories, however, have retained their clarity. Looking back into my past,

I realize the extent to which my years at Harvard deeply affected me. That period still fills me with a sense of wonder at all the new experiences (cultural and otherwise) I was exposed to.

Four names from that period (1960s and 70s) stand out as influential in the development of my thinking. The first is Erik Erikson, the well-known psychoanalyst and teacher of human development. His lectures at Harvard College were like psychodramas, hugely exciting to me. He made me realize, through his studies of transformational leaders such as Martin Luther and Mahatma Gandhi, the importance of the interface of personality and historical moment. Another person who had a huge influence on me was C. Roland Christensen, a professor of business policy who contributed enormously to the quality of teaching at Harvard. Apart from the influence he has had on my teaching style, his humanity and wisdom still touch me. His sudden, untimely death has been hard to take, although he lives on in my inner world. My main mentor during those years at the Harvard Business School was Abraham Zaleznik, professor of leadership. His influence on my way of looking at the world and at organizations has been enormous. My weekly dialogues with him taught me many things about the creative process. His seminars left me with a sense of wonder about the mysteries of the mind. The crossing of our paths very much determined my career choice, nebulous and precarious as it looked at the time. Last but certainly not least, Sudhir Kakar, listed in a recent issue of the Nouvel Observateur as the "psychoanalyst of the world," helped to shape my perspective. Who would have thought, when we first met as young men in Abraham Zaleznik's seminar, that our lives would intertwine as they have?

On a more contemporary note, I would like to thank my five program directors who work at the INSEAD Global Leadership Center: Elisabet Engellau (who is much more than a colleague), Roger Lehman, Jean-Claude Noel, Stanislav Shekshnia and Martine van den Poel. In addition, I like to express my appreciation to Konstantin Korotov, once my doctoral student and now a professor at the European School of Management and Technology (although still associated with INSEAD Global Leadership Center). Their initiative and creative thinking in making the Center the success it has become (often against all odds) is very much appreciated. It has been an incredible journey for me to learn from all of them and from the students who pass through our doors. I would also like to express my appreciation to Agatha Halczewska-Figuet, the Center's executive director and to the Center's staff, which keeps the "back office" running efficiently: Fabienne Chemin, Silke Bequet and Nadine Theallier.

During the past year I have learned the hard way that trying to both write and run the Center is extremely difficult. Therefore, the buffering roles played by my research project manager, Elizabeth Florent-Treacy, and my assistant, Sheila Loxham, have been doubly appreciated. Their heroic efforts have helped keep the random variable that I am, on track. Finally, I would like to express my gratitude to my two editors, Sally Simmons and Kathy Reigstad, for their skill in making the unreadable readable. My appreciation for these two magicians, who practice their craft not only on words but also on logic, is hard to put into words.

Carl Jung once said that "one looks back with appreciation to the brilliant teachers, but with gratitude to those who touched our human feelings. The curriculum is so much necessary raw material, but warmth is the vital element for the growing plant and for the soul of the child." How true! In this context, I want to thank my students, who have been willing to experiment in telling their stories, and in doing so, touched the listener.

ABOUT THE AUTHOR

Manfred F. R. Kets de Vries brings a different view to the much-studied subjects of leadership and the dynamics of individual and organizational change. Applying his knowledge and experience of economics (Econ. Drs., University of Amsterdam), management (ITP, MBA, and DBA, Harvard Business School), and psychoanalysis (member of the Canadian Psychoanalytic Society and the International Psychoanalytic Association), Kets de Vries scrutinizes the interface between international management, psychoanalysis, psychotherapy, and dynamic psychiatry. His specific areas of interest are leadership, career dynamics, executive stress, entrepreneurship, family business, succession planning, cross-cultural management, teambuilding, coaching, and the dynamics of corporate transformation and change.

A clinical professor of leadership development, he holds the Raoul de Vitry d'Avaucourt Chair of Leadership Development at INSEAD, France and Singapore, and is director of INSEAD's Global Leadership Center. In addition, he is program director of INSEAD's top-management seminar, "The Challenge of Leadership: Creating Reflective Leaders" and scientific director of the program "Consulting and Coaching for Change." In addition to having received the International Leadership Association's prestigious annual leadership scholar award for his "contribution to the classroom and the boardroom," he has also five times received INSEAD's distinguished teacher award. He has also held professorships at McGill University, the Ecole des Hautes Etudes Commerciales (Montreal), and the Harvard Business School, and he has lectured at management institutions around the world. He is a founding member of the International Society for the Psychoanalytic Study of Organizations. The Financial Times, Le Capital, Wirtschaftswoche, and The Economist have judged Manfred Kets de Vries among the world's top 50 management thinkers and among the top 100 most influential people in human resource management.

Kets de Vries is the author, coauthor, or editor of more than twenty books, including *Power and the Corporate Mind* (1975, new edition 1985, with Abraham Zaleznik), *Organizational Paradoxes: Clinical Approaches to Management* (1980, new edition 1994), *The Irrational Executive: Psychoanalytic Explorations in Management* (1984, editor), *The Neurotic Organization: Diagnosing and Changing Counter-*

Productive Styles of Management (1984, new edition 1990, with Danny Miller), *Unstable at the Top* (1988, with Danny Miller), *Prisoners of Leadership* (1989), *Handbook of Character Studies* (1991, with Sidney Perzow), *Organizations on the Couch* (1991), *Leaders, Fools and Impostors* (1993), the prize-winning *Life and Death in the Executive Fast Lane: Essays on Organizations and Leadership* (1995, the Critics' Choice Award 1995–96), *Family Business: Human Dilemmas in the Family Firm* (1996), *The New Global Leaders: Percy Barnevik, Richard Branson, and David Simon* (1999, with Elizabeth Florent-Treacy), *Struggling with the Demon: Perspectives on Individual and Organizational Irrationality* (2001), *The Leadership Mystique* (2001, new edition 2006), *The Happiness Equation* (2002), *The Global Executive Leadership Inventory* (2003), *The New Russian Business Leaders* (2004), *Are Leaders Born or Are They Made? The Case of Alexander the Great* (2004) and *Lessons on Leadership by Terror: Finding Shaka Zulu in the Attic* (2004). He has also developed a number of multi-rater feedback instruments: *Global Executive Leadership Inventory* (2005), *The Personality Audit* (in press) and *The Leadership Archetype Questionnaire*.

In addition, Kets de Vries has published over 250 scientific papers as chapters in books and as articles in such journals as Behavioral Science, Journal of Management Studies, Human Relations, Administration & Society, Organizational Dynamics, Strategic Management Journal, Academy of Management Journal, Academy of Management Review, Journal of Forecasting, California Management Review, Harvard Business Review, Sloan Management Review, Academy of Management Executive, Psychoanalytic Review, Bulletin of the Menninger Clinic, Journal of Applied Behavioral Science, European Management Journal, International Journal of Cross-Cultural Management, Harper's, and Psychology Today. He has also written over 150 case studies, including eight that received the Best Case of the Year award. He is a regular writer for a number of magazines. His work has been featured in such publications as the New York Times, the Wall

Street Journal, the Los Angeles Times, Fortune, Business Week, the Economist, the Financial Times, and the International Herald Tribune. His books and articles have been translated into over twenty-five languages. He is a member of seventeen editorial boards. He is one of the few Europeans who have been elected a Fellow of the Academy of Management.

Kets de Vries is a consultant on organizational design/transformation and strategic human resource management to leading US, Canadian, European, African, and Asian companies. As a global consultant in executive development, he has worked with clients such as ABB, Aegon, Air Liquide, Alcan, Alcatel, Accenture, Bain Consulting, Bang & Olufsen, Bonnier, BP, Ericsson, GE Capital, Goldman Sachs, HypoVereinsbank, Investec, KPMG, Lego, Lufthansa, Lundbeck, McKinsey, Novartis, Nokia, Novo-Nordisk, Rank Xerox, Shell, SHV, SABMiller, Standard Bank of South Africa, Unilever, and Volvo Car Corporation. As an educator and consultant, he has worked in more than forty countries.

The Dutch government made Kets de Vries an officer in the Order of Oranje Nassau in 1997. He was the first fly fisherman in Outer Mongolia and is a member of New York's Explorers Club. In his spare time he can be found in the rainforests or savannas of Central Africa, in the Siberian taiga, in the Pamir mountains, in Arnhemland or within the Arctic Circle.

CHAPTER 1

INTRODUCTION: THE CLINICAL PARADIGM

What could an entirely rational being speak of with another entirely rational being?

—Emmanuel Levinas

I have yet to meet the famous Rational Economic Man theorists describe. Real people have always done inexplicable things from time to time, and they show no sign of stopping.

—Charles Sanford, Jr.

As I grow older I pay less attention to what men say. I just watch what they do.

—Andrew Carnegie

Be master of mind rather than mastered by mind.

—Zen proverb

There's a Zen tale about a person who noticed a disturbing bump under a rug. This person tried to smooth out the rug, but every time she did so, the bump reappeared. In utter frustration, she finally lifted up the rug, and to her great surprise, out slid an angry snake.

In an organizational context, this story can be viewed as a metaphor for the occasions when, in making interventions, we deal only with the symptoms. Inevitably, despite our attempts to smooth things over, the snake beneath—the underlying cause—keeps working its mischief. Unless we pull out that snake and deal with it, it will confound our best efforts to improve organizational efficiency.

Like the woman with the rug, too many management scholars restrict themselves to a mechanical view of life in the workplace. They look at surface phenomena—bumps on the rug—rather than at deep structure. Too often, the collective unconscious of business practitioners and scholars alike subscribes to the myth that the only thing which matters is what we see and know (in other words, that which is conscious). That myth is grounded in organizational behavior concepts of an extremely rational nature—concepts based on assumptions about human beings made by economists (at worst) or behavioral psychologists (at best). The social sciences, ever desperate to gain more prestige, seem unable to stop pretending to be natural sciences; they cannot relinquish their obsession with the directly measurable [1]. For far too many people, the spirit of the economic machine appears to be alive and well and living in organizations. Although the existing repertoire of "rational" concepts has proven time and again to be insufficient to untangle the really knotty problems that trouble organizations, the myth of rationality persists.

Consequently, organizational behavior concepts used to describe processes such as individual motivation, communication, leadership, interpersonal relationships, group and intergroup processes, corporate culture, organizational structure, change, and development are based on behaviorist models, with an occasional dose of humanistic psychology thrown in for good measure. Such an approach (behind which hovers the irrepressible ghost of Frederick Taylor, the premier advocate of scientific management) guarantees a rather two-dimensional way of looking at the world of work. Many executives believe that behavior in organizations concerns only conscious, mechanistic, predictable, easy-to-understand phenomena. The more elusive processes that take place in organizations—phenomena that deserve rich description—are conveniently ignored.

That the organizational man or woman is not just a conscious, highly focused maximizing machine of pleasures and pains, but is also a person subject to many (often contradictory) wishes, fantasies, conflicts, defensive behavior, and anxieties—some conscious, others beyond consciousness—isn't a popular perspective for most business-people. Neither is the idea that concepts taken from such fields as psychoanalysis, psychodynamic psychotherapy, and dynamic psychiatry might have a place in the world of work. Such concepts are generally rejected out of hand on the grounds that they're too individually based, too focused on abnormal behavior, and in the case of the psychoanalytic method of investigation, too reliant on self-reported case studies thereby creating problems of verification.

Valid as some of these criticisms may be, the fact remains that any meaningful explanation of humanity requires different means of verification than do the so-called hard sciences. In spite of what philosophers of science like to say about this subject, no causal claim in clinical psychology (or history and economics, for that matter) can be verified in the same way as can claims in empirical sciences such as experimental physics or astronomy. When we enter the realm of a person's inner world—seeking to understand that individual's desires, hopes, and fears—efforts at falsification are as important as the truths they conceal.

GIVING THE UNCONSCIOUS ITS DUE

The best bridge from the certainties of the empirical sciences to the ambiguities of the human mind is what I call the "clinical paradigm"—a conceptual framework that not only recognizes but celebrates the human factor, building on psychoanalytic concepts and techniques. Though the notion that there's more to organizational behavior than meets the eye is anathema to many management scholars, practitioners who deny the reality of unconscious phenomena—who refuse to bring those phenomena to consciousness and take them into consideration—increase the gap between rhetoric and reality. Rejecting the clinical paradigm is a mistake, plain and simple. After all, it's individuals who make up organizations and create the units that contribute to social processes. Even en masse, however, people are subject to laws which cannot be tested by experimental physics. Moreover, like it or not, "abnormal behavior" is more "normal" than most people are prepared to admit. All of us have a neurotic side. Mental health and illness aren't dichotomous phenomena but opposing positions on a continuum. Furthermore, whether a person is labeled normal or abnormal, exactly the same psychological processes apply.

In light of these observations, management scholars and leaders need to revisit the following questions: Is the typical executive really a logical, dependable human being? Is management really a rational task performed by rational people according to sensible organizational objectives? Given the plethora of highly destructive actions taken by business and political leaders, we shouldn't even have to ask. It should be clear that many of those activities which are incomprehensible from a rational point of view, signal that what really goes on in organizations takes place in the intrapsychic and interpersonal world of the key players, below the surface of day-to-day behaviors. That underlying mental activity and behavior needs to be understood in terms of conflicts, defensive behaviors, tensions, and anxieties.

It's something of a paradox that, while at a conscious level we might deny the presence of unconscious processes, at the level of behavior and action we live out such processes every day all over the world. Though we base business strategies on theoretical models derived from the "rational economic man", we count on real people (with all their conscious and unconscious quirks) to make and implement decisions. Even the most successful organizational leaders are prone to highly irrational behavior, a reality that we ignore at our peril.

When the illusions created by the concept of homo economicus prevail over the reality of homo sapiens, people interested in what truly happens in organizations are left with a vague awareness that things that they can't make sense of are occurring. When faced with knotty organizational situations, they feel ineffective and helpless. Far too many well-intentioned and well-constructed plans derail daily in workplaces around the world because of out-of-awareness forces that influence behavior.

Those plans include all change efforts that rely on intervention techniques which focus on the rational side of human behavior to the exclusion of the emotional side. Efforts by traditional organizational change agents—men and women burdened by the legacy of homo economicus—generally come across as overly optimistic and even naïve. Only by accepting that executives just like the rest of us aren't paragons of rationality can we understand why such plans derail and put them back on track again—or better yet, keep them from derailing in the first place [2]–[4].

Experience has shown that in the case of many knotty organizational situations, the clinical paradigm can go a long way toward bringing clarity and providing long-lasting solutions. And no body of knowledge has made a more sustained and successful attempt to deal with the meaning of human events than psychoanalysis. The psychoanalytic method of investigation, which observes people longitudinally (that is, over time), offers an important window into the operation of the mind, identifying meaning in the most personal, emotional experiences. Its method of drawing inferences about meaning out of otherwise incomprehensible phenomena is more effective than what competing theories have to offer. By making sense out of executives' deeper wishes and fantasies, and showing how these fantasies influence behavior in the world of work, the psychodynamic orientation offers a practical way of discovering how organizations really function.

TAPPING INTO PSYCHOANALYTIC THEORIES AND TECHNIQUES

The fact that a growing number of management scholars are realizing that they need to pay attention to weaker, below-the-surface signals in the organizational system is noteworthy in the context of articles in the popular press asking whether Sigmund Freud is dead. People who pose this question are usually focused exclusively on Freud's own views from the early 20th century, forgetting that psychoanalytic theory and therapy have continued to evolve since that time. Psychoanalytic theory has become increasingly sophisticated, incorporating the findings from domains such as dynamic psychiatry, developmental psychology, anthropology, neurophysiology, cognitive theory, family systems theory, and individual and group psychotherapy. To condemn present-day psychoanalytic theory as outdated is like attacking modern physics because Newton never understood Einstein's theory of relativity. Although various aspects of Freud's theories are no longer valid in light of new information about the workings of the mind, fundamental components of psychoanalytic theory have been scientifically and empirically tested and verified, specifically as they relate to cognitive and emotional processes [5]–[6]. As disappointing as it may be to some of his present-day critics, many of Freud's ideas retain their relevance.

As an archaeologist of the mind, Freud believed that neurotic symptoms can be used to decode why people behave the way they do. As conspicuous signifiers of a person's inner world, they can be seen, he believed, as "the royal road to an understanding of the unconscious." I contend that this perspective can be applied, by analogy, to organizations: just as every neurotic symptom has an explanatory history, so has every organizational act; just as symptoms and dreams can be viewed as signs replete with meaning, so can specific acts, statements, and decisions in the boardroom. Likewise, the repetition of certain phenomena in the workplace suggests the existence of specific motivational configurations. The identification of cognitive and affective distortions in an organization's leaders and followers can help executives recognize the extent to which unconscious fantasies and out-of-awareness behavior affect decision-making and management practices in their organization.

Freud himself didn't make any direct observations about the application of his ideas to the world of work (although later in life he became interested in society at large), but several of his followers—psychoanalysts such as Melanie Klein, Wilfred Bion, and Donald Winnicott—applied aspects of his theories to the workplace. The ideas of these psychoanalysts have been further explored by a large number of clinically informed scholars of organizations [2]–[4]; [7]–[16]. The work of these scholars has gone a long way toward creating a deep and rich understanding of life in organizations. Their insights have also opened the way to more effective consultation and intervention in organizations.

The clinical paradigm, with its broadly integrative psychodynamic perspective, has much to contribute to our understanding of organizations and the practice of management. A psychologically informed perspective can help us understand the hidden dynamics associated with individual motivation, leadership, collusive situations, social defenses, toxic organizational cultures, "neurotic" organizations (that is, organizations tainted by the particular neurosis of its top executive), and the extent to which individuals and organizations can be prisoners of their past.

Advocates of the clinical paradigm recognize the limits of rationality and reject a purely economist, behaviorist view of the world of work. They have concluded that behavioral and statistical data-gathering experiments can supply only a partial understanding of complex organizational phenomena, contrary to what advocates of management as a natural science would have us believe. An additional dimension of analysis is needed to comprehend organizational behavior and the people working in the system: we have to factor in that which is directly observable.

Scholars of management need to recognize that organizations as systems have their own life—a life that's not only conscious but also unconscious, not only rational but also irrational. The clinical paradigm is essential to provide insight into that life, into the underlying reasons for executive and employee behavior and actions. To understand the whole picture, we need to pay attention to these presenting internal and social dynamics, to the intricate dance between leaders and followers, and to the various unconscious and invisible psychodynamic processes and structures that influence the behavior of individuals, dyads, and groups in organizations. People who dismiss the complex clinical dimension in organizational analysis cannot hope to go beyond a relatively impoverished, shallow understanding of life in organizations.

In business as in individual life, psychological awareness is the first step toward psychological health. The truth is that by denying the reality of the unconscious, by refusing to make it conscious and work with it, we have institutionalized the chasm between reality and rhetoric. Organizations can't perform successfully if the quirks and irrational processes that are part and parcel of the organizational participants' inner world aren't taken into consideration by top management. Because unconscious dynamics have a significant impact on life in organizations, organizational leaders (and followers) must recognize and plan for those dynamics.

PHILOSOPHICAL UNDERPINNINGS OF THE CLINICAL PARADIGM

Having looked at the clinical paradigm in general terms, we're now ready to examine its philosophical underpinnings. These are based on four premises:

First, the clinical paradigm argues that there's a rationale behind every human act—even those that are apparently irrational. This point of view stipulates that all behavior has an explanation. Because that explanation is often elusive—inextricably interwoven with unconscious needs and desires—one has to do "detective work" to tease out hints and clues regarding perplexing behavior. More important, though, finding meaning in seemingly irrational behavior requires emotional intelligence. Whether one is an analyst helping an individual reach self-understanding or an organizational consultant working with executives to diagnose an entire organization, effective deconstruction can take place only when the "detective's" perception is acute enough to cope with a barrage of mitigating factors, including resistances, ingrained behavior patterns, transference reactions and projective mechanisms.

The second premise on which the clinical paradigm rests is that a great deal of mental life—thoughts, feelings, and motives—lies outside of conscious awareness. People aren't always aware of what they're doing—much less why they're doing it. Though hidden from rational thought, the human unconscious affects (and in some cases even dictates) conscious reality. Even the most "rational" people have blind spots, and even the "best" people have a shadow side—a side that they don't know—and don't want to know. What's more, people work to increase their blind spots: they develop defensive structures over time that make them blind not only to their motivation for a certain dysfunctional behavior but also to the behavior itself even though that behavior may be obvious to everyone else. Regrettably, people who fail to see their own dysfunctional behavior can't take responsibility for it. Though it's not pleasant to admit that one is sometimes a prisoner of the unconscious—we cherish the illusion that we're in control of our lives, after all—accepting the presence of the cognitive and affective unconscious can be liberating, because it helps us understand why we do the things we do and how we might change for the better.

The third premise underlying the clinical paradigm is that nothing is more central to who a person is than the way he or she expresses and regulates emotions. Along with cognition, emotions determine behavior; and characteristic patterns of emotion, thought, and behavior shape personality. The emotional reactions of infancy are primarily biological, and they're tied to the most basic human need systems. From early on, however, socialization occurs through the mediation of the primary caretakers. As socialization progresses, developmental processes enable the individual to take on the various emotional "roles"—sadness, joy, and so on.

While all humans are born with a particular temperament, this constitutional quality gives us only a predisposition to certain emotions. Before we're able to express any given emotion, the imagery associated with that particular feeling-state has to be internalized. Such internalization occurs as the child grows and matures and learns from socialization. By the time adulthood is reached, the regulation of emotions has become an integral part of one's personality, and mood-state can be used as a barometer of psychological and physical well-being. How a person perceives and expresses emotions may change as the years go by, however, depending on one's life experiences [17]–[19].

The experiencing of emotions enables people to come into greater contact with themselves, to find out what they feel (as opposed to what they think) about things, what they like and dislike, and what they want and don't want. Some people are able to express emotions appropriately and comfortably, while others struggle to find words for what they feel, and associate emotions (sometimes even those that we think of as positive) with painful thoughts. Emotions color experiences with positive and negative connotations, creating preferences. Emotions form the basis for the internalization of mental representations of the self and others that guide relationships throughout one's life. Furthermore, emotions serve people in many adaptive and defensive ways, depending on the personal "script" of their inner theater.

The fourth premise underlying the clinical paradigm is that human development is an inter- and intrapersonal process. We're all products of our past, influenced until the day we die by the developmental experiences given by our caretakers [20]–[25]. Childhood experiences play an absolutely crucial role in personality development, particularly in the way people relate to others. These experiences contribute to specifically preferred response patterns that in turn result in a tendency to repeat certain behavior patterns. The psychological imprints of primary early caregivers—particularly our parents—are so strong that they cause a confusion in time and place, making us act toward others in the present as if they were significant people from the past; and these imprints stay with us and guide our interactions throughout our lives. Though we're generally unaware of experiencing "transference"—the term given by psychologists to this confusion in time and place—we may relate to our boss as we did to our mother, or to an important client as we did to our father. The mismatch between the reality of our present situation and our subconscious scenario (colleagues or clients aren't parents, after all) may lead to bewilderment, anxiety, depression, anger, and even aggression.

THE INNER THEATER

Freud focused on the human unconscious—that part of our being which, hidden from rational thought, affects and interprets our conscious reality. The impact of unconscious processes is considerable in the world outside work—in the domains of creativity, love, and friendship, for example—as most people would readily acknowledge; but it also has a considerable effect on thought, behavior, and outcomes in organizational life. Each organizational participant has to deal with what can be described as his or her "inner theater"—the programming that each person has incorporated from his or her genetic inheritance and infant experience. Although everyone from the mail clerk to the CEO has a unique theme, it's the inner theater of executives that concerns us here. Given the power that executives wield, the influence of their inner theater on the rest of the organization is considerable.

Our inner theater results from a combination of nature and nurture. Although our brains are genetically hardwired with certain instinctual behavior patterns, this wiring isn't irrevocably fixed. Through the nature–nurture interface, highly complex motivational need systems determine the unique internal theatre of the individual—the stage on which the major themes that define the person are played out. These motivational need systems are the rational forces that lie behind behaviors and actions that are perceived to be irrational. As gasoline fuels an engine, the cognitive and emotional patterns that develop out of these interrelated motivational need systems fuel our behavior. For each one of us, our unique mixture of motivational needs will determine our personality. Especially over the crucial first months and years of our life (though in later years as well, to a lesser extent), rewiring occurs in response to developmental factors that we are exposed to.

The interface of our motivational needs with environmental factors (especially human factors, in the form of caretakers, siblings, teachers, and other important figures) defines our essential uniqueness. The mental schemas that are the outcome of this interface are then carried within us for the rest of our lives, guiding our subsequent relationships with others. These mental representations of our self, others, and relationships help us make sense of all aspects of reality, serve as the standard by which we judge what we see and decide what we want, and govern our motivations and actions. These representations become the operational code that determines how we react across situations [26]–[27]. They influence how we act and react in our daily lives, whether at home, at play, or at work.

MOTIVATIONAL NEED SYSTEMS

The British philosopher Jeremy Bentham, in an effort to explain human behavior, argued that nature has placed mankind under the government of two sovereign masters, pain and pleasure. These masters govern us in all that we think, do, and say. We can take his view of human nature one step further through the notion of motivational need systems. Motivational need systems serve as the operational code that drives behavior. Each of these need systems is operational in every person beginning at infancy and continuing throughout the life-cycle, altered by the forces of age, learning, and maturation.

The importance that any one of the need systems has in an individual is determined by three regulating forces: innate and learned response patterns, the role of significant caretakers, and the extent to which the individual attempts to recreate positive emotional states experienced in infancy and childhood. As these forces and need systems interact during maturation, mental schemas emerge—"templates" in the unconscious, if you will. These schemas create symbolic model scenes (what I like to call "scripts" in a person's inner theater) that regulate fantasy and influence behavior and action [20]–[21]; [28]–[30].

Some of these motivational need systems are more basic than others. At the most fundamental is the system that regulates a person's physiological needs—that is, needs for food, water, elimination, sleep, and breathing. Another system handles an individual's needs for sensual enjoyment and (later) sexual excitement, while still another deals with the need to respond to certain situations through antagonism and withdrawal. Although these primary need systems impact the work situation to some extent, two other, higher-level systems are of particular interest for life in organizations: the attachment/affiliation need system and the exploration/assertion need system.

Let's look at the need for attachment/affiliation first. Among humans there exists an innately unfolding experience of human relatedness [31]–[34]. Humankind's essential humanness is revealed in their seeking relationships with other people, in sharing something. As the pediatrician and psychoanalyst Donald Winnicott used to say, there's no such thing as a baby, only a mothering pair. The baby can't do without the mother. That need for attachment, beginning in infancy but lasting throughout life, involves the process of engagement with other human beings, the universal experience of wanting to be close to others. It also involves the pleasure of sharing and affirmation. When the human need for intimate engagement is extrapolated to groups, the desire to enjoy intimacy can be described as a need for affiliation. Both attachment and affiliation serve an emotional balancing role by confirming an individual's self-worth and contributing to his or her sense of self-esteem.

The need for exploration/assertion also has a lot to do with who a person becomes and how that person sees him- or herself. The need for exploration—closely associated with cognition and learning—affects a person's ability to play and to work. This need is manifested soon after birth: infant observation has shown that novelty, as well as the discovery of the effects of certain actions, causes a prolonged state of attentive arousal in infants. Similar reactions to opportunities for exploration continue into adulthood. Closely tied to the need for exploration is the need for self-assertion—that is, the need to be able to choose what we want to do. Playful exploration and manipulation of the environment in response to exploratory-assertive motivation produces a sense of effectiveness and competency, of autonomy, initiative, industry, and efficacy [35]–[36]. Because striving, competing, and seeking mastery are fundamental characteristics of the human personality, exercising assertiveness—following our preferences, acting in a determined manner—serves as a form of affirmation.

As noted above, each motivational system is either strengthened or loses power in reaction to innate and learned response patterns, the developmental impact of caretakers, and the ability to recreate previous emotional states. Through the nature-nurture interface, these highly complex motivational systems eventually determine the unique internal theater of the individual—the stage on which the major themes that define the person are played out. These motivational systems are the rational forces that lie behind behaviors and actions that are perceived to be irrational. We bring to every experience a style of interacting, now scripted for us, that we learned initially in childhood. In other words, how we related to and interacted with parents and other close caregivers during the early years affects how we relate to others—especially authority figures—now in our adulthood.

CORE CONFLICTUAL RELATIONSHIP THEMES

The basic script of a person's inner theater is determined by the motivational need systems described above. Within that basic script, however, certain themes develop over time—themes that reflect the preeminence of certain inner wishes that contribute to our unique personality style. These "core conflictual relationship themes" (CCRT) translate into consistent patterns by which we relate to others [37]. Put another way, our basic wishes color our life-scripts, which in turn shape our relationships with others, determining the way we believe others will react to us and the way we react to others. People's lives may be colored by the wish to be loved, for example, or the wish to be understood, or to be noticed, or to be free from conflict, or to be independent, or to help—or even to hinder, or to hurt others.

When we go to work, we take these fundamental wishes—our core conflictual relationship themes—into the context of our workplace relationships. We project our wishes on others and, based on those wishes, rightly or wrongly anticipate how others will react to us; then we react not to their actual reactions but to their perceived reactions. Who among us doesn't know a leader who is the epitome of conflict avoidance, tyrannical behavior, micromanagement, manic behavior, inaccessibility, or game-playing? That dominant style, whatever it may be, derives from the leader's primary core conflictual relationship theme. So potent is a person's driving theme that a leader's subordinates are often drawn into collusive practices and play along, turning the leader's expectations into self-fulfilling prophecies. Unfortunately, the life-scripts drawn up in childhood on the basis of our core conflictual relationship themes often become ineffective in adult situations. They create a dizzying merry-go-round that takes affected leaders into a self-destructive cycle of repetition.

USING THE CLINICAL PARADIGM TO REWRITE DYSFUNCTIONAL SCRIPTS

As was noted earlier, there's strong continuity between childhood and adult behavior. As the saying goes, Scratch a man or woman and you'll find a child! This doesn't mean that we can't change as adults; it simply means that by the time we reach the age of thirty, a considerable part of our personality has been formed [38]–[39]. Unless we recognize the extent to which our present is determined by our past, we make the same mistakes over and over.

Organizations the world over are full of people who are unable to recognize repetitive behavior patterns that have become dysfunctional. They're stuck in a vicious, self-destructive circle and don't even know it—much less know how to escape. The clinical paradigm can help such people recognize their strengths and weaknesses, understand the causes of their resistance to change, and recognize where and how they can become more effective. It can help them recognize those elements of their inner theater that confine rather than liberate, and help them rescript those elements. In other words, it can offer choice.

It is tragic that there is such a difference between what we are and what we could be. If we want things to be different, we must start by being different ourselves.

REFERENCES

1. Popper, K. (2002). *The Logic of Scientific Discovery.* London, Routledge Classics.
2. Gabriel, Y. (1999). *Organizations in Depth.* London, Sage.
3. Kets de Vries, M. F. R., Ed (1984). *The Irrational Executive: Psychoanalytic Explorations in Management.* New York, International Universities Press.
4. Kets de Vries, M. F. R., Ed (1991). *Organizations on the Couch.* San Francisco, Jossey-Bass.
5. Barron, J. W., M. N. Eagle and D. L. Wolitzky Eds (1992). *The Interface of Psychoanalysis and Psychology.* Washington, DC, American Psychological Association.
6. Westen, D. (1998). "The Scientific Legacy of Sigmund Freud: Toward a Psychodynamically Informed Psychological Science." Psychological Bulletin 124(3): 333–371.
7. Czander, W. M. (1993). *The Psychodynamics of Work and Organizations.* New York, Guilford Press.
8. DeBoard, R. (1978). *The Psychoanalysis of Organisations.* London, Routledge.

9. Hirschhorn, L. (1990). *The Workplace Within: Psychodynamics of Organizational Life*. Boston, MIT Press.
10. Kets de Vries, M. F. R. (1994). "The Leadership Mystique." Academy of Management Executive 8(3): 73–92.
11. Kets de Vries, M. F. R. and D. Miller (1984). *The Neurotic Organization*. San Francisco, Jossey-Bass.
12. Levinson, H. (1972). *Organizational Diagnosis*. Cambridge, Mass., Harvard University Press.
13. Levinson, H. (2002). *Organizational Assessment*. Washington, DC, American Psychological Association.
14. Obholzer, A. (1994). *The Unconscious at Work: Individual and Organizational Stress in Human Services*. London, Routledge.
15. Schwartz, H. (1990). *Narcissistic Process and Corporate Decay: The Theory of the Organization Ideal*. New York, New York University Press.
16. Zaleznik, A. (1966). *Human Dilemmas of Leadership*. New York, HarperCollins.
17. Darwin, C. (1920). *The Expression of Emotion in Man and Animals*. New York, Appleton–Century–Crofts.
18. Plutchick, R. (1980). *Emotions: A Psycho-evolutionary Synthesis*. New York, HarperCollins.
19. Tomkins, S. S. (1995). *Script Theory: Differential Magnification of Affect. Exploring Affect: Selections from the Writings of Silvan S. Tomkins*. Ed V. Demos. New York, Cambridge University Press: 312–410.
20. Emde, R. N. (1981). "Changing Models of Infancy and the Nature of Early Development: Remodelling the Foundation." Journal of the American Psychoanalytical Association 29: 179–219.
21. Erikson, E. H. (1963). *Childhood and Society*. New York, W.W. Norton & Society.
22. Kagan, J. (1994). *Nature of the Child*. New York, Basic Books.
23. Kohlberg, L. (1981). *The Philosophy of Moral Development*. New York, Harper & Row.
24. Piaget, J. (1952). *The Origins of Intelligence in Children*. New York, International Universities Press.
25. Pine, F. (1985). *Developmental Theory and Clinical Process*. New Haven, Yale University Press.
26. George, A. L. (1969). "The 'Operational Code': A Neglected Approach to the Study of Political Leadership and Decision-Making." International Studies Quarterly 13: 190–222.

27. McDougall, J. (1985). *Theaters of the Mind*. New York, Basic Books.
28. Kagan, J. and H. A. Moss (1983). *Birth to Maturity: A Study in Psychological Development*. New Haven, Yale University Press.
29. Lichtenberg, J. D. (1991). *Psychoanalysis and Infant Research*. New York, Lawrence Erlbaum.
30. Lichtenberg, J. D. and R. A. Schonbar (1992). *Motivation in Psychology and Psychoanalysis. Interface of Psychoanalysis and Psychology*. Eds J. W. Barron, M. N. Eagle and D. L. Wolitzky. Washington, American Psychological Association: 11–36.
31. Bowlby, J. (1969). *Attachment and Loss*. New York, Basic Books.
32. Mahler, M. S., F. Pine and A. Bergman (1975). *The Psychological Birth of the Human Infant*. New York, Basic Books.
33. Spitz, R. A. (1965). *The First Year of Life*. New York, International Universities Press.
34. Winnicott, D. W. (1975). *Through Paediatrics to Psycho-Analysis*. New York, Basic Books.
35. Bandura, A. (1989). "Perceived Self-Efficacy in the Exercise of Personal Agency." The Psychologist: Bulletin of British Psychological Society 10: 411–424.
36. White, R. (1959). "Motivation Reconsidered: The Concept of Competence." Psychological Review 66: 297–333.
37. Luborsky, L. and P. Crits-Cristoph (1998). *Understanding Transference: The Core Conflictual Relationship Theme Method*. Washington, American Psychological Organization.
38. Heatherton, T. and J. L. Weinberger, Eds (1994). *Can Personality Change?* Washington, DC, American Psychological Association.
39. McCrae, R. R. and P. T. Costa (1990). *Personality in Adulthood*. New York, Guilford Press.

PART ONE

ENTERING THE INNER THEATER OF LEADERS

CHAPTER 2

THE NARCISSISTIC LEADER: MYTH AND REALITY

Glory is fleeting, but obscurity lasts forever.

—Napoleon Bonaparte

A narcissist is someone better looking than you are.

—Gore Vidal

I have come to warn God that I am taking his place. As he has not seen fit to avenge my enemies, I'll take his place and do it myself.

—Alexandre Dumas, The Count of Monte Cristo.

It takes a wise man to learn from his mistakes, but an even wiser man to learn from others.

—Zen proverb

A Japanese Zen master during the Meiji era received a visitor who came to inquire about Zen. The Zen master served his guest tea. He poured his visitor's cup full and then kept on pouring. The visitor watched the overflow with alarm until he could no longer control himself. "The cup is over-full. No more can go in it!" he cried out. "Like this cup," the Zen master replied, "you are full of your own opinions, beliefs, and assumptions. How can I teach you anything unless you first empty your cup?" This enigmatic little tale suggests that people who are too full of themselves—that is, who are overly narcissistic—are bound to get into trouble.

It's generally agreed that a certain degree of narcissistic behavior is essential for leadership success, a prerequisite for anyone who hopes to rise to the top [1]–[5]. Thus if we're to understand life in organizations, we have to understand narcissism. There's no place where the vicissitudes of narcissism are acted out more dramatically than on the organizational stage, where narcissistic leaders can find themselves but followers must lose themselves.

This chapter looks at narcissism generally, as an aspect of human behavior, and examines how it operates for both good and ill in an organizational context. It also scrutinizes the psychopathology of relationships between narcissistic leaders and their followers as it's manifested in the process known as transference. But first we should remind ourselves of the world's best-known account of narcissism, told in a cautionary Greek myth.

Narcissus was a beautiful young man who rejected the advances of numerous men and women who fell in love with him. The goddess Nemesis overheard some of his thwarted lovers wishing the pain of unrequited love on him and granted them their wish. Narcissus fell in love with his own reflection when he stopped to drink from a spring. Although he realized his error, he couldn't escape from his infatuation and pined to death. As his ghost was ferried across the river Styx, it leaned over the side of the boat for one last glimpse of itself in the water.

Like so many myths, the story of Narcissus draws on an element of human nature and dramatizes its excess. A certain degree of narcissism, in a spectrum that ranges from healthy self-esteem to destructive egotism, is perfectly natural and even healthy. A moderate measure of self-esteem contributes to positive behaviors such as assertiveness, confidence, and creativity, all desirable qualities for an individual in any walk of life, but particularly so for business leaders. At the other end of the spectrum, however, extreme narcissism is characterized by egotism, self-centeredness, grandiosity, lack of empathy, exploitation, exaggerated self-love, and failure to acknowledge boundaries. In this severe form, narcissism can do serious damage. This is especially true within an organization, where the combination of a leader's overly narcissistic disposition and his or her position of power can have devastating consequences.

Whether we're discussing more healthy or less healthy narcissism, we should be clearer about its source.

BACK TO THE FUTURE

A very graphic explanation of where it all begins can be found in Philip Larkin's poem "This Be The Verse," (1971)★:

> They fuck you up, your mum and dad.
> They may not mean to, but they do.
> They fill you with the faults they had
> And add some extra, just for you.

Picture the womb, where environmental conditions are perfect. Then picture the world, where from the second a baby makes its entry there's need and helplessness and the frustration of being unable to communicate. The infant mind tries to recreate the perfect bliss of life in the womb, but it doesn't have much to work with. All it can do is to create a grandiose, exhibitionistic image of itself and an all-powerful, idealized image of its parents [6]. Over time, and with "good enough" care (a term used by psychologists to denote caretaking that meets or exceeds basic physical and emotional needs), these two idealized images are moderated

★ Published with permission from *This Be The Verse* from *High Windows* by Philip Larkin and Faber and Faber Ltd.

by the forces of reality—especially responses from parents, siblings, caretakers, and teachers.

A child's sense of identity is acquired only gradually, through interaction with the environment [7]–[10]. In order to achieve normal character development, a child has to push against constraining forces and encounter both success and frustration. Moderate frustration, sometimes called age-appropriate frustration, is essential to mental health. For example, it might be frustrating for a child to have to wait a few minutes for his or her mother to finish a task before putting lunch on the table, but the level of frustration would not be inappropriate. However, if the wait extended to hours and included a tirade about the nuisance of small children, the frustration would be unhealthy and possibly even traumatizing.

Whatever the level of frustration, children deal with it as best they can by imagining themselves able to overcome any obstacle. The early years are characterized by the tension between that grandiose self-image and the helplessness that is the true state of childhood. Inadequate resolution of that tension produces negative feelings (shame, humiliation, rage, envy, spitefulness, a desire for vengeance) and a hunger for personal power and status. In most children, however, as time goes by those grandiose fantasies are modified and form the basis for well-grounded ambition, directed activity, and a secure sense of self-esteem.

A similar evolution takes place with the idealized parent image. A child's evaluation of other people becomes increasingly realistic as he or she grows. With "good enough" care, the toddler who clapped with delight when you pressed a switch and lit up a room will evolve steadily into the teenager who can accept the fact that it's pointless asking you to help with his or her physics homework.

Over time most people develop relatively stable ways of representing their experience of themselves and others. These representations are known as internal objects and are composed of pleasurable and painful experiences, fantasies, ideals, thoughts, and images that create a cognitive and affective map of the world—the internal theater [11]. The process of building this mental map involves the resolution of the relationship between real people and the idealized mental images of them retained by the developing child. The child's interactions with other people then reflect that resolution: they're in part a response to real others, and in part a response to idealized mental images.

The internal objects that an individual develops over time profoundly influence his or her affective and cognitive states, behavior, and actions. Good internal objects are generative and restorative: they keep you going when life gets tough and constitute the underpinnings of healthy functioning. Bad internal objects—or just the absence of good internal objects—can cause dysfunctions that contain the seeds of pathological narcissistic behavior.

The earliest objects of a developing child's attention are the parents. Their care, along with their ability to gauge the amount and kind of frustration appropriate to their child's level of maturity, has a major impact on the internal world that the child creates, and it determines whether that world is reassuring and affirming or confusing and turbulent. Parents who cannot or will not respond appropriately to their child's demands corrupt the developing child's internal world. Sometimes inappropriate care amounts to overt abuse. More often, though, it's the result of neglect, indifference, or ignorance. Sometimes parents use a child as an extension of themselves in their own search for admiration and greatness. This gives the child the illusion of being loved while its true needs are ignored. This sort of failure of care occurs most often with a child who has notable qualities, perhaps great physical beauty or a special talent.

When parents use a child as a way of compensating for their own disappointments, that child's pursuit of admiration can become a lifelong quest, an attempt to offset the feeling of being used rather than loved for one's own sake. This self-love can actually be a cover for self-hatred. Children troubled in this way (and the adults they become) have failed to modify or truly integrate either the grandiose self or the idealized parent images. Both representations continue in their unaltered forms, pursuing their outdated aims and preventing a cohesive sense of self. This causes incoherent behavior, problems with self-esteem, narcissistic pathology, and an imbalance in psychic structure. When symptoms such as these occur, the first place to look for a cause (as with most mental and emotional suffering) is the person's relational history.

TWO MODERN MYTHS: HEALTHY NEGLECT AND TOUGH LOVE

> But they were fucked up in their turn
> By fools in old-style hats and coats,
> Who half the time were soppy-stern
> And half at one another's throats.
>
> —Philip Larkin

With their need for power, status, prestige, and glamour, many narcissistic personalities eventually end up in leadership positions. The ability of narcissists to manipulate others and their capacity to establish rapid, if shallow, relationships serve them well as they move up the organizational ladder. They are often successful initially, despite their "handicap"—particularly in areas where they can fulfill their ambition for fame and glory. Unfortunately, power, prestige, and status are typically more important to these people than a serious commitment to organizational goals and performance. Because narcissists are motivated by selfishness, their successes are ephemeral.

Like all of us, leaders occupy a position somewhere on the narcissistic spectrum that ranges from healthy self-esteem to pathological egotism. Within that spectrum, it's helpful to distinguish between constructive and reactive narcissism. Constructive narcissism develops in response to "good enough" care. Parents who give their children a lot of support, age-appropriate frustration, and a proper "holding environment" for their emotional reactions produce well-balanced, positive children who possess a solid sense of self-esteem, a capacity for introspection, and an empathetic outlook. These individuals have a high degree of confidence in their own abilities and are highly task- and goal-oriented.

Constructive narcissists are no strangers to the pursuit of greatness, but because they're not searching exclusively for personal power, their successes are genuine. They have a vision that extends beyond themselves, and they work with great zeal to fulfill it. They take advice and consult with others before moving forward, valuing cooperation over solo performance, although they always take ultimate responsibility and never blame others when things go wrong. Constructive narcissists have the capacity to become larger-than-life figures, in the best sense of that term, serving as transformational leaders and inspiring role models. Some may seem to be lacking in warmth and consideration, substituting "the good of the company" or "the welfare of all" for reciprocal relationships, but others are charismatic.

Reactive narcissism develops in people who have been damaged in some way. It takes root when phase-appropriate development is interrupted, frustrating experiences are poorly handled, and parents are either distant and cold or overindulgent and unrealistically admiring. In those circumstances, children develop a defective sense of identity and have difficulty maintaining a stable sense of self-esteem. As adults, they remain deeply troubled by inadequacy, bitterness, anger, depressive thoughts, and lingering feelings of emptiness and deprivation. They may develop a sense of entitlement, believing that they deserve special treatment and that rules and regulations apply only to others. As a way of mastering their feelings of inadequacy and insecurity, they may develop an exaggerated sense of self-importance and self-grandiosity and a concomitant need for admiration. They typically lack empathy and are unable to perceive and understand how others feel.

Individuals with this reactive orientation frequently distort external events in order to manage anxiety and stave off loss and disappointment. They create a self-image characterized by special-ness. As adults, reactive narcissists continue to behave like babies who go unheard and lack attention. They have a strong need—sometimes conscious, sometimes not—to make up for the per-ceived wrongs done to them at earlier periods in their lives. Having been belittled, maltreated, or exploited as children, as adults they're determined to prove they amount to something. If this determina-tion stops at wanting and working to be valued, reactive narcissism can produce healthy fruit. If it turns into envy, spite, greed, gran-diosity, and vindictiveness, the fruit is sour indeed.

Although it's intuitively obvious that childhood neglect leads to reactive narcissism, it seems a bit ironic that pampering a child produces the same result. While the neglected child creates an image of specialness to compensate for an inner sense of worthless-ness, the pampered child develops an inflated self-image that's out of synch with the real world. Pampered children are led to believe that they're completely lovable and perfect, whatever they do. But because perfection is impossible—a fact that all youngsters know, having learned it the hard way—these children become anxious and insecure, unable to live up to the standards set by their parents. Parental overvaluation creates a self-image that's hard to sustain in the real world. The hard truth is this: indulgence on the part of the parents has exactly the opposite effect from what's intended. Pampered children don't feel loved as persons in their own right and develop a strong sense of inadequacy.

Excessive praise of a child produces feelings of superiority and a sense of being destined for greatness. When such early encour-agement turns out to be right—that is, when there's genuine talent—the child may be able to live up to the parents' exaggerated expectations. He or she then uses the expectations imposed on him or her as a basis for excellence as the talent is honed. Perhaps this is what Freud meant when he noted: "If a man has been his mother's undisputed darling, he retains throughout life the triumphant feeling, the confidence in success, which not seldom brings actual success along with it" [12], p. 15. In general, however, overpraised children become full of themselves and conflict-ridden. While outwardly they appear grandiose, seductive, competent, and articulate, covertly they're full of self-doubt, envious of others, and extremely vulnerable to criticism. Reactive narcissists who attain a leadership position can have marked negative effects on their organizations.

NARCISSISTIC PERSONALITY DISORDERS

The *Diagnostic and Statistical Manual of the Mental Disorders (DSM-IV-TR)*, published by the American Psychiatric Association, contains this broad definition of the various narcissistic personality disorders:

A pervasive pattern of grandiosity (in fantasy or behavior), need for admiration, and lack of empathy, beginning by early adulthood and present in a variety of contexts, as indicated by five (or more) of the following:

- has a grandiose sense of self-importance (e.g. exaggerates achievements and talents, expects to be noticed as superior without commensurate achievements)
- is preoccupied with fantasies of unlimited success, power, brilliance, beauty, or ideal love
- believes that he or she is "special" and unique and can only be understood by, or should associate with, other special or high-status people (or institutions)
- requires excessive admiration
- has a sense of entitlement, i.e. unreasonable expectations of especially favorable treatment or automatic compliance with his or her expectations

- is interpersonally exploitative, i.e. takes advantage of others to achieve his or her own ends
- lacks empathy: is unwilling to recognize or identify with the feelings and needs of others
- is often envious of others or believes that others are envious of him or her
- shows arrogant, haughty behaviors or attitudes [13], p. 717.

There are overtones of mental illness in this description. Certainly "ill" and "impaired" would describe the 1% of people that meet the American Psychiatric Association's full criteria of narcissistic personality disorders. However, many of these criteria are also applicable, to a lesser degree and not in combination, to narcissistic individuals who function more or less normally but nonetheless cause serious distress to themselves and others.

In a position of leadership, people suffering from this kind of disorder become fixated on power, status, prestige, and superiority. They overvalue their personal worth, arguing that, as exceptional people, they deserve special privileges and prerogatives. They act in a grandiose, haughty way, expect special favors, flout conventional rules, and feel entitled; they're unempathetic, inconsiderate to others, exploitative, and unconstrained by objective reality.

Despite the negativity of this description, narcissists are generally upbeat and optimistic. Unless their sense of superiority is challenged, they experience a pervasive feeling of well-being. When they're challenged, however, they exhibit irritability and annoyance with others, feelings of dejection, and outbursts of rage. When faced with setbacks or failures, they're masters of self-deception, inventing plausible reasons for their (temporary) misfortune. This fantasized rationalization helps them cope. If their rationalizations are not accepted by others, they find someone else to blame for their misfortune.

Some narcissists are motivated by the need to get even for real or perceived slights experienced in childhood. The Monte Cristo complex, named after the protagonist in Alexandre Dumas' *The*

Count of Monte Cristo, encompasses feelings of envy, spite, revenge, and/or vindictive triumph over those who wronged one. Reactive narcissistic leaders with the Monte Cristo complex aren't prepared to share power with anyone, pooling everyone into the enemy category. Such leaders rarely even consult with colleagues, preferring to make all decisions on their own. When they do consult others, the gesture is little more than ritualistic.

Whether vindictive or just reactive, narcissistic leaders learn little from defeat. Their tendency to scapegoat others when things go wrong and to get angry when things don't go their way are simply reenactments of childhood behavior—tantrums, if you will, that originate in earlier feelings of helplessness and humiliation. When people in positions of power act out in this way, the impact on their immediate environment can be devastating. Tantrums intimidate followers, who then themselves regress to more child-like behavior.

ANOTHER FINE MESSIER

Think back to the film *Wall Street*, in which the protagonist, Gordon Gekko, states:

> The point is, ladies and gentlemen, greed—for the lack of a better word—is good. Greed is right; greed works. Greed clarifies, cuts through, and captures the essence of the evolutionary spirit. Greed in all its forms—greed for life, for money, for love, knowledge—has marked the upward surge of mankind, and greed—you mark my words—will not only save Teldar Paper, but that other malfunctioning corporation called the USA. (1987)

Unfortunately, Gordon Gekko's manic, self-centred perspective isn't just the nightmare vision of an over-the-top Hollywood scriptwriter. Real executives who have lost any sense of boundaries frequently act out similar scenarios. One person whose career mirrored Gekko's rise and fall is Jean-Marie Messier, the ex-CEO of

Vivendi Universal, who on 2 July 2002 experienced his own private Waterloo when ousted from the company in disgrace.

Messier was France's most colorful and controversial business leader—not French enough for his own compatriots, yet too French for his US business partners. In his glory days he went by the nickname J6M (pronounced jeeseezem), "Jean-Marie Messier— moi-même maître du monde," which, roughly translated, means "Jean-Marie Messier, master of the world." That his nickname didn't displease him—in fact, far from it—is demonstrated by the fact that Messier used it as the title of his autobiography, *J6M. COM.*

Messier's early career was stellar. Born in Grenoble, France, in 1956, he studied at two of the most prestigious French universities, the Ecole Polytechnique and the Ecole National d'Administration (ENA), which still today turn out most of France's business and political élite. Like all good ENA graduates, Messier held a variety of senior roles in the public sector—specifically, in the French economy ministry during the 1980s—before going into investment banking. After five years at the investment bank Lazard Frères, the government called again, and in 1994 Messier agreed to take over as head of the utility group Compagnie Générale des Eaux.

Messier immediately set about transforming the 150-year-old utility group, whose core activities were collecting refuse and running sewage plants. Throwing every sound strategic consideration about the rules of diversification into the air, he decided to turn CGE into a glamorous global media and telecommunications giant. Within six years, the business had been renamed Vivendi Universal and had become the world's second largest media company (after AOL-Time Warner), with newly acquired holdings such as Universal Studios in Hollywood, the record label Universal Music, and the French TV station Canal Plus. Further acquisitions in Europe provided Vivendi with mobile telecom services, theme parks, and educational publishing businesses. The company was now a long way from the unglamorous world of the original French utility firm.

The scale of the transformation and the unabashed global ambitions that Messier revealed while still in his early 40s made him unpopular in France, where business leaders rarely display such flamboyance and brashness. His increasingly public style evoked more and more resentment among the members of the French business community and its commentators. That resentment spilled over when Messier decided to move to New York, where he lived in a €20 million apartment that was paid for by Vivendi. He then made things even worse by remarking that "the French cultural exception is dead"—a reference to the French government's practice (in his view, outdated) of subsidizing French art and culture. As a Frenchman, he should have known better than to condemn one of France's sacred cows: these subsidies were widely regarded as a barrier against the dominance of the US entertainment industry. On the business side, things were equally bad. With the decline in the economy and the onset of recession in the late 1990s, it became obvious that Vivendi's expansion had been built largely on acquisitions, many of which had been dramatically overpriced. Under Messier, Vivendi spent close to $100 billion acquiring interests in film, music, publishing, and the Internet, racking up close to $19 billion debt. Unfortunately, culture integration—the logical (and difficult) step after any buyout—was neither a priority nor a strength for Messier.

In March 2002, Vivendi Universal presented a €13.6 billion loss for 2001, resulting in a large downward revision in the value of its assets. Company shares plummeted as investors became nervous. With this development, Messier lost the confidence of the firm's important North American shareholders, including the Bronfman family, former owners of Seagram (the drinks and entertainment giant), which had merged with Vivendi two years earlier and whose family fortune had been significantly reduced by Vivendi's escapades. The company that had once been worth about $100 billion was suddenly worth less than a fifth of that amount, with some investment analysts saying that it would be more valuable if sold in pieces [14].

The situation was so grim that the board called for Messier's resignation which he finally tendered with the remark, "I am quitting so that Vivendi Universal may remain." *Time* magazine's Paris correspondent wrote:

> In France, Messier's name is now close to dirt—which also approximates Vivendi Universal's stock price. Shares have dropped around 70% since the start of the year and nearly 40% in the week of Messier's eviction. "Vivendi Universal has always been about, by and for Messier—which worked as long as markets believed in the man," says economist Elie Cohen. "When the stock declined and Messier proved incapable of reversing it, that's when market perceptions, Messier's reputation and Vivendi itself crumbled" (*Time Europe*, 15 July 2002, p. 20).

Messier was replaced at Vivendi Universal by Jean Fourtou, a man thought to be the polar opposite of Messier. Fourtou quickly set out to salvage what was salvageable of the shattered company. In the meantime, Messier decided to fight for his golden parachute, provided for in a termination clause that had been written into the American part of his contract with Vivendi. This was not an easy task. A French court immediately froze the €20.6 million severance payment, noting that the board hadn't approved it and was waiting for a vote from the shareholders. The New York tribunal to which Messier took his case ordered Vivendi to go ahead with the payment, but Vivendi and the shareholders refused, pointing out how nonsensical the payment would be when Messier was responsible for destroying the value of the company. A class action lawsuit was started in the US by Vivendi shareholders, claiming that Messier had lied to them about the company's financial health in the last months of his tenure.

Messier's own point of view remained very clear: nothing that had happened to the company was his fault. Blame lay with various people who had not left him enough time and space to take the steps needed to turn Vivendi around. Furthermore, he claimed, he was entitled to the golden parachute, since it was part of the severance package and had been agreed to at a time when the board knew to what extent he had run down Vivendi. Messier reasoned that if board members had signed the agreement despite this knowledge, it was their problem. While admitting that the size of the severance package might shock the French business community, he demanded that the promise be honoured. However, he was not his own best advocate, conveniently forgetting many previous comments he had made—comments freely accessible to anyone who read his autobiography. For example, in response to the earlier exit of one of his French colleagues, Philippe Jaffré, ex-CEO of Elf, he wrote: "If I had been on the board of Elf, I would never have agreed to the golden parachute Philippe Jaffré was given."[1] Most damaging to his own case was his condemnation of golden parachutes generally:

> The possibility of being fired by the shareholders . . . is one of the usual risks of being a business leader. . . . You are paid for that. And well paid, too. I don't think that these special compensations—the so-called golden parachutes that are so much talked about—are justified for people in this position. My contract does not include any of these. And I give my word to the Board of Directors never to negotiate one. You can't have your cake and eat it, too. . . . I am for giving leaders the possibility to become rich, but they have to accept the risks, too.[2]

[1] Messier 2002, p. 190: 'J'aurais été administrateur d'Elf, je n'aurais pas voté le golden parachute qui a été accordé à Philippe Jaffré.'

[2] Messier op. cit. 'L'éventualité d'être viré par ses actionnaires, lors d'une OPA ou pour toute autre raison fait partie des risques normaux du métier de patron. Quand on est nommé à la tête d'une entreprise, petite ou grande, on sait que l'on est révocable ad nutum, c'est à dire à tout moment sur simple décision du conseil d'administration. On est payé pour ça. Et bien payé. Les indemnités spéciales—ces golden parachutes qui défraient la chronique—ne se justifient donc pas selon moi pour les mandataires sociaux. Mon contrat ne prévoit aucune clause de ce genre. Et je m'engage vis-à-vis de mon conseil d'administration à ne jamais en négocier. On ne peut pas avoir le beurre et l'argent du beurre: des

Greed, hubris, and vanity drove Messier to build the sort of business empire no Frenchman (and few Americans) had ever achieved before. Water utilities weren't glamorous enough for this twenty-first century Napoleon, so he moved to greener pastures; but Hollywood became his Moscow. His audacity and pomposity masked incompetence and ignorance of the media business— indeed, of business in general. Worse, once he had destroyed most of the value of a number of formerly successful, independent companies with his reckless ambition and his lack of operational aptitude, he found other people to blame. And even after so much value-destruction, his greed didn't dissipate: Messier claimed an exorbitant sum of money as his right! Seldom in business history have we seen such a case of vanity and greed. And yet Messier apparently never recognized how many lives were damaged because of his antics; how many people lost their jobs.

Among the French press, the nickname J6M now stands for "Jean-Marie Messier: moi-même mis en examen" (being investigated), in honour of Messier's pursuit by the French courts for manipulation de cours, diffusion de fausses informations, and abus de biens sociaux (manipulation of the stock market, spreading of false information, and abuse of social goods). If cynicism were a crime, Messier could also be indicted for shameless lying: in his book, he declared himself a new kind of leader, one who would never, never claim a golden parachute; behaving like a spoiled child: at the general management meeting that preceded his fall, Messier, furious at having his proposal to redirect share options blocked by share holders, started procedures to cancel the meeting, arguing that the votes had been rigged.[3]

---

stock-options pour se constituer un patrimoine et un parachute au cas ou cela tournerait mal. Dieu sait si je suis partisan de donner aux dirigeants la possibilité de s'enrichir mais qu'ils en assument les risques.'

[3] 'Si le cynisme était un délit, J6m aurait aussi pu être poursuivi pour mensonge éhonté: dans son livre, il jurait être un manager de type nouveau qui ne réclamerait jamais, ô grand jamai de "golden parachute"; —caprice d'enfant

Messier's flight into grandiosity, vanity, and greed isn't exceptional in the world of business, except in degree. He's in very bad
company. His more outrageous peers include Global Crossing
Chairman Gary Winnick, whom Fortune called "the emperor of
greed." Winnick cashed in $735 million in stock over four years
while leading his company into bankruptcy. Kenneth Lay, chairman of Enron, succeeded in bringing his company crashing to the
ground (with the help of his CEO, Jeffrey Skilling, and his financial wizard, Andrew Fastow), leaving thousands of employees
jobless. Dennis Kozlowski, the toppled titan of Tyco, was found
guilty in June 2005 by a New York jury of fraud, conspiracy, and
grand larceny for looting his own company to the tune of $600
million. Bernard Ebbers, the former CEO of WorldCom, turned
a small Mississippi long-distance operator into one of the world's
biggest telecom providers before engaging in questionable accounting practices that precipitated the biggest bankruptcy in US corporate history. In March 2005 a federal jury in New York convicted
Ebbers on all nine counts of the charge that he helped mastermind
an $11 billion accounting fraud at WorldCom; they sentenced him
to 25 years in prison. All these leading executives ignored the rules
of civilized organizational behavior.

Narcissistic leadership isn't limited to the business sphere, of
course. In fact, one of the best examples of reactive narcissism
available is in the political arena. The infamous nineteenth-century
African warrior King Shaka Zulu, who achieved considerable
advances in his effort to create a great nation, illuminates the dark
side of leadership.

trop gâté: lors de l'assemblée générale houleuse qui a précédé sa chute, Jean-
Marie Messier, furieux d'avoir vu son projet d'accorder des stocks-options aux
dirigeants du groupe retoqué par une fronde d'actionnaire, avait entamé des
procédures d'annulation de l'AG, arguant que les votes étaient sûrement truqués.'
Peter Covel, Le Cordelier, 25 June 2004.

When we examine the early life of this terrifying Zulu—a man who's still held in awe in his home country—we find ample explanation for his narcissism. An unwanted child, he was expelled from his parents' tribe. Terrorized by other children, he became lonely and bitter and quickly learned to defend himself fiercely. His fighting skills brought him to the attention of a local king, who became the young man's mentor. Under this king's guidance, Shaka Zulu became the successful leader of a small Zulu tribe at the edge of the kingdom. When his mentor was killed, Shaka Zulu stepped in as his successor.

During his years as king, Shaka transformed his people's ritualistic fighting technique, introducing a deadly new stabbing spear (the assegai), an improved shield, and a devastating new form of attack. He hardened his warriors for combat, improving their endurance and success rate. In a long campaign, Shaka conquered tribe after tribe and established a large kingdom in what's now Kwazulu-Natal in South Africa. He terrorized not only those tribes not under his rule, but also his own subjects, who lived under the permanent threat of impalement (or whatever other cruel form of execution their king might choose). During Shaka Zulu's brutal reign, around 2 million people lost their lives. By virtue of military strength, persuasive religious ritual, and an effective secret service, Shaka ruled until 1828. His family members finally led a conspiracy against him, which ended in the despot's murder at the age of 41 [15].

The psychological consequences of a conflict-ridden childhood and youth go a long way toward explaining Shaka's excessive reactive narcissistic behavior, complete with vindictiveness and vengefulness, paranoia, delusions of persecution, excessive pride, feelings of rage, and an inability to develop intimate relationships. Furthermore, we can draw clear parallels between Shaka's behavior and that of other, more contemporary despotic leaders, including Hitler, Stalin, Pol Pot, Kim Jong Il, and Saddam Hussein.

As these leadership examples illustrate—Messier on a lesser scale and Shaka on a more grandiose scale—the possession of unlimited power has a negative transforming effect. In workplaces around the world, even the mildest narcissists seize the opportunity, when it presents itself, to reincarnate themselves as living gods. In that transformation, they lose the ability to distinguish between fantasy and reality. Like Messier and Shaka Zulu, reactive narcissists who head companies are preoccupied with glory, power, status, and prestige. Restless and bored when they're not in the limelight, they're flagrant attention-seekers [16]. They live in a world of instant gratification, exhibiting excesses of pomposity, arrogance, envy, greed, rage, and vindictiveness in dealing with the external environment. Their disregard for rules and the conventions of social structure leads them to engage in unethical behavior, while their tendency to blame others if things go wrong leads to a culture of fear.

The excitement generated by a charismatic narcissistic leader is temporary; it easily wears off. Too often, and too soon, the dark side of narcissistic leadership behavior overshadows the initial benefits. Narcissistic leaders frequently reveal a lack of conviction and a tendency to resort to political expediency at the cost of long-term goals. Actions that were originally interpreted as bold and imaginative are gradually exposed as short-term opportunism. Their inability to accept criticism or the free exchange of ideas, their self-righteousness and self-centeredness, their poor problem-solving, and their inability to compromise impair organizational functioning and prevent organizational adaptation to internal and external changes. In extreme cases this sends the organization into a downward spiral.

One of a leader's most important roles is to address the emotional needs of his or her subordinates. Leaders at Messier's and Shaka Zulu's extreme end of the reactive narcissism spectrum are unable to handle this. They disregard their subordinates' dependency needs and take advantage of their loyalty. This narcissistic attitude encourages submissiveness and passive dependency in subordinates, stifling their critical functions and their reality-testing skills. Narcissists' lack of commitment to others, their blithe discarding of subordinates who no longer serve a selfish purpose, their narrow self-interests, and their search for new alliances preclude a creative, innovative organizational culture. Indeed, these traits practically guarantee organizational self-destruction.

LOST IN SPACE: INTRODUCING THE T-WORD

In order to understand how the psychopathology of relationships between narcissistic individuals and others works, we have to grasp the concept of transference, introduced in the previous chapter. Transference is the name that psychoanalysts use for a patient's present-day repetition of childlike ways of relating that were learned in early life. The unconscious redirection of feelings from one person to another, transference results in emotional confusion regarding time and place [17]–[18]. In essence, it suggests that no relationship is a new relationship; every relationship one experiences is colored by the nature of previous relationships.

During analysis, the patient begins to transfer thoughts and feelings connected with parents, siblings, or other influential figures in their life to the therapist. For example, a patient who is hostile toward his father may experience that same hostility in exchanges with his therapist; a patient who is loving toward her mother may feel a parallel version of that love for her therapist. Recognizing and discussing transference helps the patient gain insight into the ways he or she relates to other people in present life.

Although the word transference conjures up images of the analyst's couch, it's a phenomenon that all of us are familiar with: all of us act out transferential (or historical) reactions on a daily basis, regardless of what we do. Understanding the process of transference is critical to being able to understand the nature of the leader-follower interface. Executives arguing in the boardroom over issues of corporate strategy are unconsciously still dealing with parental figures and siblings over issues of power. The subordinate whose inability to listen reminds the CEO of his father, or the colleague whose unpredictability reminds another executive of her mother, inspires in the adult the same feelings that those particular people inspired in the child. The psychological imprints of our early caregivers—particularly our parents—cause this time-place confusion and make us act toward others in the present as if they were significant people from the past. These imprints stay with us and guide our interactions throughout our lives.

Two important subtypes of transferential pattern are especially common in the workplace: mirroring and idealizing [16]. These traits are important to our discussion here because they're often exaggerated in reactive narcissists. Let's look at each in turn:

Mirroring. It's said that the first mirror a baby looks into is its mother's face. Starting with that first mirror, the process of mirroring—taking our cues about being and behaving from those around us—becomes an ongoing aspect of our daily lives and our relationships with others. Within organizations, the mirroring process between leaders and followers can become collusive. Followers use leaders to reflect what they want to see, and leaders rarely resist that kind of affirmation. The result is a mutual admiration society. Leaders who are fully paid up members tend to take actions designed to shore up their image rather than serve the needs of the organization. In times of rapid change, embedded mirroring processes can be fatal to organizations. When things change quickly, we all need to be able to face the new reality and evolve quickly to meet developing challenges.

Idealizing. We all idealize people important to us, beginning with our first caretakers, assigning powerful imagery to them. Through this idealizing process, we hope to combat feelings of helplessness and acquire some of the power of the person admired. Idealizing transference is a kind of protective shield for followers. Reactive narcissists are especially responsive to this sort of admiration, often becoming so dependent on it that they can't function without the emotional fix. It's a two-way street, of course: followers project their fantasies onto their leaders, and leaders mirror themselves in the glow of their followers. The result for leaders who are reactive narcissists—and the Messier case is a good example of this—is that the combination of disposition and position wreaks havoc on reality-testing: affected leaders are happy to find themselves in a hall of mirrors that lets them see only what they want to see. In this world of illusion, the boundaries that define normal work processes disappear, at least for the entitled leader, who has nothing to restrain him or her from acting inappropriately, irresponsibly, or even unethically. Any follower who challenges the leader's behavior risks triggering a tantrum.

A close relative of transference is a defensive maneuver known as identification with the aggressor. When faced with an aggressive leader, followers become anxious. To overcome that anxiety, some followers resort to a defensive process known as identification with the aggressor. When people find themselves in the presence of a superior force with the power to do unpleasant things to them, they feel a strong incentive to become like that superior force, as a form of protection against future aggression [15]; [19]. In full-fledged identification with the aggressor, individuals impersonate the aggressor, assuming the latter's attributes and gradually moving from being threatened to making (and carrying out) threats. The more extreme the actions of the leader, the more aggressive the self-defense has to be—and the more tempting it is for subjects to strengthen themselves by becoming part of the system and sharing the aggressor's power.

Although people who identified with the aggressor were the backbone of the security forces of leaders such as Shaka Zulu, Adolf Hitler, and Saddam Hussein, they can also be found skulking around the water coolers in offices headed by reactive narcissists. For them, the organizational world is starkly black and white. People are either for or against their leader. Those who hesitate or refuse to collaborate become the new villains, providing fresh targets for the leader's (and loyal followers') anger. Supporters help to deal with the leader's enemies and thus share his or her guilt for any wrongdoing—a guilt that can be endlessly fed with new scapegoats, the designated villains on whom the group exacts revenge whenever things go wrong. These scapegoats fulfill an important function: they're a point of reference on which to project everything people fear, everything perceived as bad or threatening.

DOWNSIZING THE NARCISSIST

Given the number of grandiose, vain, and greedy senior executives we have all known, it's clear that many boards of directors haven't been as effective as they could have been. While on rare occasions a board will act to disempower a narcissistic leader who's harming the organization, board members generally fail to recognize the danger signs associated with narcissistic behavior and with psychological pressures on the CEO. But organizations need not be helpless in the face of reactive narcissistic leadership. They can take action, both preemptive and follow-up. Strategies include distributing decision-making and erecting barriers against runaway leadership; improving the selection, education, and evaluation of board members; and offering coaching and counseling to executives showing signs of excessive narcissism.

The first strategy, distributing decision-making and erecting barriers against runaway leadership, is best effected through structural mechanisms—a system of leadership checks-and-balances. This entails clearly and specifically detailing the roles of the CEO and the board. Combining the roles of CEO and chairman in one person is an invitation to disaster. There are very few leaders who can resist the siren call of this sort of power.

The second strategy focuses on those who work closely with the CEO. Organizations that want to avoid the dangers of narcissistic leadership must have structures in place to guide the selection, education, and evaluation of board members. These men and women must be taught to recognize the danger signs associated with potentially destructive narcissistic behavior and be willing to tighten the reins if the CEO pulls away. Latent narcissistic tendencies suppressed by a young, high-potential executive on the way up the career ladder are likely to blossom when that person reaches his or her ultimate goal and the pressures from peers and superiors lose their power. The power of high office can make a monster out of someone who has hitherto seemed a very reasonable human being. Even constructive narcissists can go astray, though reactive narcissists are far more susceptible. Thus board members need to be on guard against collusion between predisposition and position and draw boundaries—dismissal of the CEO being the ultimate sanction—when executive behavior warrants it.

Organizations must also establish systems of accountability to encourage the participation of employees and shareholders in corporate decision-making, thereby balancing the power equation.

Actively involved shareholders, particularly institutional investors, will help solve many corporate challenges. This sort of structuring can prevent the emergence of extreme oligarchic corporate structures, in which CEOs completely control the agenda and manage (in the US at least) to be paid 500 times as much as their lowest-paid employee. Corporations that establish such countervailing powers are better equipped to create wealth and compete in global markets.

The third strategy typically comes into play only when narcissistic behavior has already been detected in an executive: offering counseling and coaching. While the wisdom of experienced board members can often modify potentially destructive behavior, a board that feels unequal to the task can turn to professional help (see Chapters 10 and 11). Unfortunately, few reactive narcissists are willing to accept professional help. Part of their self-delusion is that they're able to solve their problems by themselves.

If they do accept professional help, it will probably be because of personal pain, not board pressure. The weight of the typical symptoms—dissatisfaction with life, feelings of futility, a lack of purpose, a sense of being fraudulent, the absence of meaningful relationships, a lack of excitement at work, the inability to step out of their routines, mood swings, and hypochondria—may finally become too much. Frequently, however, the motivation is a major life event such as separation, divorce, or a significant professional setback, sometimes in conjunction with depression. It's important to recognize what these complaints represent, because they're the foundations on which individuals and organizations can build a change effort.

Since narcissists fail to take personal responsibility for their failures, intervention by a coach or psychotherapist is likely to be an uphill struggle. Narcissists see others as the source of all their problems, and the sense of personal infallibility exhibited by excessive narcissists is difficult to change. Such individuals can be masterfully seductive at inducing the therapist/leadership coach into their own mutual admiration society, attempting, sometimes successfully, to persuade him or her that the problem isn't their responsibility.

Another hindrance to psychological intervention is the narcissist's hypersensitivity to negative feedback. Even constructive feedback is perceived as humiliating criticism. Narcissistic individuals need to learn to tolerate constructive feedback about their behavior and actions. They need time to realize that most human imperfections aren't catastrophic. And they need time to learn to become more sensitive about the feelings of others, become more willing to seek out cooperative forms of social behavior, and understand that reaching out to others can be gratifying.

The key challenges for the psychoanalyst, psychotherapist or leadership coach are to enable such people to recognize their own responsibility, regardless of the mess they find themselves in, and to make them aware of the primitive defensive processes they're engaged in. Narcissists have to understand the destructive nature of their defensive behavior and reduce their reliance on infantile fantasies of power and glory. They need to be helped to construct more realistic, attainable fantasies that help to build self-esteem. There's no quick fix for the trauma of having been deceived, exploited, or manipulated at some critical early developmental period. Healing is a lengthy and difficult process. Psychopharmacological intervention may be needed to ward off depressive feelings.

In *The Seven Pillars of Wisdom*, T. E. Lawrence wrote: "All men dream: but not equally. Those who dream by night in the dusty recesses of their minds wake in the day to find that it was vanity: but the dreamers of the day are dangerous men, for they may act their dream with open eyes, to make it possible." If narcissistic behavior can be channeled into more positive directions, it can be the motor that drives a successful organization. If not, employees and shareholders, along with the defeated narcissist, may pay the price in disillusionment and broken dreams.

REFERENCES

1. Giovacchini, P. (2000). *Impact of Narcissism*. Nortvale, NJ, Jason Aronson.
2. Kernberg, O. (1975). *Borderline Conditions and Pathological Narcissism*. New York, Aronson.
3. Kets de Vries, M. F. R. (1989). *Prisoners of Leadership*. New York, John Wiley & Sons, Inc.
4. Kohut, H. (1985). *Self Psychology and the Humanities*. New York, W.W. Norton.
5. Masterson, J. F. (1988). *The Search for the Real Self: Unmasking the Personality Disorders of our Age*. New York, Free Press.
6. Kohut, H. (1971). *The Analysis of the Self*. New York, International Universities Press.
7. Emde, R. N. (1981). "Changing Models of Infancy and the Nature of Early Development: Remodelling the Foundation." Journal of the American Psychoanalytical Association 29: 179–219.
8. Erikson, E. H. (1963). *Childhood and Society*. New York, W.W. Norton & Society.
9. Kagan, J. and H. A. Moss (1983). *Birth to Maturity: A Study in Psychological Development*. New Haven, Yale University Press.
10. Winnicott, D. W. (1975). *Through Paediatrics to Psycho-Analysis*. New York, Basic Books.
11. McDougall, J. (1985). *Theaters of the Mind*. New York, Basic Books.
12. Freud, S. (1917). *A Childhood Collection from Dichtung und Wahrheit. The Standard Edition of the Complete Psychological Works of Sigmund Freud, Vol 17*. J. Strachey (editor and translator). London, The Hogarth Press and the Institute of Psychoanalysis.
13. American Psychiatric Association (2004). *Diagnostic and statistical manual of the mental disorders: DSM-IV-Tr*. Arlington, VA, American Psychiatric Association.
14. Johnson, J. and M. Orange (2003). *The Man who Tried to Buy the World*. New York, Portfolio.
15. Kets de Vries, M. F. R. (2004). *Lessons on Leadership by Terror: Finding Shaka Zulu in the Attic*. London, Edgar Allen.
16. Kets de Vries, M. F. R. and S. Perzow (1991). *Handbook of Character Studies*. New York, International University Press.

17. Breuer, J. and S. Freud (1895). *Studies on Hysteria. The Standard Edition of the Complete Psychological Works of Sigmund Freud, Vol 2.* J. Strachey (editor and translator). London, Hogarth Press and the Institute of Psychoanalysis. 3–311.
18. Etchegoyen, R. H. (1991). *The Fundamentals of Psychoanalytic Technique.* London, Karnac Books.
19. Freud, A. (1966). *The Ego and the Mechanisms of Defense.* Madison, Conn., International Universities Press.

CHAPTER 3

A PARADE OF
PERSONALITIES

I told the doctor I was overtired, anxiety-ridden, compulsively active, constantly depressed, with recurring fits of paranoia. Turns out I'm normal.

—Jules Feiffer

If from infancy you treat children as gods they are liable in adulthood to act like devils.

—P. D. James

To be normal is the ideal aim of the unsuccessful.

—Carl Gustav Jung

Be master of mind rather than mastered by mind.

—Zen Proverb

There's a Zen story of a frog that was swimming happily in a river, minding his own business. Suddenly, he heard a voice calling out to him. Swimming toward the sound, the frog saw a scorpion standing on the riverbank. The scorpion said, "I need to get across the river. Please give me a ride." The frog was skeptical. "I know your type," he said. "Scorpions sting. How do I know you won't kill me if I try to help you?" The scorpion said, "Why would I do that? If I kill you, I'll die too, because I can't swim."

This made sense to the frog, and he agreed to take the scorpion across the river. The scorpion crawled on to the frog's back and the frog slid into the water. But halfway across the river, the frog suddenly felt a sharp sting in his back and, out of the corner of his eye, saw the scorpion remove his stinger. "You fool!" the frog croaked. "Now we'll both die! Why on earth did you do that?"

"I couldn't help myself," the scorpion admitted. "It's my character."

A QUESTION OF CHARACTER

Character is the sum of the deeply ingrained patterns of behavior that define an individual. The word character derives from the Greek word meaning "engraving." Our character, sometimes referred to as our personality, is what distinguishes us from others; it's the stamp impressed on us by nature and nurture that defines who we really are [1]–[9]. It's a composite of the habits that we choose and develop, but that gradually come to drive us. There's a saying that warns, Watch your thoughts; they become your words. Watch your words; they become your actions. Watch your actions; they become your habits. Watch your habits; they become your character. Watch your character; it will become your destiny. And that's not always good: as August Strindberg once said, "Man with a so-called character is often a simple piece of mechanism; he has often only one point of view for the extremely complicated relationships of life."

Some students of psychology take pains to distinguish character from personality, maintaining that the former encompasses the deep, underlying structures that make a person distinctive, while personality involves only visible, superficial behavior. The term character often has moral connotations that personality lacks: we talk about someone having a "good" or "bad" character, for example. Certainly there's ample opportunity for confusion between the terms. In this chapter, however, character and personality are used interchangeably to signify the same thing.

Character, or personality, is central to the way people perceive themselves and to the way they present themselves in a public setting. As Carl Jung once said, "Personality is the supreme realization of the innate idiosyncrasy of a living being." Personality determines motivation and ambition and dictates the way a person relates to his or her internal and external world. It colors the nature and quality of one's relationships with others and influences the way each person pursues his or her goals in life. Personality shapes ideals, values, beliefs, patterns of information-processing, and leadership style. It also affects a person's moral compass—that amalgam of moral, ethical, and motivational principles that guides an individual through life. The above-quoted saying is probably correct: character is destiny.

As we saw in Chapter 2, early experiences influence the development of an individual's emerging psychological structures and create personality traits—constant and long-lasting aspects of an individual's way of functioning. Although the genesis of behavior, emotions, attitudes, and defense mechanisms can be traced back to infancy, personality traits tend to become more prominent in adolescence or early adulthood. They persist throughout life and affect every aspect of everyday behavior. And they do so rather predictably: specific personality types are associated with certain belief systems and behavior patterns and distinctive leadership styles.

As the years go by and a person matures, some personality traits may cause interpersonal problems. Common traits such as stinginess, generosity, vindictiveness, arrogance, and independence pervade a wide range of personal and social situations, and they're generally little more than a nuisance. If one or more of these traits become rigid and self-defeating, however, they can impair social and professional functioning. When that's the case, we say that a person suffers from a character or personality disorder—that is, he or she experiences inflexible behavior patterns that cause internal distress and significantly impair day-to-day functioning. Generally, though, these traits and behaviors are egosyntonic, meaning that they're such an intrinsic part of the personality that they're invisible to their "owner."

Those who study character look at it in a number of different ways. One group of researchers takes the construct-centered or nomothetic perspective [10]. They look at character in an abstract sense, not as grounded in the behavior of any particular person. Typically they formulate a categorical typology such as paranoid or compulsive to help clinicians make quick assessments of the way a particular individual is functioning. But categories, unfortunately, have limitations: because they tend to be fixed, they limit the number of slots into which a person can fit. As a result, strange, infrequent, or hybrid conditions have to be excluded, since they don't fit the prescribed categories.

Some researchers who object to the restrictions of the construct-centered approach favor what's called a dimensional trait profile approach. This option, which allows for a greater degree of flexibility in looking at people, looks for an underlying logic in how character traits are expressed in the external world. It sets up axes such as active/passive and self/other and then profiles an individual against those axes: Is the subject inclined to take initiative in shaping the events in his or her life, for example, or does the subject prefer to simply respond to events (active/passive)? Is the subject's emotional energy directed toward the self or toward others (self/other)? The trait approach assumes that character is built on basic behavioral matrixes such as these, which ultimately determine a person's unique imprint on the external world.

There are a number of problems with the trait approach, however. The first is how to arrive at agreement about which traits to include. There's no easy answer to this dilemma; trait theorists disagree strenuously about the nature and number of traits needed to represent a person adequately. Furthermore, there's the temptation to create configurations of traits that look suspiciously like categories—and lo and behold, the trait theorists have paradoxically arrived at the very sort of categorization their method is designed to avoid.

But whether they talk about categories or traits, any sensitive researcher, psychotherapist, or leadership coach realizes that people are far too complex to be summarized in a simple personality description. Furthermore, labeling people can be a weapon of denigration. To quote Jean Paul Sartre, "Once you label me, you defeat me." And, in any case, taxonomies provide only provisional answers at best. They're just a starting point for describing an individual and must be modified when more evidence becomes available.

Proponents of the ideographic approach take such warnings about all forms of taxonomy seriously. While the nomothetic and trait approaches ask what general observations can be made about a person, the ideographic approach asks how the person has become the unique individual he or she is and emphasizes the individual complexity and uniqueness of each person. Because every person is special (the argument goes), nobody can be understood through abstract, universal laws or by measuring dimensions of individual difference. To understand personality properly, a rich developmental approach is needed, one that reflects the person's own previous history—a biographical approach, if you will. The main drawback to the ideographic approach is that, in rejecting any form of taxonomy, it creates an indefinite number of possibilities.

I would argue that both the nomothetic and the ideographic extremes are unsatisfactory. While the nomothetic perspective fails to take into account the uniqueness of each individual, the ideographic perspective fails to consider the need for individual comparisons. I favor a variant of the nomothetic approach, looking at personality in the form of general prototypes—constructs that are flexible, without discrete boundaries [5]; [11]. A prototype delineates the most common features of people within a specific category—for example, within the category of people who are drawn to others we find the dramatic, controlling, dependent, and self-defeating prototypes. It describes a theoretical construct and establishes a standard to which others can be compared. No person matches a prototype perfectly, of course; people simply approximate one prototype (or two or even more prototypes) over others, to varying degrees. Thus prototypes are conceptual anchoring points around which facts and observations about specific individuals can cluster. They're clinical points of departure, heuristic devices used to impose order in a highly complex area by interweaving categorical and dimensional propositions.

ASSESSING LEADERS AND FOLLOWERS

It's difficult to construct a yardstick by which to judge the personality styles of leaders and followers. Personality traits that would be considered aberrant in ordinary circumstances may be essential ingredients of success for someone in a leadership or follower role. Some organizations are themselves dysfunctional, and people with highly dysfunctional dispositions can flourish in them while "normal" people would be consumed. Nevertheless it is useful to examine various styles of leading and following and attempt to conclude which offer people the greatest chance of success.

Everyone, including both leaders and followers within organizations, is engaged in a metaphorical form of theater, as I noted earlier. This theater follows specific scripts based on imagined, desired, and feared relationships between the individual and his or her significant others, both past and present. These core conflictual relationship themes, introduced in Chapter 1, profoundly influence affective and cognitive states and behavior and sometimes contribute to specific collusive relationships [12]. In these "stage activities," patterns of the past are reenacted in the present. To quote the psychoanalyst Joyce McDougall:

> Each secret-theatre self is . . . engaged in repeatedly playing roles from the past, using techniques discovered in childhood and reproducing, with uncanny precision, the same tragedies and comedies, with the same outcomes and an identical quota of pain and pleasure. What were once attempts at self-cure in the face of mental pain and conflict are now symptoms that the adult I produces following forgotten childhood solutions [13] p. 7.

Studying prototypes and analysing personality invites us to look beneath the surface and make inferences about the origin of these patterns of behavior.

The *Diagnostic and Statistical Manual of Mental Disorders* (DSM-IV-Tr) [1], published by the American Psychiatric Association, is more specific about these stage activities, and classifies different personality syndromes as a number of prototypes, according to their various distinguishing characteristics. What follows in this and the next two chapters is a brief look at some of these prototypes, largely, but not solely, based on DSM-IV-Tr. One of the DSM-IV-Tr prototypes, the narcissistic type (a self-contained prototype), I considered so important to the study of leadership that I devoted Chapter 2 to it.

For purposes of illustration and clarity, I will present fairly extreme versions of the different prototypes I deal with—that is, dysfunctional versions. Remember, though, that prototypes aren't depictions of mental disorders: each one includes the entire range of human behavior, from normal to dysfunctional, because normality and pathology are relative concepts, positions on a spectrum. Furthermore, as I said earlier, most people are hybrids, showing a mixture of the various styles, with no single style dominating to any significant extent. The prototypes, then, should be seen as useful forms of shorthand that help the reader see certain elements of personality that are often not immediately identifiable.

In describing these personality prototypes, I will expand the descriptions given in DSM-IV-Tr and refer to elements such as behavior, emotion, defensive structure, intrapsychic organization, and development, examining how effective or ineffective each style can be in an organizational setting. DSM-IV-Tr doesn't offer an exhaustive listing of personality constructs. The listing it includes was a political compromise about prototypes arrived at among psychiatrists and psychologists from many different backgrounds and disciplines. In addition, some acknowledged concepts were excluded from the listing because the psychiatric task force studying the concepts decided that some weren't sufficiently well defined to meet increasingly rigorous standards of definition and thus didn't warrant a full-blown classification in the manual. I have included a few of these, believing that certain behavior patterns are hard to pin down precisely because they're so covert, common, and widely variable.

The prototypes presented in the DSM-IV-Tr fit into a relational matrix. Generally, individuals favor one of four broad ways of relating to others: moving toward people, moving away from people, and moving against people [14], and finally narcissistic types, as discussed in the previous chapter, move against people, though they do so out of the wish that others would move toward them. Several personality prototypes fit within each way of relating. The remainder of this chapter looks at people within the first relational mode: people who are driven to move toward others. Though such individuals share a great need for attention and affection, they fall into four different prototypes: dramatic, controlling, dependent, and self-defeating. We will start with the dramatic disposition.

THE DRAMATIC DISPOSITION

Anne Murphy[1] had just been appointed senior account executive in a stellar advertising firm. This was a surprise to many of her colleagues, who thought she lacked the discipline to hold down a senior position and felt that she had already progressed in the company as far as she ever would—or should. Although good at selling herself, she made client presentations that were vague and superficial to the point of being incoherent, she had been known to deal unprofessionally with major clients, and she seemed to lack the powers of logic necessary to assess and address complex situations.

This tough assessment of Anne was consistent with her colleagues' early opinions of her. Almost from the first, she had been considered strong on impressions but weak on details, facts, plans, and logic. For example, the summaries she prepared of important discussions were so void of substance that it was difficult for others to move from the summaries to a specific action plan; her poor attention to detail made collaboration with colleagues difficult; and she forgot important facts so often that her colleagues had grown tired of covering for her.

Easily influenced by other people and the latest fads, Anne tended to play hunches and experiment with off-the-wall convictions. She was also highly volatile: one minute she would be smiling and perhaps excited; the next she would erupt into tearful sadness. She seemed desperate for attention and approval; no amount of acknowledgment ever seemed enough for her. When she didn't receive the approbation she was hoping for, she dropped her superficial charm and became rude and condescending. These shifting moods left people close to her hurt, bewildered, and repelled. Now that she had been given a more responsible role in

---

[1] All names in this book, unless otherwise indicated, have been changed to preserve anonymity.

the firm and her deficiencies had become more noticeable, many people concluded that it was safer to maintain some distance from her.

So why, despite these shortcomings, was she still on board? There were several reasons: she was able to create a strong first impression, she was good at winging it in the absence of facts and figures, and—most important—she thrived on the excitement and glamour of advertising, and was genuinely likeable. She was sociable, made friends easily, frequently went out of her way to help others, and worked to build a positive atmosphere in the office. Despite these social skills, Anne appeared to have acquaintances rather than friends: most of her relationships were relatively superficial. She seemed to draw the attention of men more than women, displaying a seductive behavior that seemed unconscious. This occasionally caused awkward and embarrassing incidents, though she was quick to cut short any advances prompted by her flirtations.

Dramatics like Anne follow a pervasive pattern of excessive emotionality and attention-seeking, and are driven by a desperate need to be in the spotlight at any cost. They actively solicit the interest of others and are uncomfortable in situations where they aren't the center of the action. Although they're outgoing, talkative, convivial, affectionate, energetic, and vigorous—all very positive characteristics—their behavior becomes problematic when the needs that generate the behavior are inflexible, repetitive, and persistent.

Typically, dramatics are some combination of the following:

- keenly alive to others' desires and moods
- unable to concentrate or focus on events
- very gullible and thus easily taken advantage of
- constantly in search of support, reassurance, and protection
- easily hurt, with a fragile sense of self-esteem
- extremely sensitive to criticism or disapproval

- exploitative of their personal attractiveness
- inclined to fantasize
- involved in superficial, short-term relationships
- intolerant of delay, frustration, and disappointment
- continually setting themselves up for failure, rejection, and frustration
- capricious, shallow, and insincere

Because dramatics focus on superficialities, they invest little time and attention in their internal life. As a result, they know themselves very little and thus often have no sense of who they are outside their identification with others. They're like chameleons, changing their attitudes and values to fit the views of significant others in their lives. Their intense observation skills are dedicated to determining what behavior, attitudes, or feelings are most likely to win other people's admiration and approval.

All too often, dramatics experience themselves as small, fearful, and deficient children who have to cope in a world dominated by powerful others. Because of this perspective, they feel absolved from responsibility for their behavior and feel entitled to be manipulative in order to force attention and caretaking on the part of others. This disposition occurs more in women than in men, although some therapists believe it's simply more often diagnosed in women because attention-secking and sexual forwardness are less socially acceptable in women.

Family environment and early relationships are nearly always at the root of dramatics' fragile self-perception and excessive need for attention. Something in their early parent-child interface created an exaggerated need for attention. Perhaps they had difficulty capturing the attention and affection of their parents while growing up. Their parents might, for example, have given the bulk of their attention to another sibling or been too busy with each other or with work. If neglected for whatever reason, they would have learned to adopt seductive strategies to secure parental attention, a way of acting that gradually became a lifelong pattern. Alternatively, perhaps they had to deal with a parent's constant dissatisfaction—attention, to be sure, but of the wrong kind. Or perhaps they had a parent who treated them as an extension of him- or herself. Children dealing with these sorts of parents typically make heroic efforts to get their attention or to appease them. Normally either ignored or punished, they find that only theatrical behavior elicits a different, sometimes positive, reaction.

When children grow up in this sort of family, they become uncertain about themselves. They present a false self to the outside world (see Chapter 14). Used to being whatever the circumstances call for, they can't identify their true feelings or their likes, dislikes, beliefs, and values. Eventually, unconsciously, they conclude that only attention-seeking behavior elicits parental approval. The broader message they absorb is that they're appreciated, cared for, and affirmed only for what they do; they aren't loved for who they are. Having failed to internalize a strong sense of who they are and what they stand for, they can't develop a realistic understanding of themselves, their own true strengths and weaknesses.

Given this poor sense of themselves, dramatics are unable to enter into deep relationships and make lasting commitments—and yet they need relationships badly, however superficial these relationships may be. Dramatics can't be alone without feeling anxious and abandoned.

THE DRAMATIC INDIVIDUAL WITHIN THE ORGANIZATION

Because they're dependent on the affirmation of others, people with a dramatic disposition suppress any urge to be assertive, argumentative, or aggressive toward authority figures. On the contrary, they respond very positively to anyone in a position of power, expecting him or her to offer magical solutions to their problems. When interacting with people they look up to, dramatics are engaging, responsive, and enthusiastic, frequently telling their mentors how wonderful, effective, and competent they are. This characteristic is typically rated positively in a work setting.

Dramatic people can be very successful in organizations, in part because they're often quite ambitious. They're particularly effective in situations where impression management is important and where the general expression of ideas is more important than precision. They're very likeable, with considerable charm and enthusiasm, which makes other people initially want to work with them. They're less effective, however, in situations where performance is measured by competence, diligence, thoroughness, and depth. Their limited attention span can mean that they under-achieve, failing to fulfill their intellectual or artistic potential. Because they're easily bored and frustrated, they may go through frequent job changes. Dramatics typically do well in fields such as acting, marketing, politics, and the arts, at times even reaching leadership positions. But because they often fail to see their own situation realistically, they're more likely to be followers than leaders.

THE CONTROLLING DISPOSITION

Gustav Krupp von Bohlen und Halbach, took on the name Krupp when he married the sole heiress of the Krupp fortune—Bertha, the "Cannon Queen". In doing so he gained a company as well as a woman. As leader of Krupp, the giant German armaments company, he developed a style that could best be compared to a machine. He was the ultimate martinet. After becoming Bertha's consort, he embraced like a long-lost friend the Generalregulativ, a compilation of regulations written and introduced by his forceful predecessor. This "constitution" described in unusual detail the rights and responsibilities of all his workers: the Kruppianer. For a man whose vacation pastime was reading railway timetables, this passion for the Generalregulativ was not surprising. His love for recordkeeping and his fascination with his stopwatch were unsurpassed. In Gustav's mind, trivia trumped substance, and ritual was more important than content, ethics, and morality. The keynote of his personality was the expectation of obedience: the obedience of the Kruppianer to the letter of the Generalregulativ and his own blind obedience to the idea of what the House of Krupp stood for. He had a similar misguided attitude toward Adolf Hitler. His company became infamous for its use of slave labor during World War II.

A good illustration of Krupp's preoccupation with regulation is found in William Manchester's *The Arms of Krupp*:

> Visitors weren't allowed to come in their own cars; their chauffeurs might be lax. Under the regulation drill, his drivers dropped them off the main entrance at 1:29 p.m. At 1:30 they entered the reception room to chat with Gustav and Bertha until 1:40, when they were led into the dining room. The moment Krupp finished a course, servants removed all plates from the table; poky and garrulous eaters were left hungry. The meal ended at 2:15, coffee at 2:29. At 2:30 on the dot, the guests stepped into the waiting limousines and were driven away. Nothing was left to chance, including the temperature of the coffee, which might have thrown everything out of whack and which, therefore, was never too hot [15], p. 287.

There are many men and women like Krupp in leadership roles in organizations today. Here is another example:

Michael Fisher, the managing director of one of the divisions of a large consumer products company, was labeled by the other members of the executive committee as a control freak. Initially, he was quite successful at building up the European operations, in spite of being very difficult to deal with. After a successful start, however, stagnation set in and his division was no longer growing. Any suggestions by the other board members for ways to change the situation fell on deaf ears. Michael saw all advice as an intrusion into his fiefdom and rejected it out of hand.

If he had listened to the grumblings of his colleagues, he would have learned that several people thought he was unable to handle and develop his people, and they saw that as the cause of his division's stagnation. Michael tended to micromanage his employees, letting them know—in no uncertain terms—when he felt that they had made a mistake. As a result, some of his best people had quit or had asked for a transfer. He dealt in the same manner with his peers. At board meetings, for example, Michael was relentless in demanding his way. At every occasion, he tried to set the agenda, deciding what actions should be taken or not. He seemed to have a driving need to run the show and call the shots. Many meetings ended in stalemate, because Michael was unwilling to bend. He often got his way, though, because the chairman of the company was conflict-avoidant.

The central theme in the life of Gustav Krupp von Bohlen und Halbach and Michael Fisher was control. That theme rules a large part of the working population. People with a controlling disposition want the world to be an ordered, disciplined place where everything is predictable. Their urge to control everything that affects their lives is a way of managing their hostile feelings toward those who controlled them in the past. That hostility, if not transmuted into submission, becomes tyranny.

Emotional and cognitive rigidity are the hallmarks of people with a controlling disposition. Common characteristics among this group are orderliness, parsimoniousness, obstinacy, rigidity, and perseverance. Rules and regulations, whether of their own devising or of others', help controllers to create an orderly world. They fear that the world will fall apart if they don't follow the highest standards at all times or if the rules aren't obeyed. Having learned early on in life that breaking the rules and regulations brings displeasure, they know that ideology and correctness come before love and loyalty.

Typically, people with a controlling disposition are:

- rigid, inflexible, and lacking in spontaneity
- stubborn
- excessively judgmental and moralistic
- self-punitive and self-denigrating
- grim, tense, joyless, angry, frustrated, irritable
- uncomfortable with emotions
- fearful of making mistakes
- easily lost in detail
- tense, inhibited, and reserved
- unduly conventional, serious, and formal

People with a controlling disposition are caught in a permanent struggle between obedience and defiance, a troubling unresolved conflict instilled by parental over-control. From childhood onward they were taught that the only good way to handle their rebellious urges was to become conforming and submissive; they had to live up to parental expectations or risk condemnation. When growing up, they were subjected to daily scrutiny and given feedback in a cold manner that was apparently unloving and unsupportive. Ironically, over-controlling parents may in fact be genuinely caring, determined to keep their child safe no matter what. However, their manner of expressing that care is to keep the child strictly in line, with punitive measures used as necessary. No good can come, they think, from the physical and emotional expression of tender feelings toward others. They use shame and guilt to enforce cooperation, with positive reinforcement contingent on following the rules. Typically they run their household like a tight ship—and the appearance of the house reflects this, well-maintained and fanatically tidy.

The growing child in this sort of household learns quickly to operate within the approved boundaries set by the parents. Fearful of deviating or taking initiative, dreading the sanctions that will follow if they step out of line, they're on a constant quest for perfection to obtain parental approval. Later, as adults, they still live under the persistent fear of making a mistake and being accused of imperfection. They always feel that they could do better, or do more. They're obsessed with "shoulds" and "musts" and the need to drive themselves harder. The internalized image of harsh, judgmental parents is ever-present, haunting them and feeding a punitive inner conscience. Strong feelings of guilt, self-criticism, irritation, and resentment are the inevitable legacies of over-controlling child-rearing.

Many of the characteristics of the controlling disposition—achievement orientation, high standards, strong moral principles, prudence, thrift, caution, a desire to do things properly, a sense of responsibility—are positive attributes. They help people move forward in life and contribute to successful careers. But the pendulum can easily swing too far, at which point the need for control becomes too much of a good thing. Industriousness and efficiency give way to rigidity and inflexibility, characteristics that sabotage true effectiveness. Likewise, the excessive emotional control that holding the pendulum in this balance demands can be a serious handicap in the world of work and their personal life.

Because keeping the pendulum in line—managing the unresolved struggle between obedience and defiance—takes so much energy, people with a controlling disposition resort to psychological defenses—for example, intellectualization/isolation of affect, reaction formation, displacement, and sublimation as follows:

- Controllers intellectualize matters, preferring to think about issues rather than react to them emotionally. In a related defense, they split feelings from thoughts so as to remain emotionally detached.
- They deal with diametrically opposing thoughts and feelings about obedience and defiance with the help of reaction formation—for example, an executive who has hostile feelings towards his boss instead shows extreme deferential behavior.

- They blame others for perceived wrongs, using this displacement to avoid dealing with the real cause of their problems.
- They sublimate their unacceptable level of hostility, expressing it in a socially acceptable way—for example, through the choice of profession. Judges, police officers, soldiers, nurses, and surgeons show a high incidence of the controlling disposition.

THE CONTROLLING INDIVIDUAL WITHIN THE ORGANIZATION

People with a controlling disposition see their relationships in terms of dominance and submission, superiority and inferiority, and their behavior is dependent on their position in the pecking order. Because they relate to others in terms of rank or status, they're more comfortable with an authoritarian than an egalitarian style. They're respectful, deferential, ingratiating, even obsequious to superiors (with whom they identify), while at the same time being autocratic, condemning, uncompromising, and demanding toward subordinates. Working with controllers is like working in a minefield: you never know when you're going to trigger a mine and pay a heavy emotional price for violating some rigid standard.

Controlling personalities are often excessively devoted to their work and productivity, to the exclusion of pleasure and personal relationships. As workaholics, they sacrifice their family and friends to their job. But hard work isn't necessarily smart work. Preoccupied as they tend to be with trivial details, rules, order, organization, schedules, and procedures, they may not see the big picture. Because they operate in a world of regulations and hierarchies, their perceptive abilities are restricted and their creative talents are underdeveloped. They tend to be mediocre performers in situations that demand more than careful planning or attention to detail, and they stifle innovation and risk taking in others.

When it comes to leadership, people with a controlling disposition would at first glance seem to be the ideal bureaucratic personalities. Some degree of control is necessary for the effective and efficient operating of any enterprise, after all. Controllers are dependable and disciplined, extremely industrious and efficient, organized, respectful, and conscientious. They won't rest until their assignment is completed. They're generally extremely loyal to their superiors and to whatever cause they're asked to pursue. But if control itself begins to take control, as often happens as one's responsibilities mount with each step up the career ladder, it begins to eat away at organizational effectiveness.

Because controlling personalities see the world in black and white their way of doing things and the wrong way of doing things—they tend to inhibit both creativity and relativistic judgments. They may be so prudent, self-controlled, and intolerant of deviance that they can't function effectively among "normal" people, with their many and varied imperfections. They may have difficulty incorporating new and changing information, in which case learning takes place only over a great deal of time and with a great deal of effort. Furthermore, controllers often become so consumed by perfectionism and order they fail at task completion, unable to finish projects because they can't meet their own overly strict standards. And yet they're typically reluctant to delegate tasks or to work with other people.

Perhaps the trait that most condemns people with a controlling disposition to failure in positions of leadership is their indecisiveness. Torn between their desire to comply with the wishes of others and the desire to follow their own wishes, they may become blocked. Plagued by a nonspecific fear of making mistakes, they substitute procrastination for action. Some of them become the Hamlet of their organization, their modus operandi indecisiveness.

Others follow their own wishes indirectly, resisting authority via furtive, withholding behavior. People dominated by such characteristics are obviously unsuitable for leadership positions.

THE DEPENDENT DISPOSITION

Although Eric Thornton, chairman of the Santon Corporation, didn't mind people looking up to him and coming to him for advice and reassurance, he felt that there should be a limit to such encounters. This thought triggered his irritation with Ray Vernon, his staff assistant. Ray seemed bright enough, he wrote good reports, and he had satisfactorily completed a number of complex special projects, but he couldn't seem to take wing and fly on his own. Not a day went by without Ray coming to Eric's office to give him a progress report about his latest project and ask him if what he was doing was satisfactory. Eric felt that someone in Ray's position should be able to decide such things for himself. Ray's need to constantly check and recheck the correctness of his work was like a never-ending soap opera. However positive Eric's feedback, it never seemed good enough: Ray was insatiable.

Eric had told Ray repeatedly to figure things out for himself, to solve his own problems, but Ray always came back for more. Had Eric made a rod for his own back when he told Ray that he was a hands-on executive who wanted to be kept informed? For some issues, he did want that. But Ray was giving him more than he'd bargained for. He was treating his boss like a nursemaid. Eric had scheduled a performance appraisal session with Ray during the upcoming week. What was he going to tell him? In previous conversations, he had talked about giving Ray a line job—the logical next career step—but that now looked risky. What was Eric going to do with him?

This example demonstrates how people with a dependent disposition want others to assume responsibility for major areas of their lives because of their inability to function independently. People like Ray want to be taken care of. They remain childlike throughout their lives, unwilling to grow up. Extremely reluctant to act on their own, they base their self-esteem largely on the support and encouragement of others. Dependents are self-denigrating and fearful of the disapproval of other people. Given their hunger for approval, criticism can have a devastating impact.

We all like to be taken care of from time to time. But when this need becomes a compulsive, pervasive, and excessive craving, it's troublesome. It produces clinging, stifling, humiliating, or submissive behavior built on a foundation of insecurity. Dependent individuals of this kind build their lives around others, believing that they have to be subservient to maintain their supporters' goodwill. Their often charming façade masks their dependence on the appreciation of others. Dependents fear that they will be completely helpless if left on their own.

Typically, dependents:

- feel helpless, inadequate, powerless, and ineffectual
- can function only when supported by others
- are extremely insecure
- make urgent and inappropriate demands for immediate attention
- are prone to outbursts of affection or anger
- are anxious and somewhat depressed
- display fatigue and lethargy
- don't feel much joy in living
- are pessimistic, discouraged, and dejected
- are prone to food, alcohol, and drug problems
- are hypochondriacal
- are noncompetitive, self-effacing, compliant, and obsequious
- see themselves as ineffective, incompetent, or even stupid

Occasionally, we find examples of dependent personalities who go so far that they willingly give up their own identity as independent human beings. They lose themselves in another person, becoming as it were his or her extension or double, fused and entwined with the other. It's as if they can feel complete as a human being only by creating this kind of attachment. This is a defense mechanism known as introjection. By diffusing the distinction between themselves and the significant other, dependents prevent the painful awareness of separateness and the threat of loss. A secondary defense mechanism is denial: dependents typically smooth over uncomfortable interpersonal events or hostile impulses by pretending that they never happened.

Not surprisingly, in occupational and social life people with a dependent disposition have difficulty making everyday decisions without excessive advice and reassurance from others. They go to great lengths to ingratiate themselves with others, to the point of volunteering to do things that are unpleasant. Because they see themselves as powerless, they prefer to play an inferior role, from which they can encourage or allow others to make most of their important life decisions for them. Whenever possible, they subordinate their own needs to those of others on whom they depend, to avoid the risk of having to rely on themselves.

Dependents avoid conflict whenever possible. They experience great difficulty expressing disagreement with others because of their fear of loss of support or approval. Their niceness is in part a defense, however, and it can conceal a considerable amount of hostility. Afraid to express that hostility for fear it would lead to rejection (and thus isolation and loneliness), they remain loyal no matter what the circumstances—even despite abuse and intimidation.

We generally find one of three kinds of parenting styles at the root of this behavior pattern: overprotective, authoritarian, or genuinely unloving. Although the child-rearing patterns are different, all three approaches can lead to a similar outcome. Let's look at overprotection first. An anxious mother generally plays the major role in creating an overprotective environment. The child may be the only one she has, or perhaps was ill during pregnancy and still fears that she could "lose the baby." Both parents may be extremely anxious that the child will be hurt when venturing out solo. Thinking they are protecting the youngster, they may put numerous obstacles in his way to prevent him from doing things by himself. This gives the child very little opportunity to learn from his mistakes and doesn't prepare him to cope with life on his own. On the contrary, it perpetuates a deeply rooted symbiotic relationship with the parents. The legacies of this sort of child-rearing are feelings of vulnerability and helplessness and a fear of desertion.

Similar effects can be produced by controlling parents who don't permit their child to grow up. They always take over, giving the child no opportunity to learn from mistakes. As a consequence, the child develops a strong belief that she can't function without the guidance and protection of others and that the best way to obtain approval and maintain relationships is to acquiesce to requests, expectations, and demands. This authoritarian pattern of child-rearing reinforces dependent behavior in children and prevents them from developing independent, autonomous behavior. The inability of certain parents to allow their child to go through the process of separation-individuation stifles the development of the individual as a differentiated human being. Children raised in this way maintain their childlike sense of helplessness and believe that they will be all right only as long as a strong figure is supporting them.

The third explanation for the dependent disposition is a family constellation in which a child's bona fide dependency needs are highly frustrated. Parents who have no interest in their children as individuals, who have so many children that they simply can't attend personally to all of them, or who either choose or are forced by circumstances to work so much that child-rearing falls by the wayside, can't love their children the way people need to be loved—individually and genuinely. Growing up in a family where there isn't enough love to go around instills a feeling of rejection that sets the pattern for a lifelong search to make up the deficit.

THE DEPENDENT INDIVIDUAL WITHIN THE ORGANIZATION

Dependents aren't likely to be leaders of people. Lacking initiative, unwilling to act independently, insecure, afraid of change, and unassertive, they prefer a reactive rather than proactive role. They have difficulty initiating projects and doing things on their own because of a lack of confidence in their judgment or abilities.

Whenever possible, dependents abdicate responsibility. They prefer having others take the lead, perceiving their colleagues and friends as much more capable than they of shouldering life's responsibilities, navigating the complex world, and dealing with the competitions of life. Given their need to please, they rarely even make good sounding boards, having a tendency to simply echo what others are saying. If they find a supportive figure in the organization, however—someone willing to feed their craving for approval—they may function surprisingly well. Many dependents successfully play a subordinate role in an executive constellation, for example. With the right support, they may even turn into overachieving workaholics!

Because of their need for support and care, dependents are unlikely to question authority or dispute orders from others. Such ingratiating behavior sometimes elicits positive reactions from people in leadership positions, who see it as a sign of loyalty. There can be some overlap between the dependent and the dramatic disposition. However, people whose personal disposition includes a strong component of dependency are unlikely to be leadership material. Dependents simply don't have the self-confidence and competitiveness needed to assume such a role.

THE SELF-DEFEATING DISPOSITION

Many writers have been fascinated by people exhibiting the self-defeating disposition. A good illustration can be found in the interchange between Charles Dickens's David Copperfield and his Uriah Heep. Take the following:

> Would you like to be taught Latin? I said briskly. I will teach it you with pleasure, as I learn it. . . .
>
> Oh, indeed you must excuse me, Master Copperfield! I am greatly obliged, and I should like it of all things, I assure you; but I am far too 'umble. There are people enough to tread upon me in my lowly state, without my doing outrage to their feelings by possessing learning. Learning ain't for me. A person like myself had better not aspire. If he is to get on in life, he must get on 'umbly, Master Copperfield!

The writer Franz Kafka wasn't much better than Uriah Heep, apparently. In his famous Letter to His Father he says the following:

> Never I thought, would I make it through first grade; but I did, I even got a prize. I certainly won't pass the high-school entrance examinations; but pass I did. I'll definitely fail in my first year in high school; but no, I didn't fail, I succeeded in passing, time and time again.
>
> Success, however, did not inspire confidence; on the contrary, I was always convinced . . . that the more I accomplished, the worse off I would be in the end. In my mind's eye I often saw a terrifying conclave of teachers (the Gymnasium merely provides the most cogent example, but they were all around me) meeting to discuss this unique, this absolutely outrageous case, to wit: how I, the most incompetent, certainly the most ignorant of all, had managed to sneak from first into the second gymnasium grade, then into the third, and so on up the line. But now that I had at last aroused their attention, I would of course be immediately thrown out, to the immense satisfaction of all righteous men delivered from a nightmare [16], pp. 93–95.

This passage gives a glimpse into Kafka's tendency to wallow in guilt and his need for self-flagellation—or, as he would put it himself, his "death wish." Throughout his actions and his writing there's a strong streak of masochism. Suffering was central to his personality; life was a form of martyrdom. And no one was more talented at extorting sympathy through illness than Kafka [17].

As an employee of the Workmen's Accident Insurance Institute in the early 1900s in Prague, a position he held for sixteen years, Kafka was reasonably effective, although he viewed his work as a way of killing time. His relationships with his parents and women, on the other hand, could not be labeled effective: making a commitment was difficult for him. Wallowing in self-pity, he could never reach decisions, and he seemed to go out of his way to avoid happiness. With his masochistic outlook on life, he appeared almost to welcome as a form of salvation the discovery that he had tuberculosis.

As the examples of Uriah Heep and Franz Kafka illustrate, there's considerable similarity between the self-defeating and the dependent disposition. In fact, the two often go together. What distinguishes the self-defeaters is the masochistic quality of their thought and behavior. Although these people are capable of making great contributions to society through service to others, their self-sacrificing behavior tends to be excessive. In this prototype we find people who make unrealistic, perfectionist demands on themselves, are unwarrantedly pessimistic, have unfounded health concerns, are troubled by helplessness, and depend on others for emotional support and decision-making. Self-defeating individuals engage in self-devaluation and even self-damaging behavior. They prefer to be unrecognized for their achievements. They store up and harp on injustices done to them, rather than try to correct them, because behind their complaints they hide a satisfying sense of moral triumph about their self-imposed suffering.

Like the dependent group, people with a self-sacrificing disposition are inclined to put themselves in an inferior position. But believing that by inviting and enduring pain they will forestall some greater anguish, they also go out of their way to prove themselves unlovable, to emphasize their own worst features, and to find excuses to debase themselves. They also reject or render ineffective others' attempts to help them, and ignore or push aside people who treat them well. This poor treatment of others reveals a sadistic tendency that self-defeaters hide. The guilt at having sadistic feelings, however, turns these feelings inward to self-sadism, or masochism. Thus self-defeaters need people upon whom they can transfer their sadistic tendencies: in other words, they seek out victimizers in order to themselves be victims.

Some self-defeaters single out people and situations that lead to disappointment, failure, or maltreatment even when better options are clearly available. Moreover, by relating to others in a self-sacrificing manner, they encourage and invite people to take advantage of them. They voluntarily give others the shirt off their back without waiting to be asked. In the process, they create a system of emotional and obligatory dependence, drawing others into their self-destructive web, dominating and controlling them through self-sacrifice. In a subtle, possessive way, they bribe others to love them.

Typically, self-defeating people:

- have a strong sense of injustice
- enjoy self-imposed suffering
- put themselves in inferior positions
- willingly accept blame for things for which they aren't responsible
- have a sadomasochistic orientation
- are self-sacrificing
- feel forlorn and mournful
- oscillate between feelings of love, rage, and guilt toward themselves and others
- court failure and disgrace

- reject opportunities for pleasure
- are drawn to situations and relationships where they're subject to humiliation, suffering, and distress
- are physically accident-prone

The root of self-defeating behavior seems to be parental indifference or hostility, which stimulates the young child's desperate wish to establish some form of contact, whatever the price. As time goes by the child learns that only by being miserable will she get a reaction from her parents—in other words, that her parents will be kind to her only when she isn't doing well. Thus occasions of suffering provide respite from an otherwise indifferent or hostile family environment. It's as if the child said to her parents, "Please love me. See how miserable I am, how much I suffer. I know that I'm really bad."

Apart from internalizing a sense of misery, the child also internalizes a sense of parental reproach. The internalized parents become permanent inner persecutors. Self-defeating prototypes are torn by guilt: guilt at their own anger at finding themselves in this situation and guilt at not living up to parental expectations. Although the desire for punishment that such feelings produce is usually subconscious, self-defeaters grow up feeling gratified only when they're victimized. This kind of self-handicapping behavior typically becomes noticeable first in school, though it continues into work and other areas of social functioning, where self-defeaters repeatedly become involved with people or situations destined to have a bad ending.

Paradoxically, masochistic behavior gives self-defeaters a modicum of power, both as children and as adults. Because they enjoy their suffering, their tormentors have only limited power over them. This is a rather contorted way of denying one's helplessness, but it brings relief nonetheless. They continue to hold the reins even as they defer to others: although at first glance they may seem to be self-sacrificing and concerned about the welfare of others, they're really preoccupied with themselves and working to satisfy their own internal goals.

THE SELF-DEFEATING INDIVIDUAL WITHIN THE ORGANIZATION

In an organizational setting, self-defeating people can be an asset. They're generally extremely helpful and considerate in their dealings with other people; they tend to be noncompetitive and unambitious, comfortable playing a role in the background; they're ethical, honest, and trustworthy; and they have a sense of humility and are self-effacing, neither boastful nor proud. Because they don't like being the center of attention and feel uneasy in the limelight, they're better followers than leaders.

As followers, however, they sometimes engage in a kind of sadomasochistic tango, drawn to bosses who inflict psychological pain on their subordinates. Such bosses typically have a narcissistic, controlling, abrasive, or antisocial disposition and know an easy victim when they see one. The general tenor of the resulting superior/subordinate relationship is inevitably dominance and submission rather than congeniality and cooperation.

As noted earlier, some self-defeating people always select situations that will lead to failure. They fail to complete tasks even when they're perfectly able to, for example, because completion would mean success. They seem to seek out or even fabricate impediments to successful performance, preferring to be the author of their own downfall. Naturally, extreme self-defeaters such as this are poor candidates for a leadership position. Their self-deprecatory behavior, lack of self-confidence, fear of standing out, and passive modus operandi make them more suited to be followers.

Erich Fromm once said, "Man's main task in life is to give birth to himself, to become what he potentially is. The most important product of his effort is his own personality." As the examples have shown, the creation of what we call personality or character involves a very complex developmental process during which hiccups can occur at any stage. And as we have seen in the case of people who are driven to move toward others, the outcome of this process is sometimes bizarre and self-defeating.

REFERENCES

1. American Psychiatric Association (2004). *Diagnostic and Statistical Manual of the Mental Disorders: DSM-IV-Tr.* Arlington, VA, American Psychiatric Association.
2. Carver, C. S. and M. F. Scheier (2001). *Perspectives on Personality.* New York, Allyn & Bacon.
3. Kaplan, H. I. and B. J. Sadock, Eds (1985). *Comprehensive Textbook of Psychiatry.* Baltimore, Williams & Wilkins.
4. Kets de Vries, M. F. R. and S. Perzow (1991). *Handbook of Character Studies.* New York, International University Press.
5. Millon, T. (1996). *Disorders of Personality: DSM IV and Beyond.* New York, John Wiley & Sons, Inc.
6. Pervin, L. and J. E. Oliver, Eds (2001). *Handbook of Personality: Theory and Research.* New York, The Guilford Press.
7. Reich, W. (1933). *Character Analysis.* New York, Farrar, Straus, and Giroux.
8. Shapiro, D. (1965). *Neurotic Styles.* New York, Basic Books.
9. Stone, M. H. (1993). *Abnormalities of Personality: Within and Beyond the Realm of Treatment.* New York, W.W. Norton.
10. Allport, G. (1937). *Personality: A Psychological Interpretation.* New York, Holt.
11. Millon, T. (1986). *A Theoretical Derivation of Pathological Personalities. Contemporary Directions in Psychopathology: Toward the DSM-IV.* Eds T. Millon and G. L. Klerman. New York, The Guilford Press: 639–669.
12. Luborsky, L. and P. Crits-Cristoph (1998). *Understanding Transference: The Core Conflictual Relationship Theme Method.* Washington, American Psychological Organization.
13. McDougall, J. (1985). *Theaters of the Mind.* New York, Basic Books.

14. Horney, K. (1945). *Our Inner Conflicts.* New York, Norton.
15. Manchester, W. (1970). *The Arms of Krupp.* New York, Bantam Books.
16. Kafka, F. (1987). *Letter to His Father.* New York, Knopf.
17. Pawell, E. (1985). *The Nightmare of Reason: A life of Franz Kafka.* New York, Vintage Books.

CHAPTER 4

LEADERS AND FOLLOWERS: MOVING AWAY FROM PEOPLE

Once you label me, you defeat me.

—Jean-Paul Sartre

There is no detachment where there is no pain. And there is no pain endured without hatred or lying unless detachment is present too.

—Simone Weil

If a man be gloomy let him keep it to himself. No one has the right to go croaking about society, or what is worse, looking as if he stifled grief.

—Benjamin Disraeli

All of the significant battles are waged within the self.

—Zen proverb

There was once a monk who had made a vow not to become attached to anyone or anything. At a very early age he broke all ties with his family in order to concentrate on meditation. He believed that relationships would hinder his studies to become a

Zen master. He became a mendicant, wandering the world so that he wouldn't become attached to any particular place. One day, a traveler met him in the mountains and decided to follow him. They walked some way in silence, and then stopped under a tree to rest. The traveler offered the monk his pipe, which the holy man accepted out of friendship. After a while, he commented how pleasant smoking was, and the traveler immediately offered him another round of tobacco. After smoking contentedly for some time, the monk astonished the traveler by suddenly throwing both pipe and tobacco away. "I was enjoying it too much," he explained. "Pleasure disturbs meditation."

Some years later, when he was 28, the monk settled down for a time and studied Chinese calligraphy and poetry. He grew so skillful that his teacher praised him. He stopped immediately: "If I'm not careful," he said, "I'll be a poet, not a Zen master." He never wrote another poem.

This Zen monk represents a particular personality type, someone who resists attachment. All his life this holy man distanced himself from other people and from pleasurable experiences. This behavior contrasts sharply with that of the personality dispositions dealt with in the previous chapter. That particular parade of personalities has a tendency to move toward others, with self-esteem determined by the perceptions of others. This chapter deals with individuals who tend to move away from people. Their aim is the active avoidance of others. In one way or another, they fear that all relationships will ultimately lead to conflict, frustration, and a bad end. People who fit this prototype fall into one of two categories: detached disposition and depressive disposition.

THE DETACHED DISPOSITION

Peter Prince, an executive working in the IT department of an insurance company, was overheard to say, "I don't dislike people.

I just seem to feel so much better when they're not around." This attitude toward his colleagues didn't endear him to his immediate boss, Joan, who had plans to groom him for a more general management position. But after Peter participated in a 360-degree feedback exercise conducted as part of his performance appraisal, Joan—who had been asked to read some of the written comments—realized that he had great difficulty building relationships and responding to others emotionally.

Some of his colleagues commented on his wariness, his inability to open up. Others mentioned that they would like him to be more outspoken at meetings and wondered why he was always so silent and detached. One of his colleagues, clearly irritated, compared him to Gollum from *The Lord of the Rings*, a creepy character with solitary habits, spiteful behavior, odd interests, emotional changeability, nervousness, and difficulty in forming friendships. This colleague's notes made it clear that he felt that Peter, like Gollum, was interpersonally disengaged. Others commented that on the rare occasions when Peter did communicate with others, his remarks were unfocused; he would wander from topic to topic and lose the attention of his audience.

In discussing with Joan the feedback about how he was perceived, Peter said that maintaining relationships was just too much trouble; it simply wasn't worth the effort. She commended the written and organizational components of his work but pointed out that by keeping his distance, he handicapped his capacity to learn from experience, increase his self-awareness, and develop potentially rewarding relationships with other people.

Peter was clearly a gifted individual, excelling at most hobbies he tried, whether playing the violin or thinking up chess moves. At work, however, he was no standout. Apparently not ambitious to move up in the organization, he had twice refused a promotion, arguing that he liked the work he was currently doing and had no interest in trying something different. He seemed to be happiest on his own, playing the violin or solitary chess, or surfing the Net and playing computer games. But while engaging in these lonely pursuits, he sold short his potential, replacing the expectations of society, where he didn't seem to fit in, for those of a more imaginary world.

Individuals like Peter are toward the extreme end of the spectrum of the detached disposition. According to the *Diagnostic and Statistical Manual of Mental Disorders (DSM-IV-Tr)*, this disposition can be subdivided into two separate prototypes: schizoid and avoidant. Schizoid individuals—the more unusual of the two prototypes—may have emotional or cognitive deficits that make them incapable of establishing close relationships. They seem to be genuinely indifferent to others and have no wish to become closer. In contrast, avoidant personalities are actively detached—that is, their detachment is more self-protective. Circumstances have put them on a path away from people, but they would like to move closer [1]–[4].

We might call the schizoid subgroup aloof loners and the avoidant group lonely loners. While the former don't seem to care about relating to others, the latter do care. Put two avoidants together and they're like hedgehogs trying to get warm during a cold night, wondering how close they can get to each other without being hurt. Looking for closeness, avoidants are painfully alert to the minutest signals of rejection from others, interpreting even the most neutral events as evidence of disdain or ridicule. Concerned about their social inadequacies and afraid that other people will find them uninteresting, they maintain their distance. Although they would like to be closer to others, they have learned to be wary about reaching out. To many of them, intimate relationships are just plain frightening.

The fear of rejection that both subgroups of detached people experience is grounded in reality. They have painful memories of early attempts to move closer to people that ended badly—attempts that taught them to engage in protective withdrawal. While the schizoid subgroup has given up trying for intimacy, the avoidant group may still make the occasional effort. Both groups, however, actively (though not necessarily consciously) work to drive away people who would like to be closer to them. Although this seems self-destructive, it provides detached people with a modicum of control over their lives. They choose to actively push people away rather than risk being rejected by them. In other words, they anticipate the distance and maintain it on their own terms. Fatalistic about human relationships, they find their hermit-like behavior safe and comfortable.

People in the schizoid subgroup show little desire for social involvement; they restrict social relationships out of fear that contact may become disruptive and painful. In contrast, members of the avoidant subgroup are less self-contained. Thus although both subgroups are very private people, those who fit the more schizoid sub-prototype can tolerate isolation with comfort, while those with an avoidant personality are more distressed by their isolation and experience loneliness. Avoidants remain willing to reach out to others in spite of past disappointments, but they're always on edge in any social encounter, caught between their deep-seated desire for affection and acceptance, and their fear of intrusion and ridicule. Both subgroups perceive the world as an unfriendly, cold, and dangerous place. Not surprisingly, people with a schizoid disposition rarely seek professional help in overcoming their fear, while individuals with an avoidant disposition may do so.

People with a detached disposition are inclined to go their own way, but they do so without obvious defiance or a need to demonstrate their independence. Although they may be nonconforming, they keep a low enough profile to avoid sanctions, both at work and in general society. When they do have contact with others—in comparison with the avoidants—they don't seem to be genuinely involved or to care (at least on a conscious level) what others think of them. On the other hand, they're very sensitive to any form of intrusion and will withdraw from external pressure whenever possible.

By preference, they engage in solitary activities, opting for mechanical or abstract tasks. Creative work is also an adaptive response to their detachment: creative activity is a confirmation of their originality and uniqueness. Because they're more comfortable in a world of fantasy and introspection, they may engage in extremes of eccentric thinking and be fascinated with concepts such as ghosts, UFOs, and reincarnation.

Given their difficulties in relationship-building, detached people are unlikely to marry. With their problems in reaching out, they're prepared to enter into relationships only if they're given unusually strong assurances of uncritical acceptance. Love and sex imply closeness and entrapment, situations fraught with danger for the detached personality. They may prefer to live with siblings or other relatives in comfortable but non-intimate stability. If they do marry, their relationship is typically similar to that of room-mates, with limited intimacy and rare or no sexual relations.

Typically, people with a detached disposition are:

- alienated from themselves and others
- repressed and isolated
- vague, emotionally absent, and indifferent to praise, criticism, and the feelings of others
- undemonstrative and passive
- bland and lacking in personality

When faced with the need to respond to emotional or problematic situations, they generally:

- withdraw into fantasy
- deflect response through rumination, rambling speech, intellectualization, and conflict avoidance
- diminish emotional events

In fact, their observable mood changes are slight and their emotional range restricted. They show no demonstrative feelings, either of rage or affection, and react passively to adverse circumstances. They're likely to find it hard to respond appropriately to important events both in their own lives and in a wider context (for example, natural disasters).

There are a number of factors that contribute to the detached disposition. The detached adult often has a history of grossly inadequate early parenting characterized by distancing, devaluation, rejection, humiliation, and loss. The parents of children who opt for detachment as adults generally lack emotional expressiveness. For example, they don't give cuddles or other affective forms of expression that are the staples of a healthy childhood. As a result of distancing, children feel helpless, isolated, and abandoned. They fear that they're not wanted, that they can't please anyone, or even that they're hurting those to whom they feel attached.

The family constellation that breeds detachment compounds routine emotional distancing with periodic episodes of outright rejection. Traumatic childhood experiences involving scorn and ridicule are the norm in such households, and they create the expectation that all relationships will be painful and that all human interaction ends badly. Repeated rejection crushes a child's natural energy and optimism and creates persistent feelings of self-deprecation and social isolation. Children growing up in such a climate don't acquire the emotional and social cues needed to be able to relate to others. Therefore, as adults they're reluctant to share their feelings. For them, intimacy is synonymous with vulnerability. It's no wonder that they have relationship problems!

The defensive outlook that detached children learn in their early years is accentuated by rejection by peer groups at school. If the child of rejecting parents encounters positive, reinforcing experiences outside the hostile home environment, early parental rejection is not so damaging; the child may bounce back and recover. However, if rejection by parents and siblings is

compounded by rejection from a peer group, the problem is aggra-
vated. Failure at sports, drama, or social tasks such as finding a
partner for the school prom validate parental rejection.

If they're humiliated and rejected by their peers, detached
individuals begin to wonder what's wrong with them. Why do
others reject them? What makes them so unlovable? Predictably,
they blame themselves for their predicament. Thus their feelings
of loneliness and isolation are compounded by their own harsh
self-judgment. Because social ineptitude feeds on itself, the intensified feelings of inferiority and worthlessness that plague detached
people exacerbate their tendency to withdraw from others.

While rejection by parents and peers is the number-one cause
of detachment, a number of other family dynamics can contribute
to this behavior pattern. One is the fear of losing one's identity as
a separate individual because of the intrusiveness or domination
of primary caretakers. Children in this situation use distance as a
defense against engulfment, a defense that can turn into a lifelong
pattern. Children who fear engulfment have typically been infan-
tilized by their parents, never permitted to grow up as they should,
and thus they suffer from a developmental imbalance. Victims of
learned social incompetence, they subsequently have difficulty
relating to people outside their family in a mature, self-confident
manner. They develop a habitual pattern of dealing with other
people regressively, displaying an overly dependent, awkward
manner that makes people who don't know them feel ill at ease
and want to keep their distance from them. Detached people
quickly learn, from such reactions, to likewise keep their
distance.

This attitude can be exacerbated by persistent advice from
parents, peers, teachers, religious leaders, and even the media to
be on guard against the evils of the world. When children can't
turn anywhere for validation, withdrawal is the likely outcome.
Some of the outward manifestations of detachment—an even-
tempered, calm, dispassionate, unflappable front presented to the

world—are advantageous. But the negatives outweigh the positives: the intense need for private space that detachment indicates results in repeated failures of intimacy and pervasive feelings of isolation.

THE DETACHED INDIVIDUAL WITHIN THE ORGANIZATION

People with a detached disposition can adapt well to life in certain types of organizations, if they're able to find a niche that suits their personality makeup, but they'll never be among the movers and shakers. Their emotional isolation restricts them to low-level, low-visibility positions that require little interpersonal contact. Given their lack of social skills, detached individuals can't build the organizational networks that are indispensable for getting things done, they alienate whatever social support they might initially have, and they can't deal with the inevitable conflicts of organizational life. In stressful situations, they may withdraw into their imaginations, perhaps fantasizing or playing computer games. That same lack of social skills—in particular, their lack of personal presence and their inability to assess the subtleties of human behavior—makes them incapable of energizing others and helping them to improve their own performance. Inexpressive, disengaged, and apathetic, they're the antithesis of organizational cheerleaders. They don't do much for themselves either: because their behavior isn't typically goal-directed, their career management is likely to be poor or nonexistent.

So how does a person who has to work with detached individuals influence and manage them? How does someone build a relationship with people whose psychological agenda is to remain totally uninvolved? The first step is to provide the right job and setting: detached individuals function quite well in selected occupations—usually relatively low-status positions such as a night clerk, a movie projectionist, or a night watchman, or higher-status positions such as university researcher or financial analyst.

Ironically, the many advances in voyeuristic technology have proved a bonanza for these people, enabling them to get closer to others (albeit clandestinely) without having to relate to those others in person. This is well illustrated in the gripping television series *24*, a techno-thriller starring Kiefer Sutherland as federal agent Jack Bauer, head of a counterterrorist unit. Jack is helped by a group of nerdy characters who snoop on other people's lives using sophisticated monitoring equipment. This particular pathology was dramatized earlier in Francis Ford Coppola's film *The Conversation* (1974). Surveillance expert Harry Caul, played by Gene Hackman, is hired by a wealthy executive to spy on his wife and her lover. As the film progresses, we discover that the main character in the film is as obsessed with maintaining his own privacy as he is motivated by intruding secretly in the life of his clients. Harry Caul's statements are indicative of his state of mind:

> I would be perfectly happy to have all my personal things burned up in a fire because I don't have anything personal. Nothing of value. No, nothing personal except my keys, you see, which I really would like to have the only copy of . . . Listen, if there's one surefire rule that I have learned in this business it's that I don't know anything about human nature, I don't know anything about curiosity. That's not part of what I do. (Harry Caul in *The Conversation*, Francis Ford Coppola (1974))

Film scripts don't come out of a vacuum. They're generally grounded in reality. The character of Harry Caul has a kindred spirit in the real-life person of George Perkins, the CEO of a company providing information-based business solutions to the government. His expertise lay in finding solutions to technical problems. As CEO, he played a rather symbolic role, since he was machine- rather than people-oriented.

George had a background in math and computer science. After earning his doctorate at MIT he was hired as an assistant professor in the computer science department. His teaching career was short-lived, however, because he couldn't communicate with his students. George then tried to make a living working for a mid-sized consulting company specialized in IT. His task was to help the partners provide innovative business solutions for their clients. His knack for gathering information and finding new business solutions made him good at the work, but his poor communication skills led to problems with the partners. The resulting conflict made him decide to work on his own, but he found it difficult to acquire and keep clients in spite of his obvious talent.

His luck changed after a chance encounter with David, an old roommate from his college days. David had just quit his job with a large consulting firm and was looking for a new challenge. When George explained his predicament—that he had good ideas but was having a hard time selling them—David suggested that they team up. George was willing to give it a try, given that they had always gotten along in college. He knew very well that he himself wasn't very good at leading and persuading people, and he knew that David was much better in that role. Together, they functioned as a highly effective executive team, making for the beginning of a very profitable business partnership. George's brilliance in designing new information technology packages and David's salesmanship turned out to be an extremely successful combination. Going public ten years later made both of them rich beyond their wildest dreams.

As noted earlier, it's unusual for detached people to gain leadership positions. George was able to be a successful exception because he didn't have to deal much with either customers or employees; he led the way in the technical arena only. It was up to his partner to do the essential people-work of addressing the emotional needs of subordinates, setting out expectations, and giving feedback about accomplishments. Only with such an executive role constellation can a detached leadership style succeed. Otherwise, detachment must be mixed with another style to create leadership effectiveness.

THE DEPRESSIVE DISPOSITION

"It's snowing still," said Eeyore, gloomily.

"So it is."

"And freezing."

"Is it?"

"Yes," said Eeyore. "However," he said, brightening a little, "we haven't had an earthquake lately."

This quote from A. A. Milne's *Winnie the Pooh* is indicative of the mindset of people with a depressive disposition. But characters like Eeyore aren't to be found only in children's tales; in many organizations we can find people with a similar mindset.

To illustrate, Roger Holden, the CEO of a global consumer products company, was concerned about John Green, the executive in charge of a recently acquired beverage firm. John had been running the company for many years before Roger's company made a bid for it. Although the post-merger integration process was successful, Roger began to worry about John, who no longer seemed like the person Roger had met when the negotiations began. Although John from day one had come across as serious, he now seemed devoid of vigor and focus. He was morose and low-spirited, with a defeatist and fatalistic attitude about almost everything. He painted everything in the blackest light, invariably expecting the worst. Furthermore, he was extremely critical and judgmental of others. His attitude was affecting the atmosphere at the office, where several people had intimated to Roger that John was increasingly difficult to work with. He was certainly not the energizer the company needed to climb out of a market downturn. Roger wondered if he should keep John in his present position or terminate his contract, at a significant financial loss.

People with a depressive disposition are governed by the belief that they're bad. They see themselves as inconsequential at best and anywhere from reproachable to contemptible at worst. Believing that they deserve to be criticized and derogated, they indulge in acts of self-denial, self-punishment, and self-torment. They see their lives as a series of failures and themselves as helpless victims, manipulated by forces beyond their control. Not surprisingly, then, they give off a sense of permanent hopelessness and wretchedness [5]; [6]. Against this black background, depressives see life as a system of duties and responsibilities, and they repudiate pleasure and all forms of play and frivolity.

Defeatist and fatalistic about almost everything, depressives offer the gloomiest possible interpretation of any event, despairing that things will improve in the future. Whatever the situation, they invariably focus on its negative aspects (often assuming blame for whatever went wrong). Deploring the past and fearing the future, they believe there's no bright side to look on. The only interesting news is bad news, and bad news is reassuring because it represents reality.

For depressives, memory represents only emptiness and nothingness. Life's early experiences suggest a desert, barren ground. It's the pain rather than the pleasure of the past that predominates. Early recollections seem drained of any richness, joy, or meaning. A major defense mechanism to deal with painful memories is repression—that is, subduing distressing feelings at as low a level as possible. But this is a Faustian bargain, because it results in lifelessness. As with memories, so in the present: depressives have a limited emotional repertoire. When faced with conflict, they don't know how to react.

Typically, depressives demonstrate:

- a sense of helplessness, hopelessness, and worthlessness
- a poor appetite and weight loss
- sleeping problems
- loss of energy and chronic fatigue
- general apathy
- lack of sexual interest
- inability to concentrate
- irritability
- dejection and joylessness
- guilt, remorse, and wretchedness
- recurring thoughts of death and suicide

When at their lowest point, depressives sometimes kill themselves as a final, desperate act of defiance—a gesture that demonstrates initiative in a way that their general behavior does not. Suicide can also be chosen as retaliation toward others, an indictment suggesting that nobody cared.

As with all the other prototypes we're looking at in these chapters, the depressive disposition is an outcome of nature and nurture; biogenic (or constitutional) factors interact with psychogenic factors to produce depression. Depressives typically learn their self-defeating ways of looking at the world during early childhood, generally as the result of extremely adverse parenting. The most salient contributing factor is early loss of emotional support, sometimes as the result of an overwhelming external circumstance that causes a disruption in caretaking. The death of a major figure in a child's life, for example, causes feelings of abandonment and desertion; so do less dramatic circumstances such as divorce, exposure to marital conflict, or living with a depressed parent. Consistently, a major contributing factor to the depressive disposition is a child's perception of loss, lack of comfort, and feelings of isolation.

The reason that this sort of disruption is so traumatizing to a child is that it happens just at the stage in life when the child is determining whether the environment is caring or indifferent. During those years when the need is greatest, such a disruption robs the developing child of a comfort-providing caretaker, leaving feelings of loss and disappointment that linger for decades. In the absence of needed comfort, the child (and then adult) internalizes painful, self-critical, and self-destructive thoughts, believing him- or herself worthless and undeserving of care. As time goes on, the individual's self-image becomes greatly distorted, churning out feelings of ineptitude, inadequacy, and helplessness. These people continue to feel unlovable throughout life.

Depressives also feel responsible for their circumstances. If a parent leaves the home, it's the child's fault (so he thinks) for not being lovable enough. This state of mind creates feelings of help-lessness and hopelessness. Prolonged exposure to unhappy events that are beyond one's control leads to apathy, pessimism, and loss of motivation. As a result of their childhood experiences, individu-als with a depressive outlook acquire what psychologists call learned helplessness, a belief that they can't control the outcome of events in their lives. This contributes to their feelings of worthlessness and low self-esteem. They see themselves as inconsequential, guilty, and undeserving of warmth and care. All their aggressive impulses are turned inward on themselves and expressed through self-denigrating comments.

Self-deprecation brings depressives some respite from their inner pain. One unconventional interpretation suggests that it's actually a tactic (though not necessarily a conscious one) for dealing with feelings of anger and resentment. Depressives present them-selves—not without reason—as victims: vulnerable, defenseless, abandoned and deserted. Unfortunately, this isn't the kind of self-projection that makes others want to reach out to them.

There are, however, situations in which depressives themselves can reach out successfully. Their familiarity with suffering helps them identify with the suffering of others. One thinks of the late Diana, Princess of Wales, whose public statements about her feelings of empathy for the victims of AIDS and landmines met de-rision and admiration in equal parts. However, there's no doubt that her activities on behalf of international organizations working in these areas—including personal contact with sufferers—helped her through difficult times in her own life by proving her genuine usefulness to others. Such instances are rare, because depressives are generally reluctant to show that side of themselves. They prefer to obtain sympathy from others, although their attempts are fre-quently self-defeating, since many people are turned off by their behavior.

Another interpretation of this kind of behavior is that it's a cry for help. Self-denigration can bring what psychologists call second-ary gain in the form of attention and help from others. There are always some people who respond to a cry for help, people from whom this kind of behavior evokes nurturing, reassuring, protec-tive responses. Such responders try to convince depressives that they have value, that there's hope. Perversely, that sort of positive response can actually encourage the perpetuation of misery, since misery brings the sufferer the attention he or she craves.

There are also times when a depressive style gives people a way out of difficult situations, absolving them from unpleasant duties or unwelcome responsibilities. It can also be used as a strategy to rationalize poor performance. Because depressives openly admit their worthlessness, they have the perfect excuse when things go wrong. It may also enable them to blame others for not having been sufficiently helpful.

DEPRESSIVES WITHIN THE ORGANIZATION

People with a truly depressive disposition have constricted interests and difficulty understanding different lifestyles or points of view. They're poor bets for leadership positions because of their lack of spontaneity, their indecisiveness, and their inability to take initiat-ive. Because of their pessimism, they're inclined to overestimate their difficulties and underestimate their capabilities. Hypochondriacal and anxious, they adhere to routine and don't allow themselves to be distracted by impulses and passion. Their negativity hinders both their productivity and their progress within an organization: even if things are going well, they're continually preparing for the worst. Constantly anticipating disaster, they're by definition not problem-solvers. Furthermore, anticipating failure can turn into a self-fulfilling prophecy and threaten the future of the enterprise.

The same sense of vulnerability that makes them see the world as a dangerous place leads them to seek constant assurance from others that they're good enough, that they're coping. This can be oppressive to co-workers, especially since if reassurance isn't forthcoming, depressives may retreat into silence and guilty self-reproach. Furthermore, in craving sympathy they may overplay their helplessness and make their colleagues feel guilty.

Their negativity also makes them extremely critical and judgmental of others and therefore incapable of motivating people to exceptional achievements. At work, which they see as unpleasant drudgery, a duty to be fulfilled, their skepticism and cynicism create a downbeat, discouraging, destructive atmosphere. Not only are they very hard on themselves, but they put considerable pressure on others. They expect the people who work for them to take on a great deal of work, and they nag about getting things done while simultaneously criticizing their subordinates' performance.

Depressive tendencies in a leader create a negative and non-communicative organizational culture. Constantly fearful that they will fail in their duties and responsibilities, depressive leaders react with intense self-flagellation to any setback. An innocuous remark may set in motion a seemingly endless process of worrying. Knowing this, colleagues will be inclined to minimize their interactions.

As we've seen in our discussion of people who move away from others, there's often a fine line between normalcy and dysfunction, humor and anguish, laughter and sorrow, comedy and tragedy. For many people the tragedy of life is not that it ends so soon, but that they wait so long to begin, stuck as they are on a treadmill of dysfunctionality. But maybe the most poignant observation of mankind in all its foibles is one offered by Albert Schweitzer, who once said, "The tragedy of life is what dies inside a man while he lives."

REFERENCES

1. Barlow, D. H., Ed (2001). *Clinical Handbook of Psychological Disorders.* New York, The Guilford Press.
2. Beck, A. T. and A. Freeman (2004). *Cognitive Therapy of Personality Disorders.* New York, The Guilford Press.
3. Millon, T. (1996). *Disorders of Personality: DSM IV and Beyond.* New York, John Wiley.
4. Millon, T. and G. S. Everly (1985). *Personality and its Disorders.* New York, John Wiley & Sons.
5. Beck, A. T., A. J. Rush, B. F. Shaw and G. Emery (1979). *Cognitive Theory of Depression.* New York, The Guilford Press.
6. Solomon, A. (2001). *The Noonday Demon: An Atlas of Depression.* New York, Simon & Schuster.

CHAPTER 5

LEADERS AND FOLLOWERS: MOVING AGAINST PEOPLE

I have been up against tough competition all my life. I wouldn't know how to get along without it.

—Walt Disney

My mom never saw the irony of calling me a sonofabitch.

—Jack Nicholson

I find it rather easy to portray a businessman. Being bland, rather cruel and incompetent comes naturally to me.

—John Cleese

Only those who are extremely pliable and soft can be extremely hard and strong.

—Zen proverb

There once lived a great warrior. His reputation extended far and wide throughout the land, and many students gathered to study under him. Though quite old, he was still able to defeat any challenger.

One day a young fighter arrived at the warrior's village. He had a long history of success in combat and was determined to be the first person to defeat the great warrior. Along with his considerable strength, he had the uncanny ability to spot and exploit any weakness in an opponent. His strategy was to wait for his adversary to make the first move, revealing a weakness, and then strike with merciless force and lightning speed. No one had ever lasted beyond the first strike in a match with him.

Against the advice of his students, the old warrior accepted the young warrior's challenge. As the two squared up for battle, the younger man began to hurl insult after insult at the old warrior, and then at his family. Getting no response, he supplemented his insults with dirt thrown in his opponent's face. For hours, he verbally assaulted the old warrior with every curse known to mankind, pausing now and again to spit in his face. The old warrior merely stood there motionless and calm, smiling at the young man. Finally, the young warrior had totally exhausted himself. Defeated and shamed, he left.

Disappointed that their master hadn't fought the insolent youth, the students gathered around him and asked, "How could you endure such indignity? How could you stand it? What did you do to drive him away?"

The master's response was simple: "If someone comes to give you a gift and you don't accept it, to whom does the gift belong?"

In this chapter we will deal with people whose habitual pattern of interaction is to move against people—that is, people who try to affect others negatively. Unfortunately, most such people aren't exposed to the sort of learning opportunity offered by the old warrior. Instead, they create a self-fulfilling prophecy: their negative behavior is responded to in kind, prompting further negativity right back, thereby creating a vicious cycle of anger, hostility, and vindictiveness. For many such individuals, life is perceived as a struggle for survival. They believe that they live in a dog-eat-dog world and have to behave accordingly. Other people are to be exploited, belittled, and controlled. These people typically have one of the following four dispositions: abrasive, paranoid, negativistic, or antisocial.

THE ABRASIVE DISPOSITION

Heinrich Himmler, the head of Hitler's SS and a classic example of the abrasive disposition, once said, "The best political weapon is the weapon of terror. Cruelty commands respect. Men may hate us. But we don't ask for their love: only for their fear." To most of us today this seems an extreme statement, but the behavior of many renowned business executives suggests that they went to school with Himmler. One notorious abrasive from the work world is Al Dunlap, also known as "Chainsaw Al," "Rambo in Pinstripes," and "The Shredder," who, ironically, was once viewed as one of the most effective executives in North America. He earned his later reputation as one of the meanest executives in the United States by ruthlessly eliminating thousands of jobs. He was renowned for his ability to restructure and turn around troubled companies, but in the process he succeeded in driving many of those companies into the ground.

However, not even his harshest critics could have predicted the eventual disastrous outcome when Dunlap first strode into Sunbeam. The day after Sunbeam announced that it had hired the self-styled turnaround artist and downsizing champion as its CEO, the company's shares soared dramatically: at Scott Paper, Dunlap's previous CEO assignment, he had more than doubled the value of the shares in 18 months, increasing the company's market value considerably.

Dunlap's rallying cry was shareholder value. His philosophy was to make extreme cuts—massive layoffs in all areas of operations, if necessary—to streamline the business. The concepts of teamwork and group dynamics seemed foreign to Dunlap, whose actions suggested that people were completely dispensable. He would even fire employees who had been with the company for many years the instant they cost more than he felt they were worth. He saw making money for the shareholders, at whatever price, as his sole responsibility. He had no time for ethical concerns.

At the first meeting with his key executives Dunlap began by shouting that the old Sunbeam was over. He continued: "This is the best day of your life if you're good at what you do and willing to accept change, and it's the worst day of your life if you're not." Afterwards the stunned executives reported that "he just yelled, ranted and raved. He was condescending, belligerent, and disrespectful" [1].

Dunlap's leadership pushed managers to the breaking point. They often compared working for him to trench warfare. The pressure was extremely high, the hours exhausting, and the casualties numerous. Dunlap had imposed such unrealistic goals on the company that most Sunbeam managers believed he was engaged in a short-term exercise to pretty up the business for a quick sale. No wonder the employees were relieved when "Chainsaw Al" was thrown out because of "creative accounting," his brutal reign having been disastrous for the company.

People like Dunlap pride themselves on their self-reliance, fearlessness, lack of sentimentality, and hard-boiled competitive values. There are many Dunlaps to be found in the business world, crude bullies whose demeanor toward others is aggressive, manipulative, and demeaning. They take pleasure in the psychological or physical suffering of others, and may even use violence to establish dominance in a relationship. Cold-blooded and detached, they behave as if they are unaware of the harm they cause.

Quick to resort to threats or punitive action, they favor making preemptive strikes, turning the passive into the active by doing to others what they fear may be done to them. Abrasives see most other people as devious, controlling, and punitive. Viewing the world in this way absolves them of feelings of shame and guilt about their own irresponsible, aggressive actions. Once they displace these feelings to others, they act recklessly and impulsively, justifying anger and vengeful behavior by claiming that they need to be the aggressor in order to keep the upper hand. Anyone who challenges that upper hand is severely punished. Abrasives don't hesitate to sacrifice other people in their pursuit of their goals. The end always justifies the means, in their view, no matter how harsh those means might be [2]–[5].

The primary defensive mechanisms used by abrasives are isolation, projection, and rationalization. They're pros at remaining untouched by the effects of their own unpleasant activities (isolation), scapegoating others when things go wrong (projection), and finding excellent reasons why they're not themselves to blame (rationalization). It's no wonder that people with an abrasive disposition are rarely able to sustain lasting, close relationships with others.

Typically, people with an abrasive disposition are:

- strongly opinionated, narrow-minded, unbending, and obstinate
- authoritarian, intolerant, and prejudiced
- energetic, competitive, and power-oriented
- rigidly self-disciplined
- perfectionist, setting extremely high standards for self and others
- fascinated by violence
- harsh, cruel, and domineering
- prone to outbursts of rage
- given to humiliating or demeaning others
- fearful of the dominance of others
- vindictive
- quick to take offense

At the origin of this kind of behavior we can usually find a convergence of various hereditary and biogenic factors. For example, there's often a history of misplaced parental rejection or hostility—that is, the child has been the inappropriate recipient of parental anger. As the most vulnerable member within the family system, the child is the most convenient outlet for displaced aggression, easy to scapegoat and label as "bad." This sort of treatment leads to feelings of resentment. Some children, faced with the powerlessness of this situation, simply give up. Others confront it, deny their powerlessness, and attempt to gain the upper hand through provocative, belligerent behavior [6].

In some cases parental antagonism is triggered by a child with a choleric temperament, prone to hostility and outbursts of rage. These tendencies initiate a vicious cycle in which the child not only prompts aggression from others but also learns to expect it. As a result, the child becomes extremely guarded, alert to anticipating and warding off denigration, malice, or deception. Chronic exposure to parental rejection, in the form of teasing, belittlement, or humiliation, becomes the template for behavior later in life. Eventually, this type of family dynamic hardwires children to be negativistic, quarrelsome, and defiant. Physical and verbal aggression becomes their sanctioned standard of behavior. When hindered, these children have temper tantrums, become angry, cruel, and mean-spirited, and occasionally even persecute others to get their own way. Because of this learned behavior, such children are unlikely to experience and express tender feelings. They regard authority figures as tough, dangerous, and abusive. Having internalized this model of hostile interaction growing up, as adults they reject authority but, paradoxically, are willing to take on positions of leadership and then abuse others.

ABRASIVES WITHIN THE ORGANIZATION

In organizations, abrasive types can be impulsive, unpredictable, and even self-destructive. They carry a chip on their shoulder and are always spoiling for a fight, which makes them extremely difficult to work with. Explosive and undisciplined, they can't handle planning. Guided by their own dogmatism and hardheadedness, their attitude is "my way or the highway."

Preoccupied with command, power, and dominance, this personality type is more commonly found in leaders than followers. Abrasives want to gain and retain as much power as possible to prevent others from controlling and harming them. They need to be in command: if there's harming to be done, they want to be the ones doing it. Although such people may have certain workplace competencies, they lack one important quality necessary for effective leadership: the ability to create networks and build alliances with others.

Frequently, abrasives pride themselves on being oriented toward getting the job done. A focus on results becomes an excuse for hostile, hurtful actions. The interests and feelings of others—so say abrasives—can't be allowed to interfere with the accomplishment of their goals. Restructuring, downsizing, and other change processes often give people with an abrasive disposition an opportunity to engage in downright hostile behavior. Such processes are the perfect occasions to humiliate people who are in a poor position to defend themselves.

Totally dedicated to work, abrasives refuse to be distracted by family considerations, health concerns, or the need for relaxation. They seem to be prisoners of their personality, having only a minimal understanding of the forces that propel them to do what they do. They devalue sentimentality, intimacy, tenderness, and social cooperativeness and have no talent for intimate relationships. Unable to express softer feelings, they inspire no such feelings in others, thereby continuing that vicious cycle.

Abrasives lack sympathy for the weak and oppressed, whether clients or co-workers, and are contemptuous of those who express compassion and concern for the underdog. They can be extremely self-righteous, rationalizing their actions by saying that what they're doing is for the common good and in the interest of the organization. Given a socially sanctioned power base—i.e., a management position—they may play the role of strict disciplinarian, turning the workplace into a gulag.

The bullying behavior that characterizes people with an abrasive disposition can take various forms. It can be directed toward people they see as vulnerable and powerless—minority groups or women, for example—and expressed as racism or sexism. If nobody at a more senior management level is prepared to challenge the bullying and set boundaries, they will get away with it. Worse, if senior management abdicates responsibility and doesn't interfere, bullying can become a generally accepted part of organizational behavior. In companies where abrasive behavior has become the accepted way of doing things, you will often hear exculpatory platitudes about "the struggle for global competitiveness" and such things. A high level of internal competition and a politicized climate makes some organizations particularly prone to bullying.

One illustration of this is the corporate culture created by senior management at Enron before its fall, where bullying was viewed as an effective way to get the job done. Enron had Ken Lay—a distracted, hands-off chairman—a compliant board of directors, and an impotent staff of accountants, auditors, and lawyers. This loose oversight—combined with the relentless push for creativity and competitiveness by its CEO, Jeff Skilling, and an imaginative CFO, Andy Fastow—fostered a growth-at-any-cost culture, drowning out voices of caution and overriding all checks and balances of prudent business management. Through Skilling's hiring practices, the company became increasingly staffed by ruthless, aggressive trader types. There was no place for the sentimental. It was a dog-eat-dog environment. The reward system—"rank and yank"—epitomized the company culture that developed. Employees would spend about two weeks annually ranking fellow employees' value to the company, on a one-to-five scale. The process could be brutal, and often led to employees downgrading their peers to make themselves look better. Each division was forced to rank a fifth of the employees as fives. This behavior made a mockery of the language that defined the company's values in the annual report: respect, integrity, communication, and excellence [7].

As the Enron case illustrates, some performance-related reward systems, such as ranking, may enhance aggressive behavior. Promotion following the successful harassing or sabotaging of colleagues' work is likely to reinforce a self-perpetuating pattern. Moreover, organizations, when hiring, may single out people with an abrasive disposition for fast-track positions. Over time, these fledgling executives (modeling their behavior on senior executives) become socialized into a more toxic organizational culture, where abrasive behaviors are the acceptable way of doing things.

Abrasive people who attain a leadership position may have suppressed or temporarily suspended aspects of their dark side to facilitate their rise to the top. They may subdue their personalities for short periods of time, but they're most unhappy doing so. They're like steamrollers that can't be stopped for more than a second: they resume their abrasiveness the moment they reach a position of power, generally taking full opportunity to take revenge for real or perceived injustices encountered on the way.

Although abrasive executives can find a home in neurotic organizations, this style of leadership doesn't make for long-term success. Because of the way abrasives deal with others, eventually they or the company will run into problems. Toxic organizational cultures are notoriously unstable, and frequent job changes are common for abrasive individuals, who are the sort of people who will impulsively walk out of a job without having made provisions for another. In extreme cases, people with this particular disposition may even refuse to accept social norms, breaking the law or failing to honor their obligations, as Al Dunlap and the senior management at Enron unfortunately demonstrate.

THE PARANOID DISPOSITION

In 1988 Fortune magazine commented that "Mars' assets are often underestimated because the company is as loose with its information as . . . the CIA." Forrest Mars Sr., the one-time head of a company so obsessively private that turnover figures are still a matter of guesswork, led an organization that was characterized by its abusive, quirky, paranoid, and furtive corporate style. Forrest's father, Frank Mars, had founded the confectionery business that still bears his name, but he didn't care for the aggressive expansion plans his son outlined in the 1930s: "I told my father to stick his business up his ass," Forrest remembered. "I wanted to conquer the whole goddamned world."

And in his way he did, building an empire that produced M&Ms, Snickers, Milky Way, and Mars (of course), as well as pet food and Uncle Ben's rice. He made millions on the basis of a $50,000 buyout from his father and the right to market Snickers overseas.

Hoping to benefit from a little industrial espionage, Forrest Mars left his native US and went to work for the Swiss masters Tobler and Nestlé. Then he opened a small factory in England, where he manufactured Mars bars and developed a distinctive management style. In return for unquestioning loyalty from his staff, he rewarded them with profit-sharing and salaries way above the usual rate for the industry. This compensated in part for his temper tantrums, which he threw (along with boxes of chocolate) if he noticed a defect in manufacture. Returning to the US, he bought back the Mars company from his father's widow and expanded it hugely, buying up competitors and moving into gourmet pet food manufacture. It was said that he never forgot an insult. He ran his empire like a totalitarian state, firing workers for the smallest transgressions. Bad printing on a single M&M was an excuse for discarding millions of the sweets. Managers at the pet food plant had to taste the product, as part of the systematic quality control.

Mars's management style was repeated at home. Although he was one of the richest men in the US, Forrest's children had to work for their pocket money, and when his daughter failed to win first place in a riding competition, Mars took away her pony. However, when he retired from the company in 1973, his sons, Forrest Junior and John, continued to run Mars in their father's style. But Forrest was not finished. He started a new company, Ethel M. Chocolates. Living above his office, he watched his staff through two-way mirrors. In 1992, despite his no longer being associated with the Mars company, he tried to create a merger deal between Mars and Nestlé behind his sons' backs [8].

The example of Forrest Mars is but one of many. The paranoid disposition is rife in organizations. Paranoia operates on a spectrum that goes from normal vigilance toward potential threats in the environment, through transitory paranoid behavior and inter-personal suspiciousness (known as paranoid personality disorder), to delusional states. Essentially, paranoia can be seen as an ongoing, unwarranted suspiciousness and distrust of people. People with a paranoid disposition experience a polarity in their self-image: even though their behavior may be grandiose and arrogant, they're vulnerable to shame, and vacillate between the impotent, despised self and the omnipotent vindicated self.

The outstanding and consistent feature in the behavior of people with a paranoid disposition is their pervasive and unwar-ranted suspicion of other people. They're unshakably convinced that most people, governed by hidden motives, say one thing and mean something else. The paranoid worldview says that given a chance, others will take advantage of them and they will be vul-nerable, losing control over their lives. They believe, for example, that it's unsafe to confide in others, because confidential informa-tion will be used against them. People with a paranoid disposition tend to misread the actions of others, questioning their loyalty and expecting trickery and deception everywhere. Consumed by mistrust and the anticipation of betrayal, they expect the worst of others and are accordingly apprehensive, suspicious, uncompromising, and argumentative.

People with a paranoid disposition are unbelievably touchy, magnifying even minor slights into major offenses. Hypervigilant, they constantly scan the environment for signs of threat and take elaborate precautions even where none are needed. That hyper-vigilance, in conjunction with the expectation that all people are driven by hidden motives, leads to a distortion in perceptions, thoughts, and memories. Even when no confirmation of their suspicions is found, they act as if it had been, moving forward on the assumption that they're right. To others, paranoiacs look intensely guarded and secretive, while they see themselves as faithfully guarding their independence, superiority, and autonomy [4]; [9]–[10].

Paranoiacs favor three defense mechanisms: splitting, which is the tendency to divide the world into two camps (good versus evil, us versus them, for example); projection, which is blaming others for feelings that originate within themselves, and for faults and errors that are rightfully theirs; and denial, which is negating the reality of a particular situation. They may also engage in fantasy, deceiving themselves through the fabrication of unrealistic schemes to ward off deep feelings of helplessness.

Typically, people with a paranoid disposition are:

- hypersensitive
- reluctant to confide in others
- quarrelsome and quick to anger and lash out
- self-righteous
- prone to nitpicking
- tense, and unable to relax
- lacking a sense of humor
- unforgiving of insults, injuries, and slights
- making mountains out of molehills

At the heart of the paranoid disposition—as with the other proto-types—there's frequently a negative childhood experience. As children, paranoid individuals may have been exposed to an extremely intrusive parenting style that fostered feelings of inadequacy or helplessness. Shame and humiliation may have been used by parents as controlling devices. Early experiences of being spied on, demeaned, depreciated, and/or taken advantage of lay the foundation for a lack of basic trust, creating a need for vigilance at all times to safeguard against trickery, deception, and attack.

Children growing up in an intrusive domestic environment have difficulty creating their own psychic space. They have an uphill struggle achieving any level of autonomy or individuation, because the attempt is often perceived as an attack by the rest of the family. As a result, children feel persecuted and have huge uncertainty both about their own identity and about where their identity ends and the identity of the other begins. They become obsessed with understanding the hidden motives of others.

Given these early experiences, paranoid individuals are inherently suspicious of people in authority. They have learned that it's unwise to put their trust in others, fearing (rightly) that their trust will be abused. As a way of fighting feelings of helplessness, they indulge in thoughts of omnipotence and in defensive, highly rigid ideas of self-importance. They often inflate themselves through the creation of grandiose and persecutory fantasies. When under great stress, they may experience a bursting of this inflated bubble of self-importance, leading to highly explosive reactions. When the effects of all these forces are taken into account, it's easy to see that the reality-testing ability of paranoid people can be seriously impaired.

Like individuals with a detached disposition (see Chapter 4), paranoiacs are often interested in mechanical devices, electronics, and automation. This interest may symbolize a reaction against their childhood feelings of being controlled by uncontrollable forces. Mechanical devices help them to monitor their environment, warning them of any sign of threat.

THE PARANOID DISPOSITION WITHIN THE ORGANIZATION

An extreme example of paranoid behavior on a global scale can be found in Stanley Kubrick's Cold War masterpiece, the film *Dr. Strangelove, or How I learned to stop worrying and love the bomb.* It's a hymn to paranoid thinking in a nuclear world. This film, with its darkly hilarious vignettes involving gungho soldiers, wacky generals, spying Russians, drunken premiers, battles with soda machines, fights in the War Room, and the Russians' top-secret Doomsday Machine, demonstrates how prone people are to paranoid thinking. The film seemed even more plausible when it first came out, because its exaggerations were based on then-current rhetoric and events (such as the Cuban missile crisis) that already had an air of horrific exaggeration about them. The film was able to tap into the deep fears and anxieties that emerged in a society that lived with the hydrogen bomb.

The film opens with the paranoid General Jack Ripper declaring a "Code Red," which in effect means that he has authorized the annihilation of planet earth. He seals off Burpelson Air Force Base and orders his B52 bombers (which are at their failsafe positions) to engage in a nuclear attack on the Soviet Union. When his assistant, RAF Group Captain Mandrake, advises moderation, Ripper replies that he intends to launch a preemptive strike on Russia to stop a suspected Communist infiltration—namely, fluoridation, which Ripper sees as a plot to contaminate the red-blooded American water supply. Worried that it will sap Americans' precious bodily fluids, he will drink only grain alcohol and rainwater; likewise, fearing that the culmination of the sexual act with women will drain him of his essence, he eschews intercourse. To foil this dastardly plot, Ripper seals off his high-security defense bunker, overriding the authority of Congress and the President. In his view, no one can be trusted, including men who are wearing the same uniform and saluting the same flag. Although Ripper is a caricature, the film offers a very good description of the dangers of the paranoid mind and a paranoid culture.

The US President (Peter Sellers) and Dr. Strangelove (again, Peter Sellers), the latter a wheelchair-bound Nazi nuclear scientist who has bizarre ideas about man's future, work with the Soviet premier in a desperate effort to save the world. The President orders the army to attack Burpelson Air Force Base and asks someone to get General Ripper to call him. Since the base is on "Condition Red," it's defended by security personnel against any and all attempts by any unit to gain entry to the base. General Ripper himself pulls a machine gun out of a golf bag and orders Group Captain Mandrake to help him repel the army attack.

The Soviet premier, having been informed by the US President of the dramatic situation, remains suspicious and sets into motion Russia's dreaded Doomsday Machine, a defensive system that (when triggered by the dropping of even a single bomb on the USSR) automatically launches buried Soviet nuclear weapons, thereby unleashing a destructive capacity so great that the world would be engulfed in fallout for more than ninety years. The Soviet ambassador explains that they built it because they had read in the New York Times that the US was working on a similar device and they were afraid of a doomsday gap. The President assures him that this had not been the case.

Ripper's assistant Mandrake, meanwhile, tries to cajole his boss into telling him the recall code. Ripper, determined that his plan be carried out, calmly goes into the washroom and shoots himself. By the time the Army takes over the Air Force Base, Mandrake has figured out what the recall code is, and he contacts the President, who implements it. The recall code works for all the bombers except for one, the "Leper Colony," whose radio equipment is damaged and is unable to receive the vital information. Led by Major "King" Kong, an old-fashioned, gung-ho cowboy type (complete with cowboy hat and Texas accent), these men are as loyal and anti-Communist as they come. Unfortunately, the "Leper Colony" is losing fuel and has to divert to the nearest target of opportunity. When Major Kong reaches his target, he realizes that the hydrogen bomb he needs to drop has become jammed due to an earlier skirmish. He dislodges the bomb manually and climbs aboard the deadly weapon, riding it to destruction like a bronco-buster.

Despite Major Kong's efforts, the explosion triggers the Russian Doomsday Machine. Just before the end of the world, the US President and Dr. Strangelove fritter away precious time discussing how society's male élite and a proportionately larger contingent of beautiful women might survive the nuclear holocaust in underground hideouts, thus eventually repopulating the planet. In the final scene, in which we hear Vera Lynn singing "We'll Meet Again," the doomsday shroud forms a halo around the film's last image: the billowing cloud of the hydrogen bomb and the extinction of life.

While General Ripper and Dr. Strangelove are figures of fiction (although some people have suggested that the real Dr. Strangelove was Dr. Edward Teller, the "father of the H bomb"), the paranoid disposition is alive and well and living in organizations. The ideal repositories of paranoia, organizations are havens for people who act in similar, albeit not as catastrophic, ways. And paranoiacs cluster at the top: because they are very aware of the dynamics of power, they strive for leadership positions in order to be better able to protect themselves. They want to strike out aggressively and shape their own destiny. Unfortunately, leadership positions further accentuate paranoid characteristics, because they increase vulnerability.

As the *Dr. Strangelove* example caricatures, leaders are especially vulnerable to paranoia because they really do face genuine dangers, both obvious and hidden, in the form of opponents who want to get rid of them. You can't be an effective leader without rubbing some people up the wrong way. There will always be people who dream of (or enact) retaliation, just as there will always be followers who envy a leader's power and plot to attain it. For leaders, healthy suspiciousness is an adaptive mechanism, a rational response to a world populated by real and not just imagined enemies. Vigilance in the presence of perceived or likely danger is simply an extension of the survival instinct. If suspicion isn't moderated by a sense of reality, however, it slips over into paranoia. Effective leaders ground their behavior in sound political practices that limit and test danger, and they rely on trusted associates to help them stay safe and sane.

Unfortunately, leaders with a paranoid disposition are often too isolated to engage in constructive reality-testing. Preoccupied with details, they pay insufficient attention to the bigger picture, seeing hidden meanings and secret coalitions everywhere. We can find many examples of this disposition among political leaders— including despots such as Stalin, Pol Pot, Kim Il Sung, Saddam Hussein, and Robert Mugabe—and among the top management of organizations.

The direct cause of failure for many paranoid leaders is faulty information-processing, a result of paranoiacs' confusion between subjective and objective reality. Others are brought down (sometimes with their organization) by their resistance to change. Still others so contaminate their environment that it destroys them: as their personal suspicion becomes a suspicious corporate culture, the organization starts to resemble a police state more than a creative enterprise, and the end soon follows.

THE NEGATIVISTIC DISPOSITION

David Post, the new president and CEO of Lotar, a large department store chain, was wondering what to do about Lawrence Neilson, one of his vice-presidents, who (like David himself) was relatively new to the job. David was becoming increasingly annoyed at how Lawrence ran his department and how he related to David. Too many meetings were being canceled at the last moment, and too many reports were either left unfinished or completed very late, in spite of promises to the contrary. Worse, a number of projects had been canceled halfway for no good reason, greatly demotivating the people who had been working on them. David was tired of Lawrence's asking for extensions to deadlines and avoiding responsibility when something was late or went wrong. But with Lawrence's genuine talent for finding excuses, it was difficult to fault him: he offered a plausible reason for everything that went wrong.

Lawrence's mixture of apparently helpful cooperativeness and thinly disguised contrariness was infuriating, but it was hard to know how to be angry with someone who sent such mixed messages. What do you say to someone who tells you he's doing his utmost but fails to produce the report you requested? There were times when David thought Lawrence's helpfulness was just a piece of theater. After all, he never showed much enthusiasm when he received an assignment.

Out of curiosity, David requested a check on Lawrence's background. After some prompting, Lawrence's two previous employers revealed that he had been fired from both jobs for failing to pay enough attention to detail and for making costly mistakes. They also commented on his lack of urgency in finishing projects.

Lawrence Neilson exemplifies a major characteristic of people who fit the negativistic prototype: a subtle resistance to demands for performance. They agree to do whatever is asked of them but then fail to perform. Although there's some controversy about the exact makeup of negativistic people, generally they show a contrariness and disinclination to do as others wish, combined with capricious impulsiveness, irritable moodiness, and an unaccommodating, fault-finding pessimism. People with a negativistic disposition are likely to respond inappropriately to any given situation. Wartime psychiatrists coined the term "passive-aggressive" in the 1940s to describe this sort of behavior when they found themselves dealing with reluctant and uncooperative soldiers who followed orders but did so with chronic, veiled hostility and smoldering resentment [11].

There's a big difference between the passive-aggressive conduct that all of us display occasionally, when we're obliged to do something we don't want to do, and ingrained, habitual passive-aggressive behavior like that of Lawrence Neilson. But even in its milder forms this behavior pattern can be a maddening blend of evasiveness and contrition, affability and impudence.

Typically, people with a negativistic disposition are:

- stubborn
- passive
- defiant and provocative
- inefficient
- critical of authority figures
- overtly compliant and cordial
- covertly aggressive
- ambivalent about everything
- prone to procrastination
- emotionally confused
- fearful of commitment
- unsure of their own desires
- reluctant to express their feelings
- indecisive
- contrary

- discontented, sulky, and moody
- irritable and argumentative
- pessimistic

Negativistic people use three main defensive strategies: displacement, externalization, and opposition. The most common is displacement, a strategy by which they shift their anger away from powerful targets to those who are less able to retaliate or reject them. Negativistic people also externalize their problems, meaning that they attribute them to other people, because they can't accept blame for their own shortcomings. They strengthen their autonomy through devious opposition to authority figures while simultaneously seeking favor from them. They're afraid that following rules will compromise their freedom, but they try to keep their rebellion covert enough to maintain a sense of safety and allow themselves to deny any malicious intent. They also tend to "forget" obligations.

Negativistic people devote their energy to protecting themselves from what they perceive as unreasonable, arbitrary authority. The childhood roots of this behavior lie in a youngster's cognitive and emotional inability to assess clearly what's expected of him or her. The contrary, sulking, and verbal nitpicking behaviors that characterize negativists may have their origins in unending power struggles with parents. Those children who are destined to become negativistic adults are brought up in an environment where external consistency and control are lacking. For example, parents may confuse their children by constantly fighting over expectations, each parent undermining and disqualifying every statement the other parent makes. Children internalize the inconsistent and erratic behavior of their parents over time, eventually overdosing on arbitrary, double-bind communications. Witnessing overt behavior that doesn't match covert behavior, they understand at some level that their parents are saying one thing while meaning another. It's very hard for children to accuse their parents of not meaning what they say. As comparatively helpless beings, they can rarely confront such issues in a direct way. They have to resort to indirect, confusing tactics such as passive resistance.

Growing up, these children learn what kind of behavior pays off, and it's not what the rest of the world tells them. How can they get their parents' attention? It doesn't take them very long to learn that negative behaviors (nail-biting, bed-wetting, eating problems, procrastination, pouting, obstruction, stubbornness, and inefficiency) gain them more and prompter attention than obedience. Not only do such behaviors work, they're in daily use by primary role models: negativistic children imitate their parents' erratic, capricious, and conflicting demands, actions, and attitudes. After kids have completed their contradictory training at home, they take their learned behavior into the workplace with them, dealing with authority figures in a way that causes them problems throughout life.

Though the roots of negativism are in the home, the first indications of problems may emerge when these children go to school. Unable to thwart their more powerful parents, they instead exercise their antipathy to authority figures by sabotage and the circumvention of rules. Their contrary, erratic behavior provokes fights with other children, and by their teenage years such kids may have developed antisocial tendencies such as delinquency, drug abuse, and theft.

Though generally there are inconsistent, arbitrary, and manipulative parents behind negativism, sometimes negativistic behavior stems from a more positive, socially protective need—to keep peace at home and avoid costly mistakes. Children who grow up in loving but demanding families that give them unmanageable responsibilities may turn negativistic. First-born children are more prone to this than others, because they're often expected to take on a good share of their siblings' care. Unable to express their feelings about what they perceive as unreasonable demands, they begin to resent the parents' expectations while not daring to defy them. Although they don't protest, they feel that they will be unable to meet their parents' expectations and so begin to find ingenious ways to fail. In such circumstances, behavior that's cautious and self-protective at heart can be interpreted as insolence or sabotage.

Whatever the family dynamics, people who develop a negativistic disposition inevitably perceive authority figures as arbitrary, unreasonable, and unfair. This perception, learned early, becomes an emotional template that's directed at any authority figure who makes demands on them, whether it's a teacher, spouse, or boss. The sense of independence achieved by responding negatively, however, is a Pyrrhic victory: it leaves negativists with a legacy of contrariness, irritable affectivity, interpersonal ambivalence, and a discontented self-image.

Because people with a negativistic disposition have a basic conflict concerning their self-worth, they oscillate between self-loathing and a sense of entitlement or moral superiority. They're capable of being self-deprecating and feeling guilty for failing to meet expectations in one situation while demonstrating stubborn negativism and resistance in another. If things are going well, negativistic people often go out of their way to derail them. By snatching defeat out of the jaws of victory, they create the disillusionment they anticipate.

Negativists suffer from a range of intense and conflicting emotions that surge quickly to the surface due to weak controls and lack of self-discipline. In spite of an often agreeable façade—they know that it's safer not to show hostility directly—they're unpleasant to work for or with. Their unpredictable, conflicting, and vacillating behavior is extremely difficult to deal with in social situations as well. Predictably, negativists become stuck in a vicious cycle, constantly making enemies instead of friends and making a mess of interpersonal relationships.

THE NEGATIVISTIC INDIVIDUAL WITHIN THE ORGANIZATION

There are occasions when mild negativistic behavior pays off in the workplace. For instance, it can be an effective means of avoiding potentially costly confrontations. A good example of negativism used in that way is described in Joseph Heller's book *Catch 22*. The novel follows a fictional World War II US Army Air Corps bombardier Captain Yossarian, who is based on the island of Pianosa, west of Italy. The following interchange takes place between Yossarian and his crew while on a bombing mission:

"Bomb bay clear," Sergeant Knight in the back would announce.

"Did we hit the bridge?" McWatt would ask.

"I couldn't see, sir, I kept getting bounced back here pretty hard and I couldn't see. Everything's covered with smoke now and I can't see."

"Hey, Aarfy, did the bombs hit the target?"

"What target?" Captain Aardvaark, Yossarian's plump, pipe-smoking navigator would say from the confusion of maps he had created at Yossarian's side at the nose of the ship. "I don't think we're at the target yet, are we?"

"Yossarian, did the bombs hit the target?"

"What bombs?" answered Yossarian, whose only concern had been the flak.

"Oh well," McWatt would sing, "what the hell." [12]

As this antiwar, anti–irrational bureaucracy novel illustrates, insolence directed toward unreasonable, arbitrary authority can be a form of adaptive behavior and provide some protection from extreme pressure to conform to unreasonable demands. In the case of the servicemen in Heller's novel, passive-aggressive behavior is an effective survival strategy.

Generally, however, a passive–aggressive attitude compromises organizational life. Although negativists tend to avoid open conflict, their querulousness, obstructive behavior, and scornful attitude toward authority work against them. They make poor leaders, because in addition to their own inadequate performance, they aren't able to bring out the best in others or encourage people to higher levels of performance. They do best as low-level employees in settings where there are relatively few consequences for nonproductive behavior, or where there are either few rewards or rewards that are distributed arbitrarily. In such situations they may get away with foot-dragging slowness and inefficiency. But their unwillingness to get things done means that they won't last long in most organizations. Those who do last generally don't advance well. Their confusion about what they want from life means that they're poor at career planning, and their behavior is clearly not conducive to career progression.

THE ANTISOCIAL DISPOSITION

Joe Wright didn't know what to do with Al Dover, one of the senior traders in the investment bank where Joe held a top management position. Al produced undeniably great results, but Joe was bombarded with complaints about the way he went about getting them. Like the complainants, Joe was worried about Al's aggression and apparent need to control others. Al seemed to have a total disregard for other people's rights. As far as Joe could tell, Al demonstrated a remarkable lack of insight into the effect his behavior had on others. Discussions they'd had about it had gone nowhere; Al denied everything. But with so much smoke, there had to be a fire somewhere.

Joe also had a hunch that Al wasn't abiding by the rules set by the investment community and had been ignoring the boundaries of confidentiality. He had been accused of trading for personal profit, but the evidence was flimsy and his reputation as a star producer had allowed him to get away with it. Joe had supported him through that but remained concerned about the way Al had rationalized his actions. Joe had suggested that Al would profit from having a leadership coach, but Al's reaction was that any problems he was involved in were of others' making.

Matters came to a head when a female research analyst complained that Al had responded with verbal intimidation when she confronted him with an accusation of insider trading. That intimidation, if the complaint was valid, could cost the bank dearly. Al claimed that he couldn't remember the incident, even though it was allegedly very recent, and he also denied the charge of insider trading. Listening to him, Joe was suddenly reminded of the story of Dr. Jekyll and Mr. Hyde. Al's charm just didn't fit with some of the stories Joe had heard about him. Was he being manipulated? Was Al disregarding the bank's ethical guidelines? Was Al another Nick Leeson (the trader who had bankrupted Barings Bank) in the making?

People with an antisocial disposition like Al's fail to conform to social norms, rules, and obligations. They have a callous disregard for the rights and safety of other people, along with an easily triggered temper and a capacity for violence. They show no remorse when their actions hurt others. Despite their bravura, however, they're quite insecure, with low self-confidence and self-esteem. To cover their insecurities, they resort to defense mechanisms such as scapegoating, rationalization, projection, and denial, all strategies designed to shift responsibility away from oneself and onto others. Not surprisingly, they're accomplished liars [2]; [13].

Typically, people with an anti-social disposition are:

- impulsive and reckless
- self-centered
- independent
- suspicious of intimacy

- callous and abusive
- charming and manipulative
- dishonest and amoral
- aggressive to the point of violence

Sustained neglect and abuse in childhood often result in antisocial behavior in adults. Looking back, we might expect to find asocial parents who were inconsistently available or were impulsive and erratic, perhaps in combination with criminal influences and violence. Over time, children raised in this sort of environment develop contempt for the rules of what they see as a hypocritical society. But deprived and abusive environments aren't the only breeding grounds for this kind of behavior: children from privileged backgrounds can also be antisocial. The main factor is a perception of neglect and deprivation within the family system. Generally, the first indications of antisocial behavior begin to emerge in childhood or adolescence.

Broken homes and homes where the parents have a history of substance abuse or mental illness nurture antisocial behavior. Children who grow up with violence and abuse adopt the behavior that has been modeled for them and typically turn to fellow lost souls in a desperate attempt to establish solidarity, to find a place in a hostile, uncaring world. Lacking guidance and care when growing up, these people never acquire a basic awareness of other people's feelings. Unlike the abrasive prototype, however, they're not driven by vengeful feelings. They simply know no better; they have never learned to care.

Typical elements of antisocial behavior in childhood and adolescence include lying, stealing, and fighting, behaviors that help to relieve tension, irritability, and boredom. There may also be issues with authority and the law, cruelty to animals, pyromania, academic failure, and aggressive sexual behavior. More than any of the other prototypes we've looked at in this and recent chapters, people with an antisocial disposition are drawn to crime, sensation-seeking, and high-risk behaviors such as excessive drinking and drug abuse.

As adults, antisocials have a great need to control others. Once they have power, they are prone to humiliate and dominate others. When they're hindered in exerting control, they exhibit violent tempers that can flare up quickly and without regard for others. Not surprisingly, then, antisocials tend to have poor interpersonal relationships. Fearful of their own inadequacies, unwilling to take responsibility for their behavior, they're always on the attack, always the aggressor, always prepared to victimize others. Deprived of the lessons of caring in childhood, their capacity to love—even simply to relate intimately and affectionately with another person— is markedly impaired. Without the compassion, sincerity, and ethical and moral values that characterize most human beings, they experience only superficial and shallow emotional reactions (though some can produce an empathic façade), and their relationships have little depth. Their only emotional strength is hostility.

ANTISOCIALS WITHIN THE ORGANIZATION

People with an antisocial disposition, known in their extreme form as sociopaths, are generally intellectually able but morally color-blind, unable to differentiate between acceptable and unacceptable forms of behavior. Like moths to a flame, they're attracted to power, prestige, and money and have few difficulties infiltrating the world of business. They know how to bend the rules to their advantage and can be convincing, compulsive liars when called to account. They lack a sense of responsibility for their actions and are devoid of any sense of remorse.

There are many antisocial people to be found in organizations; compulsive liars who can be charming while excelling at deception and evading accountability; predators who, refusing to acknowledge the contributions and achievements of others, twist, distort, and misrepresent everything others do. They're capable of theft and plagiarism. Like abrasives, antisocials do best (and may even thrive) in organizations where authority is weak and senior management fails to erect boundaries against this kind of behavior.

Restructuring is a favorite tactic of antisocials who have reached a senior position in an organization. The chaos that results is an ideal smokescreen for dysfunctional leadership. Failure at the top goes unnoticed, while the process of restructuring creates the illusion of a strong, creative hand on the helm.

The story of Lord Conrad Black, who is a real-life parallel to the protagonist in *Citizen Kane*, exemplifies many of the antisocial (and abrasive) personality characteristics outlined here. At one point Black was the third-largest media magnate in the world. Apart from the *Citizen Kane* resemblance, there were also uncanny parallels between Black and Dennis Kozlowski of Tyco. But optimists would say that at least Kozlowski managed to make some money for his shareholders, whereas investors in Black's flagship company, Hollinger International, weren't so lucky. With the acquiescence of lawyers, accountants, and directors who refused to challenge him, Black and a few cronies allegedly skimmed off 95% of the firm's profits through "management fees" (on top of salaries and bonuses) in the last six years of his reign (to say nothing of the luxury cars, mansions, private jets, and other perks they accumulated) [14].

Black's leadership style has been described as ruthless, volatile, and vindictive. Shareholder activism and corporate governance counted for nothing: Hollinger International was run as a personal fiefdom. Eventually, however, Black's hubris led to his downfall.

Throughout his life Black acted as if he was too important for the rules of law and etiquette that apply to ordinary people. From an early age he was fascinated by power, studying the lives of historical figures and developing friendships with some of the world's leading politicians. Through his newspapers he tried to position himself as an intellectual force of right-wing conservatism. He seemed to want to use the media to reshape the political culture of society. As time went on, however, the money and fame that came with the newspapers wasn't enough for him. He wanted a title. By renouncing his Canadian citizenship, he made himself eligible for the British discretionary peerage. When the Canadian Prime Minister Jean Chrétien moved to block his entrance into the House of Lords, Black went so far as to sue him.

Conrad Black was born into a wealthy Canadian family. His father was the president of Canadian Breweries, an international brewing conglomerate. The older man's dying words to his son were allegedly, "Life is hell, most people are bastards, and everything is bullshit." At an early age, Black demonstrated his entrepreneurial spirit by selling exam papers at his private school, Upper Canada College, after which he was promptly expelled. He rose to national prominence through a series of ingenious takeovers and the restructuring of holding companies. By the early 1990s the Hollinger group controlled over 400 newspapers in North America.

Black was reputed to be an extremely hands-on proprietor. To him, newspapers weren't a public good, and when it suited him he would intervene in editorial policy-making. He strongly believed that he had the ultimate responsibility for what the newspapers he owned had to say. Disagreeing with Black wasn't an option. Excessively litigious, he would sue whenever he was obstructed and succeeded in intimidating many journalists.

On 17 November 2003, Black announced that he would step down as CEO of Hollinger. The move followed findings by a special committee that Black and other senior executives had received $32.15 million in unauthorized payments. The private jet and the cars, the homes in London, New York, and Palm Beach, the FDR memorabilia—even the philanthropic donations to hospitals and arts institutions—almost all had been paid for by shareholders. Black was accused of improperly diverting tens of millions of dollars of corporate assets from Hollinger International. However, he denied any wrongdoing, maintaining that the committee's report contained numerous inaccuracies and misrepresentations.

Whatever the outcome of the legal issues, Black has been irrevocably toppled from his perch, his empire has been broken up, his name has been horribly tarnished, and his network of high-powered friends has dissolved. Few believe that Black will ever run a public company again.

PROTOTYPES AND BEYOND

Richard Freely, the president of a faltering company in the electrical appliance industry, seemed increasingly unwilling to face the declining profit position of his company. One month before the banks eventually took control of the firm, he held meetings during which he discussed nonexistent orders, the development of revolutionary new machinery, and the introduction of innovative products. These new developments were supposed to turn the company around and dramatically change its position in the industry. Richard dismissed the dismal profit-and-loss picture, inefficiencies in production, and poor sales performance, attributing them to unfair industry practices by competitors or even sabotage, and assured his managers that change was imminent and that the company would shortly be out of the red.

Richard wasn't doing much better than his company. Always a loner, he became more and more detached as the stressfulness of his situation increased. He became unapproachable: anyone who seemed likely to bring bad news couldn't get an appointment with him, and even sycophants had to be careful. It didn't take much to arouse his suspicions that someone was conspiring against him. If any subordinate questioned him, Richard indulged in an outburst of coruscating, humiliating anger and then fired the dazed employee. The evil spell was broken only when the banks took control.

In Richard Freely we see a mixture of styles: elements of the paranoid disposition in the way he blamed unfair competition or sabotage for his problems, elements of the detached disposition in his increasing isolation, and elements of the abrasive disposition in his anger management (or lack of it). In fact, hybrids—mixtures of all these styles and others—are the rule rather than the exception, and a "normal" personality recognizes elements of many of the styles in his or her behavior. Anyone trying to analyse their own or a leader's style, then, should remember that "pure" prototypes are fairly rare. Because of the blending of styles, diagnoses are often very difficult to make. An overview of the different personality styles described here and in Chapters 2, 3, and 4, and the likelihood of finding each style in leaders and followers, is given in Table 5.1.

As I've indicated, certain combinations of personality style tend toward leadership, and others mean that people will be followers. Some mixtures of styles can be winning combinations,

Table 5.1 An overview of the spectrum of personalities

Disposition	Leadership Tendencies	Follower Tendencies
Narcissistic	Very high	Low
Dramatic	Medium	High
Controlling	High	High
Dependent	Very low	High
Self-defeating	Very Low	High
Detached	Medium	Medium
Depressive	Low	Low
Abrasive	Medium	Low
Paranoid	High	Medium
Negativistic	Very low	Medium
Antisocial	High	Low

while others can be extremely dysfunctional. For example, narcissism and a controlling disposition create a complementary combination that can be highly successful. On the other hand, as the example of Richard Freely shows, combining paranoia with detachment and abrasiveness spells disaster.

Although certain prototypes are more likely to make successful leaders than others, as the table indicates, it's all a matter of degree. While moderation in mixtures of style may have no ill effects, excess almost certainly will.

In our discussion of prototypes, we've seen that the acquisition of a specific personality disposition is a duet between nature and nurture. Personality doesn't develop in isolation, but in a complicated context of people and places and events. It's a process that we all go through. Like rain, it leaves nobody untouched. Assessing personalities is also a complex process. Many very subtle indicators need to be taken into consideration. In some ways, people are like books, and it takes time to read them and work out the plot. The more "books" we read, the more we discover that "normal" and "abnormal" are just stations on a spectrum of possibilities. Paradoxically, even being too normal—a normopath, we might say—can be a problem. We learn too, as I've noted here, that most of us represent a variety of different dispositions; though we may favor one, we can't be slotted into any one specific prototype.

Most important, as noted earlier, personality is destiny. All of us like having a personality of our own; we like being unique. That's what the narcissism of minor differences is all about. However, none of us wants to be too different. Maintaining that balance remains a challenge to us all.

REFERENCES

1. Byrne, J. A. (1999). *Chainsaw: the notorious career of Al Dunlap in the era of profit-at-any-price*. New York, HarperCollins.

2. Barlow, D. H., Ed. (2001). *Clinical Handbook of Psychological Disorders.* New York, The Guilford Press.
3. Hamstra, B. (1994). *How Therapists Diagnose: Seeing though the Psychiatrist Eye.* New York, St. Martin Press.
4. Millon, T. (1996). *Disorders of Personality: DSM IV and Beyond.* New York, John Wiley.
5. Stone, M. H. (1980). *The Borderline Syndromes.* New York, McGraw-Hill.
6. Kets de Vries, M. F. R. (2004). *Lessons on Leadership by Terror: Finding Shaka Zulu in the Attic.* Cheltenham: Edward Elgar.
7. McLean, B. and P. Elkind (2003). *The Smartest Guys in the Room: The Amazing Rise and Scandalous Fall of Enron.* New York, Penguin Books.
8. Brenner, J. C. (2004). *Emperors of Chocolate: Inside the Secret World of Hershey and Mars.* New York: Broadway Books.
9. Comer, R. J. (2003). *Abnormal Personality.* New York, Worth Publishers and W. H. Freeman and Company.
10. Shapiro, D. (1965). *Neurotic Styles.* New York, Basic Books.
11. Wetzler, S. (1992). *Living with the Passive-Aggressive Personality.* New York, Fireside.
12. Heller, J. (1996). *Catch 22.* New York: Simon & Schuster.
13. Millon, T., P. H. Blaney and R. D. Davis, Eds (1999). *Oxford Textbook of Psychopathology.* New York.
14. McNish, J. and S. Stewart (2004). *Wrong Way: the Fall of Conrad Black.* New York, The Overlook Press.

CHAPTER 6

ELATION AND ITS VICISSITUDES

No great genius has ever existed without a touch of madness.

—Aristotle

The history of the world's great leaders is often the story of human folly.

—Voltaire

It's a terrible thing to look over your shoulder when you are trying to lead—and find no one there.

—Franklin Roosevelt

The quieter you become, the more you can hear.

—Zen proverb

Noh, a form of play that originated in Japan in the 14th century, is one of the oldest existing forms of theatre. Originally an entertainment for religious festivals, Noh developed further under the protection of medieval shoguns. Noh performances are typically a combination of song, dialogue, music, and especially dance, with themes addressing human destiny rather than specific events. They often feature restless ghosts who are compelled to return to earth to retell their stories in a sacred space.

Noh plays are performed in a restrained, highly stylized manner; the actors, like Zen priests, are inscrutable, their gestures abstracted by simplification as is typical of Zen communication. Along with elaborate costumes, the actors wear masks to convey their characters. The masks help ensure that an actor's facial expression never varies from that which the playwright intended (though an actor may change his mask in mid-performance, as dictated by the play). Along with the other components of Noh, masks help the actors concentrate on the essence or soul of the people they're representing.

Noh is a truly timeless art form: it speaks to modern audiences as it did to the noblemen and women of a much earlier period. As indicated above, there are parallels between Zen and Noh, the former having had considerable indirect influence on the latter. Both Noh art and Zen are underpinned by imbalance and paradox. The early Noh producers and actors worked primarily for an audience whose aesthetic standards were those of Zen; and whatever may be said of the literary content of the plays, their structure and the atmosphere of their presentation were in full accordance with the canons of Zen taste.

A comparable Zen-like stylized theater, but of a very different form, can be found in Leni Riefenstahl's *Triumph des Willens* (or *Triumph of the Will*). Presented as a film, this recording of the annual Nazi Party Congress at historic Nuremberg in September 1934 may be the most controversial documentary ever made, being both despised and admired. Considered the greatest propaganda film of all time, *Triumph of the Will*'s sense of spectacle made it a visual icon to Nazism. The film is not only a full-blown celebration of the power of the Nazi regime, but in particular a glorification of Adolf Hitler. It chronicles the week of events at the Nazi rally, culminating in a speech by Hitler. As with watching a Zen-influenced Noh play, seeing *Triumph of the Will* is a remarkable experience, due to its artistic quality—its lyrical, dance-like cinematographic rhythm and its light and dark movements. Nazi symbols—swastikas, eagles, flags, and banners—are highlighted from different angles, making for a great sense of drama. People are blended into the background or filmed as part of a group: we see anonymous masses of soldiers marching, carrying Nazi flags, and saluting the Fuehrer. Vast faceless masses appear to be an essential part of the film's construction; Hitler is the only non-faceless persona—but given the way he comes across, he could be a Noh actor with a set of masks.

This black-and-white documentary, with a mastery of technique that's both breathtaking and sinister, brilliantly captures the Wagnerian grandeur and meticulous choreography of the Nazi rally. To give the documentary real momentum, Riefenstahl opens it with Hitler descending in a plane from the skies above Nuremberg to an enthusiastic reception from Nazi supporters on the ground. From Hitler's arrival all the way to the end, the film shows an incredibly orchestrated spectacle featuring tens of thousands of extras. This remarkable documentary takes great pleasure in the Teutonic architecture of Albert Speer, the formal precision of marching cadres, and above all, the almost religious exaltation of Hitler as the mystical personification of the dreams and ideals of his people. The film is like a love song celebrating Hitler's charismatic talents.

People obviously believed what they saw in the Noh-like images they were shown in *Triumph of the Will*—believed in the elaborate glorification of a dark leader and in the staged beauty of dictatorship. The ranting of Hitler, with his frightening tirades about the glory of Germany, the stultification of people used to being addressed by blaring intonation rather than common sense—the result is a mesmerizing experience. At the end of the documentary, after Hitler has delivered an impassioned speech that stirs up his enthralled audience, admiring aide Rudolph Hess takes the microphone, points to Hitler (as if emphasizing the ultimate abdication of self), and says, "Adolf Hitler is Germany and Germany is Adolf Hitler. He who takes an oath to Hitler takes an oath to Germany!" Few people at that rally would have been able to prevent themselves from being swept away in the maelstrom of visual, symbolic, and emotional forces. The enthusiasm with which the Germans threw themselves into an orgy of violence and self-destruction is a testimony to the mesmerizing qualities of charismatic leadership—in this case, of the darkest sort.

The term "charismatic leadership" is often used to describe the compelling effect some people have on those in their employ or constituency. Charismatic leaders, like pop stars, have the ability to leave their audience spellbound and inspired. As a consequence, they have the potential to help transform others: charismatic leaders, through language, attitude, and action, help people transcend their normal way of doing things. But as the movie *Triumph of the Will* demonstrates dramatically—and as Zen teaching emphasizes—these charismatic, inspirational qualities can also be a cause for great concern. The shadow side of this form of leadership has been a source of inspiration for Zen masters, psychoanalysts, and leadership coaches alike. While the ability to inspire others can be used for the good, it can easily be used for the bad, as the example of Hitler demonstrates. Charismatic leaders can be like the Pied Piper, entrancing those around them and leading them to their doom. Many charismatic people engage in self-destructive behavior, and when they draw others with them, the consequences can be far-reaching and even deadly.

THE GIFT AND CURSE OF CHARISMA

In the previous chapters I've presented various character prototypes and discussed how personality can affect leadership style. In this chapter I'll be looking at personality from a different angle, introducing the emotional addict—a person characterized by serious mood swings—as the latest in our personality parade. The reason for singling out this particular behavior modality is that it's often aligned with charismatic behavior and leadership. Moreover, it's especially common among leaders who lead their organizations and their people astray. Thus a better understanding of the psychological functioning of the emotional addict will help us better understand the psychodynamics of people in organizations.

Charisma is a special characteristic that some people, and most truly effective leaders, possess. The term charisma comes from the Greek word kharisma, or gift. Although it's generally used to describe the ability to charm or influence people, it also has religious connotations, meaning "of the spirit" or "inspired"—that is, having God's light shining through one. People with charisma are seen as possessing invisible energy that creates highly visible effects. Not surprisingly, as the case of Hitler shows at the negative extreme, many people feel attracted to charismatic leaders. Such leaders gather followers by dint of personality and charm, rather than via external power or authority. But what makes them so attractive can also be their downfall, and that of the people associated with them.

When we put aside charisma's religious associations, what are some of its qualities? Why is it such a mysterious force? What makes it so special? At a purely descriptive level we can list adjectives such as visionary, energetic, unconventional, exemplary, and theatrical. We have to go deeper, though, to decode the mystery. If we adopt a clinical orientation and draw on the concepts of transference (as described in Chapter 2), the enigma of charisma becomes less murky. We then recognize that followers respond to their leaders as they would have done to their parents or other authority figures while growing up. In fact, this process is part of a general developmental matrix that repeats itself, to some extent, in most leader-follower relationships. As the past is transferred to the present in the interaction between a dynamic leader and his or her followers, it sets the stage for "charismatic attribution," reactivating former developmental interaction patterns and bringing a hunger for idealization to the fore once again.

It's clear that charisma can be a gift, but as many followers can attest, it has the potential to be a curse as well. As noted earlier, charismatic leaders can cause a contagion of enthusiasm and excellence. They can also trigger contagion of a far more negative sort, drawing their followers into collusive relationships. Some of the leader-follower collusions can be summarized by the term "folie à deux," or shared madness, a form of mental contagion [1]–[4]. In folie à deux situations, both parties get stuck in a process of mutual projective identification—there's a hefty psychological term for you!—that hampers growth and development.

Projective identification, an attempt to apprehend and influence another person's subjective world, is a complex, subtle, almost mystical process whereby a part of the self is expelled and "deposited" into someone else. As an interpersonal process, it can be interpreted as an intrusive, primitive form of communication whereby the initiator gets the receiver to experience a set of feelings similar to his or her own. Through this process of projective identification, both parties—be it consciously or unconsciously—are drawn together. The person who does the projecting evokes in the recipient of the projection feelings parallel to the ones projected. In other words, the recipient, who then experiences similar feelings, understands the initiator [5].

In the case of folie à deux, leaders whose capacity for reality-testing has become impaired shift their delusions and unusual behavior patterns to their subordinates, who in turn often not only take an active part in, but also enhance, and elaborate on the delusions. The recipients of these delusional ideas start to behave in accordance with the projected fantasies (rather than simply understanding them). In some situations the initiator uses the recipient as a kind of "garbage disposal," trying to make him or her the recipient of the initiator's own undesired qualities.

Given the power dynamics of organizations, colleagues and followers who aren't willing to "play" with a delusional leader aren't likely to last. Followers who want to remain employed may need to engage in mental acrobatics to stay in the orbit of their leader; they may need to twist and stretch reality a little or a lot in order to stay close to the center of power. If they want to minimize conflict and disagreement, they must be willing to sacrifice the truth on the altar of intimacy, maintaining a connection with the leader even though that person has lost touch with reality. (The phenomenon of projective identification isn't purely negative, however, because it forms the basis for empathy, intuition, leaps of nonverbal synchronicity, experiences of mystical union with another person, and the ability to "read" another person's mind.)

"Mental gridlock" often occurs in situations of folie à deux, because once people fall into dysfunctional interaction patterns, they can't find their way out. In fact, they can't even see the rut that they're in. Given that projective identification is an unconscious process, both leader and follower in a collusive relationship would almost certainly deny the collusion. The players lack the ability to see their relationship objectively; they can't see that they're trapped in a "parasitic" bond. And they certainly wouldn't acknowledge that their collusion is a sign of arrested development, though it's an attempt to deal with deep-seated, unresolved childhood experiences and conflicts.

A famous example of folie à deux between two individuals is found in the literary relationship between Don Quixote and Sancho Panza in Miguel de Cervantes' masterpiece. Don Quixote, a nobleman, has completely lost touch with reality: he fights windmills that he thinks are his enemies, and he sees virtue and beauty in a woman whom society has rejected as a prostitute. His squire, at the outset a reasonable, sane man, ends up sharing the delusions of his master, becoming equally mad.

When collusive relationships, with their impaired reality-testing, develop in an organizational setting, they can have various outcomes—all negative. What starts on a small scale—the leader and a single follower—can lead to the full-blown contagion of groupthink and folie en masse. The result is typically the self-destruction of the leader, professionally speaking, and the demise of the organization. If before the ultimate "fall" some of the organizational participants recognize that the leader is out of touch with reality and sense the dangers of collusion, the endgame may include a "palace revolution" whereby the leader is overthrown.

Important as transference (expressed in an extreme way in folie à deux) is to charisma, it alone doesn't always fully explain that phenomenon. Even among charismatic leaders there are some who stand out as especially influential and magnetic, or who at times take on a special fervor. At the root of their charisma is what psychologists call hypomania, or elation, a close relative of manic-depression. When they're in an elevated, expansive mood state, their energetic behavior becomes even more compelling, making them highly attractive to others and thus more able to confer their perceptions and mood states on others.

Although most of us have heard about manic-depressive illness, with its devastating consequences to the sufferer and to friends and family, many are unaware of milder temperamental variants of this condition—patterns of behavior, including hypomania, that aren't as easily identified. People whose behavior is hypomanic are prone to mildly manic states rather than the extreme highs and lows of full-blown manic-depressive illness [6]–[9].

THE SIRENS OF HYPOMANIA

An example will help illustrate the complex nature of hypomania. A few years ago, I received a phone call from an acquaintance, the non-executive chairman of Novorex, a large consumer products company. He was interested in talking to me because the board he headed had just forced the resignation of David O'Connor, a man in his mid-forties who had been the CEO of the company for just over three years. Initially, according to my acquaintance, all the board members had been very pleased to have David at the helm of Novorex. He had been a highly attractive candidate for the position; his charm, energy, and positive thinking had won over everyone on the board. More important, he had been full of ideas for revitalizing the company, which had been in a slump for quite a few years.

Soon after being hired by the board, David had gone on an acquisition spree to improve Novorex's global product/market position. Although his logic for the different acquisitions was convincing at the time, the acquisition policy soon put Novorex in dire financial straits and saddled it with a portfolio of poorly matched enterprises. The promised synergies weren't materializing.

My acquaintance confessed somewhat sheepishly that he and the other board members felt considerable responsibility for the present sorry state of the company; they regretted not having been more vigilant in monitoring and questioning David about his moves. He explained that the board had been entranced by David's vision of the future; his intensity, his energy, and his self-assuredness had been almost intoxicating. David really knew how to induce enthusiasm in other people, according to my acquaintance. As a result, the board had gone along with David until it was almost too late. Even after the board members had commissioned an external consulting report and learned that most of the acquisitions were lemons—a fact confirmed by the financial results and stock prices over the last two years—they had been reluctant to act.

My acquaintance explained that he and the other board members had waited so long to intervene because they really wanted to believe David's claim that—in spite of poor financial results—a turnaround was just around the corner. However, a costly strike at their major distribution center, the result of a number of poorly executed cost-cutting measures, had convinced them otherwise. That development surely meant another year of serious losses and a further fall in the share price. With some of their larger institutional shareholders becoming vocal in their concerns, the strike had left them no alternative but to pull the plug and ask for David's resignation.

It was clear from my acquaintance's comments that his sense of responsibility extended beyond the company to the colleague who had been asked to resign. He implied that, by allowing themselves to be caught up in David's personal magnetism, they had failed not only the company but the man they had hired. He felt that David, in his present state, needed some help and asked me if I would see him. I told him that I would be happy to do so. When I received a call from David later that same day, we set up an appointment a couple of days hence.

On the basis of my acquaintance's description of David, I had expected a very different type of person than the man who kept that appointment. It wasn't easy to recognize, in the man slumped in my office chair, the energetic, self-assured individual I had heard described previously. As a matter of fact, David made exactly the opposite impression: I saw a person who felt sad and empty, who had little interest or pleasure in anything. When I probed a bit, David complained about his inability to sleep, his loss of appetite, and his general sense of fatigue.

David explained his present mood state as a consequence of his dismissal. Having had time to reflect on the matter, he acknowledged that the board's decision wasn't completely unreasonable—an acknowledgment that grieved him. His behavior and actions may have given them cause, he admitted: his acquisition policy may have been too bold; he may have painted too optimistic a picture of the expected results; he may have been a bit too cavalier with the figures; he maybe should have heeded the advice of some of his more "sober" executives rather than attempting to sweep them away with his enthusiasm. He confessed that he had ignored a consulting report that showed more depressing numbers than the ones he had presented to the board, and had rationalized the dramatic fall in share price as just temporary.

Though David described his mood state as rooted in his dismissal, it soon became clear from the conversation that he had been prone to mood swings since childhood. He mentioned that there had been many periods in his life when he had been wildly out of control—dominated by soaring highs and melancholy lows. Almost a decade earlier he had consulted a psychiatrist for help in controlling his unstable behavior, and she had prescribed medication that had helped him for a time; it had made his life more balanced. However, he had found that life with lithium wasn't as rich as life without; the antidepressant had resulted in an emotional dampening of his experiences, making his existence more "flat," less exciting. Missing the highs of hypomania, he had stopped taking the medication, and he remained off it to this day, preferring the occasional state of euphoria (and the lows that were part of the package) to the more middle-of-the-road state he had attained with the help of medication.

David tried to explain to me how he felt when flying high. While in that state, he said, he perceived everything much more intensely. A simple thing like walking in the local park, for example, became an almost mystical experience. With all his senses fully operating, his awareness of all the objects in his environment was intensified. Whatever he did—be it looking at a tree or a flower, listening to a bird, or talking with an associate—he did more deeply.

It became clear from the conversation that David was addicted to his high moods. Being in an elevated state brought him a great deal of satisfaction and seemed to benefit his work as well. It increased his own productivity and helped him energize his colleagues and actualize the various projects they were involved in. He said that getting others excited about his ideas made him feel alive. When that high-spiritedness left him, life had a dead and deadening quality.

Upon further questioning, David mentioned that before his marriage he had been something of a Don Juan, dating a steady supply of girlfriends. Women had seemed to flock to him back then, drawn by his ebullience. While not many stayed around long, he had enjoyed their company, craving the intensified sexual feelings he had experienced when in an elevated mood state. David's ability to attract women seemed to have had an addictive quality to it—the more women he dated, the more he felt the urge to meet new women—but it had also had a destabilizing influence, making him more prone to mood swings.

His marriage at the age of twenty-six had helped somewhat in balancing his moods. His wife had given some stability to his life. Recently, however, with the children in college, his wife had embarked on a full-time career. Their equilibrium changed as they saw less and less of each other. With his wife preoccupied with professional concerns, David began to spend more time at the office and on travel, and he had affairs whenever tempted, making little effort to conceal the evidence from his wife. Gradually, his preoccupation with other women ate into their marriage. He and his wife had been separated for over a year, but he was only now coming to realize how much the decrease in interaction with his wife had affected him.

It also became clear from the conversation that David was no stranger to substance abuse. He often resorted to help from a bottle when he was feeling up, because alcohol prolonged and intensified the euphoric effects. When asked, he denied that he was an alcoholic, but he admitted that he drank a few whiskeys each day. He also admitted that he had experimented with a few drugs, including cocaine.

Before joining Novorex, David had been the chief operating officer of another company in a related industry, working closely with the CEO—a man whom David described as exerting a stabilizing influence on his life. They had been very successful as a team, in part because their temperaments offset each other: the conservative CEO had modified David's expansive ideas into more manageable proportions. David had succumbed to the temptations of a headhunter, however, and accepted the job at Novorex. He thought that serving as CEO would give him the opportunity to really show his worth. And for a while it had; he had been really flying—until the present crash.

The symptoms that David described suggested a relatively mild variety of manic-depressive or bipolar disorder. Bipolar illness encompasses a wide range of mood disorders and temperaments, varying in severity from cyclothymia—which is characterized by noticeable (but not debilitating) changes in mood, behavior, and thinking—to full-blown, life-threatening manic-depression. What makes the behavior of people with any of the bipolar variants unique is the cyclical nature of their illness. These people constantly swing back and forth between two opposite poles of emotion.

In the *Diagnostic and Statistical Manual of the Mental Disorders, DSM-IV-Tr* [10], mood disorders are listed according to their intensity. Broadly speaking, a distinction is made between, in descending order of severity, Bipolar I Disorder, Bipolar II Disorder, and Cyclothymia. True manic-depressive illness, or Bipolar I Disorder (characterized by one or more manic episodes), isn't something to be taken lightly. The mood disturbance of the true manic-depressive is sufficiently severe to cause a marked impairment in occupational functioning and in social activities and relationships. Some manic-depressives also experience psychotic episodes characterized by delusional thinking, hallucinations, and/or bizarre behavior. Occasionally manic-depression is extreme enough to require hospitalization, to prevent harm to self or others. Without medication, all manic-depressives have difficulty functioning normally. With medication, however, even those with a tendency toward psychosis generally don't become psychotic. Any bouts of madness they do suffer are generally temporary, seldom progressing to chronic insanity.

Of the three bipolar subcategories—Bipolar I Disorder, Bipolar II Disorder, and Cyclothymia—it's the latter, less severe two that are more commonly found in organizational settings. Instead of engaging in truly manic behavior, with its increasingly explosive highs and potentially suicidal lows, Bipolar IIs and cyclothymics are prone to hypomanic behavior, or "mildly" manic states.

These hypomanic episodes alternate with depressive episodes during which people lose interest and enjoyment in normally pleasurable acts and events. They may also experience changes in appetite or weight, problems with sleeping (too much or too little), decreased energy, apathy, lethargy, hopelessness, a sense of emptiness and futility, feelings of worthlessness or guilt, difficulty thinking, an inability to concentrate or make decisions, and recurring thoughts of death and suicidal fantasies. It should be noted that these mood disturbances aren't due to the physiological effects of drug abuse or medication.

While hypomanics in the depressive state are bereft of energy, the opposite can be said of them when they're in the manic state. It's easy to see how executives in a hypomanic mode can revitalize and move organizations. Possessing qualities that are often described as charismatic, these people are energetic, flamboyant, and expansive. They know how to pull others under their spell with their unflagging and intoxicating enthusiasm. They're positive thinkers, undefiable optimists in the face of adversity; for them the glass is always half-full. Furthermore, they dare to tread where others fear to go; they easily assume risks and are willing to make bold moves. They crave stimulation, novelty, and excitement. Life is filled with meaning for them: they have a purpose, and there are many things to be done. They make enormous efforts to make their dreams come true and take others with them in their search for adventure.

While they're in manic mode, their speed of mental association, fluency of thought, elevated mood, and strong sense of wellbeing can be infectious, as can their sense of euphoria and their pronounced enthusiasm. They radiate self-confidence about the things that they're trying to set into motion (although that confidence is often later revealed to have been misplaced). Their high moods bring with them a sense that everything is possible. Given that belief in ultimate possibility, it's not surprising that following the rules isn't their forte. They know how to beat the system, finding creative ways around it. However, they often underestimate the effort needed to get projects on their way.

Hypomanics, when in their manic state, usually have an inflated sense of self-esteem, as well as an unbending conviction of the correctness and importance of their ideas. Although this sense of conviction can be used for the good, it can also have disastrous consequences. The "I'm always right" way of thinking and behaving tends to disregard valuable alternatives and thus contributes to poor judgment; this in turn can lead to chaotic patterns of personal and professional relationships. The grandiosity of hypomanics often leads them into impulsive involvement in questionable endeavors, ideas coming so quickly that one scheme follows on the heels of another. Hypomanics are often easily distracted as well; incapable of screening out more relevant from less relevant information, they change activities as the urge hits them. There's a certain volatility to their behavior, and they can be extremely impatient.

They're also extremely social when manic, ready to engage whomever they encounter. Consequently, they may get caught up in intense and impulsive romantic or sexual liaisons, even with workplace colleagues. Compared to more common mortals, upbeat hypomanics seem to need very little sleep. A "good" night's rest isn't for them; there are too many things to be done. Because their thoughts may race, often at a rate faster than can be articulated, their speech pattern may be louder and more rapid than is usual.

What are the organizational consequences of this cluster of elevated-mood characteristics in hypomanics? The increased energy and expansiveness, the intensified perceptual awareness, the willingness to take risks, and the fluency of thought associated with hypomania often result in highly productive and creative periods. As a result, hypomanics can be a real asset to their organizations. They can be very imaginative and creative, and are generally high-achievers. As a matter of fact, a considerable body of research indicates a strong relationship between bipolar disorders and intellectual and creative achievement. A much higher than expected rate of bipolar disorders appears to exist among exceptionally creative artists and writers. One study concluded that 38% of a sample of eminent British writers and artists had been treated for mood disorders [8]. While extreme fluctuating mood states can contribute to creative imagination and expression, the research findings also show that they can be a highly destructive force. For example, a large percentage of people suffering from bipolar disorders have a history of some kind of substance abuse or dependence. People with bipolar disorders are also far more likely to be suicide-prone.

The precarious balancing act of these people can be observed in business settings as well as in the creative realm. As indicated earlier, these people can make a major creative contribution to their organization. At the same time, their expansiveness, unwarranted optimism, grandiosity, impulsiveness, and poor judgment while in an elevated mood state can lead to the undertaking of extremely risky ventures. So caught up in their grandiosity that they overestimate their capabilities, hypomanics may engage in more activities than they can handle—more than are humanly possible. Yet they don't take well to suggestions about cutting back. Indeed, they can become extremely irritable when their wishes are thwarted. An irritable underpinning may characterize their behavior across the board. Instability of mood, alternating between euphoria and irritability, is frequently seen in hypomanics.

The fact that hypomanics tend to deny that their behavior can be problematic complicates interactions with them; they often resist all efforts to be helped. And people who haven't seen them in their most manic state are prone to concur, because hypomanics put on a good front; they can be very convincing in assuring others that there's nothing the matter with them. They avoid unpleasant ideas and perceptions, along with the emotional consequences of reality—the anxiety that would overwhelm them if the warded-off depressed feelings and images were permitted to flood them—by immersion in a mood state that varies from good humor to exultation; but only the good humor is readily apparent to outsiders.

SURVIVING THE "MANIAC"

With the knowledge gained from this excursion into the vicissitudes of hypomania, let's return to David. What can be done to help him? What are his options? What would be the appropriate form of intervention? Generally speaking, what can be done to contain the contagion of this form of charismatic behavior before it destroys leaders, followers, and organizations?

As we consider treating this disorder, we have to take several things as givens.

Hypomania is a chronic condition; it won't simply go away, even with treatment. In fact, there seems to be a genetic basis to manic-depressive illness, as demonstrated through studies of twins. Data from identical twins show that if one twin is manic-depressive, it's very likely that the other, if not manic-depressive, will have a cyclothymic nature [11].

Manic-depressive illness is relatively common. This is bad news, to be sure, but there's good news to balance it.

No other form of mental disorder has been more profoundly affected by advances in neurophysiological research than the bipolar disorders. Lithium and related drugs are highly effective in controlling the devastating effects of the more serious forms of this dysfunctional state, allowing people to lead relatively normal lives. Many people have taken these medications with good results.

While drugs tend to be the first line of defense against the bipolar disorders, it's not clear to what extent such medications—both those already in use and the many under development—limit the creativity and productivity of people with bipolar disorders. Present research shows conflicting findings on the effects of medication on creative achievement. Although it can be said that there are real problems in giving pharmacological treatment to people with mood disorders—as David noted, medication may affect their intensity of experience—the consequences of not doing so are far worse. If nothing is done about bipolar illness, there's a strong probability that it will progress, the mood swings becoming increasingly frequent and severe. Depression may intensify, increasing the risk of suicide. Modern medicine permits relief from the extremes of despair and chaotic behavior, thereby allowing bipolars choices that they didn't previously have.

Psychotherapy or leadership coaching in combination with medication can be a very effective means of treatment. Medication frees the person from the devastation caused by extreme depressive and manic episodes. Psychotherapy, for its part, helps the person deal with the disorder, assisting him or her to understand the psychological implications of mood swings and their aftermath and convincing him or her of the need to take medication to prevent a recurrence. Psychotherapy or leadership coaching can also be seen as a form of preventive maintenance: the hypomanic client takes steps, as a life strategy, to mitigate the expected fluctuations.

Of course, suggesting psychotherapy or leadership coaching is easier than initiating it, because hypomanics are rarely the best of listeners. While in a hypomanic state, whether up or down, they rarely have genuine insight into either their condition or how they're perceived by others. Furthermore, as noted earlier, denial is a common defense mechanism among hypomanics—a mechanism that seriously impairs their critical faculty. Especially when they're in an elevated mood state, hypomanics tend to deny that there's anything the matter with them; they're reluctant to admit the maladaptive nature of their behavior. When depressed they tend to be a bit more realistic about their abilities and possess more insight; for that reason, they're more easily reached when down.

What can be done to help a colleague who exhibits hypomanic characteristics? Colleagues can take on the "container" role; that is, they can psychologically "hold" the person while he or she is on a high or low, reining him or her in when necessary. Executives who recognize a hypomanic among them and sense the intoxication of a hypomanic's behavior can partner that person with someone of an especially sober mind, and they can work to create an overall executive role constellation whereby several other executives can exert a balancing influence. Colleagues can then caution the person before he or she plunges into ill-conceived business activities. Even the hypomanic who resents such warnings may heed them. In the case of the hypomanic who heads an organization, the role of non-executive board members as a balancing power is critical.

David would do well to familiarize himself with the nature of hypomania, as described in the previous pages, and to work with a mental health professional to put together a treatment package. He can begin with a couple of common-sense steps toward stability. First, given his vulnerability to mood swings, he should pace himself; the potential for drama in his life is great enough as it is. Second, in both his private and his public lives, he should avoid situations that aggravate his condition and create situations that do not.

Beyond these self-help measures, psychotherapy or leadership coaching may be of some help to David, as suggested above. Medication, while a more extreme measure, should also be considered if his severe mood swings continue. The combination of psychotherapy and medication may help him stabilize his life. Later, when he has attained a more balanced mood state, these interventions may no longer be needed. While David may regret that he no longer has the extreme highs, he will be spared the crash that follows.

To synthesize treatment modalities, David should also evolve a life strategy that allows his wife to have a balancing influence. Taking that step, while easier said than done, will likely expedite therapeutic interventions. If the marriage is irreparable, he should find another life partner—a woman who shares his wife's "containment" capabilities and can bring him to earth when he's flying too high. At work, he likewise needs checks and balances in the form of other executives, as I've noted—people who can calm him down when his hypomanic behavior takes over, who can exert a sobering influence without destroying his creative potential.

Executives caught up in the frenzy of Dionysian ecstasy dance a fine line between creative achievement and business catastrophe. Their decisions and actions, interpreted as bold and imaginative at the outset, may lead to disaster. However, hypomanics who learn from their mistakes, who nurture their reflective capacities, who are able to put on the brakes when the alarm bells ring, who create life situations that have a balancing influence—these people can be a great asset to any organization. Their capacity to dream and set high goals, their positive attitude in the face of adversity, and their ability to inspire and energize go a long way toward giving their organizations a competitive advantage.

Clearly, then, hypomania isn't something to be obliterated. Samuel Beckett, in Waiting for Godot, said, "We are all born mad. Some remain so." And maybe that's a good thing. In spite of dark forces that can run out of control—voices of unreason that can lead people to ruin—it's to be hoped that we all retain a touch of madness. And we shouldn't hide what madness we have, because it can be the source of much creativity. But we should try to contain it. One could even argue that too much sanity is itself a sign of madness. After all, without a degree of madness, life in organizations would be pretty dull. And such dullness would lead to complacency, making us less prepared to deal with life's discontinuities.

REFERENCES

1. Deutsch, H. (1938). "Folie a deux." *Psychoanalytic Quarterly* 7: 307–318.
2. Enoch, D. and H. Ball (2001). *Folie à deux (et Folie à plusieurs). Uncommon psychiatric syndromes.* H. Ball. London, Arnold.
3. Kets de Vries, M. F. R. (1979). "Managers can Drive their Subordinates Mad." *Harvard Business Review*: 125–134.
4. Laseque, C. and J. Fabret (1877). "La folie a deux ou folie communique." *Ann. Med. Psychologie* 5 serie (T. 18).
5. Ogden, T. H. (1982). *Projective Identification and Psychotherapeutic Technique.* New York, Jason Aronson.
6. Fuller Torrey, E. and M. B. Knable (2002). *Surviving Manic Depression: A Manual on Bipolar Disorder for Patients, Families, and Providers.* New York, Basic Books.
7. Goodwin, F. K. and K. R. Jamison (1990). *Manic-Depressive Illness.* New York, Oxford University Press.
8. Jamison, K. R. E. (1993). *Touched with Fire.* New York, The Free Press.
9. Mondimore, F. M. (1999). *Bipolar Disorder: A Guide for Patients and Families.* Baltimore, The Johns Hopkins University Press.
10. American Psychiatric Association (2004). *Diagnostic and Statistical Manual of the Mental Disorders: DSM-IV-Tr.* Arlington, VA, American Psychiatric Association.
11. Murphy, M., R. Cowan and L. Sederer (2004). *Blueprints Psychiatry.* Malden, Mass., Blackwell.

CHAPTER 7

THE IMPOSTOR SYNDROME: THE SHADOW SIDE OF SUCCESS

When you aim for perfection, you discover it's a moving target.

—Geoffrey Fisher

The first and worst of all frauds is to cheat one's self.

—Philip James Bailey

I do not fear failure. I only fear the "slowing up" of the engine inside of me which is pounding, saying, "Keep going, someone must be on top, why not you?"

—General George Patton

If you cannot find the truth right where you are, where else do you expect to find it?

—Zen proverb

There's a story about a duplicitous traveler who, while passing through a village, pretended to be a Zen master. His false sanctity easily fooled the credulous villagers, prompting them to exalt him to saint-like status and provide for all his needs. Life was going smoothly for the impostor-sage until the day he made the acquaintance of a vain, gullible, but highly attractive woman who kindled his desire. To get his way, the impostor told her that he had lately been visited by the mountain spirit that protected the village. He explained to her that this spirit had so much fallen under her charm that he desired to enjoy her physically through his body. The woman, unable to resist this flattery, submitted to his wishes. Many nights in a row, the impostor succeeded in taking advantage of her.

Unfortunately, the gullible woman wasn't very discrete. She bragged to her friends about her special experiences with the mountain spirit. She told them how every evening the mountain spirit would fly down from the mountain to make love to her on account of her special beauty. Her friends, too, found this news too exciting to repress. The story moved like wildfire through the village. Soon the news reached the ears of the woman's husband, who wasn't pleased. He decided to find whether the story was true, the proof he sought being the mountain spirit's capacity to fly.

And "fly" the mountain spirit did when the husband burst into the room where his wife was in deep embrace with the impostor who was able to make a quick getaway, not by really flying, but by jumping out of the window. In spite of his dramatic exit, the husband and the other villagers managed to hunt him down. When they caught the impostor, they almost killed him. Luckily for him, he was saved by a passer-by, the abbot of the local monastery. This abbot gave him sanctuary but kept him in captivity, forcing him to study Zen to find the true way. Pretending to be what he wasn't was no longer an option.

As in this Zen story, people leading fraudulent lives or engaging in fraudulent activities have always held a great deal of fascination for the general public. Many case histories of impostors and con men can be found in the psychological literature as well [1]. Most of these case histories (as in the case of the false Zen master) explore the lives of "real" impostors or liars—that is, people on the far end of the imposture continuum, who are engaged in objectively fraudulent activities. When studying the lives of these impostors, we discover that psychological gratification is much more important to most of them than the material advantages they gain. Whatever financial benefit they accrue is simply icing on the cake.

True impostors seem to reject and devalue their own identity, despite having genuine gifts. Instead of using their considerable talents to develop a solid career identity, they use them to engage in imposturous activities. Clinical psychologists have tried to explain this kind of behavior by suggesting that such people, for various reasons, have been forced into an adult role prematurely [2]–[10]. More insecure as children than most people, future impostors need an audience to help them establish a realistic sense of who they are. In order to capture and hold the admiration of grownups, these children develop astounding talents in mimicry— most noticeably the ability to imitate adult behavior. Unfortunately, the price of that distorted developmental track is often the lack of a well-formed separate self, a poor sense of identity, and poor reality-testing. These children may even start to believe their own fabrications. As stories about and experiences with being taken in by impostors suggest, one of the most common ways in which they use their talent for mimicry is the manipulation of language: they often exhibit a great facility with both words and the ability to listen. Like many writers of fiction, they understand how to fabricate illusions and how to make their illusions convincing.

The relationship between impostors and their audience is to some extent mutually reinforcing. Symbolically, impostors take on the role of the archaic, all-caring mother figure, satisfying oceanic longings, gratifying an almost forgotten but never really relinquished childhood desire for total attention and care—hence their effectiveness at convincing others of the particular role they're playing. To their audience, impostors represent someone who understands all their needs, relates to their deepest desires, and is prepared to take care of them.

To the true impostor, the greed of the audience for more of the same—more attention, more wish-fulfillment—is a constant stimulus. The fantasy world of the audience, once the impostor has successfully penetrated it, contains infinite demands for the gratification of desires. Thus impostor and audience are linked by a compatibility of interests in an unconscious, collusive conspiracy. As the comedian W. C. Fields once said, "You can't cheat an honest man." The audience is kept happy by the expectation that it will have its demands met, while the impostor uses the audience to counteract an inner sense of emptiness and reaffirm his or her identity (however elusive that identity may be).

Feeling or acting like an impostor isn't an all or nothing matter. It's a matter of degree ranging from true impostors (bona fide con artists) to people who just feel like frauds. Given that so many people suffer from this latter problem, and take their concerns into the workplace, let's put this group of people under the microscope.

BEING A FRAUD VERSUS FEELING FRAUDULENT

One reason for our interest in imposture is the element of universal recognition: impostors show us aspects of ourselves that we may prefer not to see. Imposture is part of a continuum, as suggested above. At one end of the spectrum are people engaged in genuinely imposturous activities—that is, people who deceive, cheat, and take on false identities in order to deceive others. At the other end of the spectrum are people troubled by the subjective experience of feeling fraudulent. To the outside observer, these latter individuals appear very accomplished and successful. What they themselves see, however, is a charlatan: in their inner world, they have the subjective experience of being a fraud. While "true" impostors deliberately base their identity on impersonation, "neurotic" impostors, genuinely successful in their field, simply feel as if they're sailing under false colors. Though the latter have achieved great success, they believe, deep down, that they don't deserve it.

To some extent, of course, we're all impostors—we all play roles when on the stage of life, presenting a different public self than the private self we share with intimates, and morphing both selves as circumstances demand. Displaying a façade and misleading our audience are defensive behaviors learned early. Showing our true self, laudable as this can be, is dangerous at times. Societal pressures to conform and achieve—whether those pressures come from parents, teachers, people at work, or peers—make us don a new persona. One of the reasons that neurotic imposture is so widespread is that these pressures combine to put great emphasis on effectiveness with very little room for making mistakes.

Some of the best research into the phenomenon of neurotic imposture was conducted in the 1970s by two clinical psychologists, Pauline Clance and Suzanne Imes, who tried to explain why some individuals don't appreciate their own success and feel fraudulent in the absence of genuine fraud [3]. According to Clance and Imes, whose research was limited to women, people exhibiting this pattern or syndrome attribute their achievements to external factors, not to their personal efforts and abilities.

Not everyone who ties achievement to external factors is an impostor, however. From a career management point of view, underplaying one's achievements is sometimes a protective career strategy. Directing attention away from the self may lower other people's expectations, a useful strategy in case of future failure.

Furthermore, it can convey the notion of modesty, thereby inviting encouragement and support from others. While such strategies are deliberately manipulative, neurotic impostors have a different motivation: they look to external factors because they suffer from deeply rooted anxieties about their exact place in life. Their feelings of distress are genuine.

These particular high achievers are unable to internalize their successful experiences. They view their achievements as being undeserved or purely accidental, and they describe those achievements in much harsher terms than any other person would. Troubled by a constant feeling that they've fooled everyone, in their heart of hearts they strongly believe that they aren't as intelligent and competent as others make them out to be. Because they can't shake a disturbing feeling of intellectual inauthenticity and dishonesty, they attribute their accomplishments to luck, compensatory hard work (making up for their lack of talent), or superficial factors such as physical attractiveness, likeability, or simply being in the right place at the right time. Convinced by their own arguments, they seriously question their ability to repeat past successes. Despite public evidence that they're very accomplished and talented, they live with the constant dread of being exposed as the incompetents and frauds they really are.

Though examples of neurotic impostors abound in the research literature, they aren't restricted to textbooks. My experience discussing this topic with large groups of senior executives has shown me that feelings of imposture are alive and well and thriving in today's organizations. In interviews with highly successful senior executives in many industries (particularly consulting firms and investment banks) I have discovered, time and time again, the prevalence of this phenomenon. And it has consequences far beyond the workplace. As human beings, we need a firm sense of our own identity so that we can relate to others. The problems with self-esteem and identity that typify neurotic impostors taint every relationship such people enter.

THE FEAR OF SUCCESS

In a society obsessed by success, failure is looked at as a catastrophe, and to some extent we all fear it. The fear of failure as an activating mechanism for feelings of insufficiency and incompetence is intuitively understandable. Ironically, we're also driven by the fear of success—a much more mysterious force. Sigmund Freud tried many years ago to demystify some of the dynamics behind this fear in an essay called "Those Wrecked by Success." He noted that some people become sick when a deeply rooted and long-cherished desire comes to fulfillment [11]. He gave as an example a university professor who cherished a wish to succeed his teacher. When eventually this wish came true and the individual succeeded his mentor, depression, feelings of self-deprecation, and work inhibition set in.

One explanation of this phenomenon—an explanation that shows the extent to which our unconscious can play strange tricks on us—is that for some people success becomes equated with a symbolic victory of doing better than the parents of childhood. This is particularly true for those individuals who have never satisfactorily resolved rivalrous feelings toward parents and siblings. For such individuals, to be successful and to have tangible accomplishments is an outcome both desired and feared.

The heart of the problem is that success makes people stand out and be noticed. When successful, they may imagine—unconsciously, for the most part—that fame and fortune will hurt them in some way. They may think that family, friends, and others will like them better if they stay "small." They may fear that climbing the ladder to a top position will arouse envy and resentment. As Ambrose Bierce said in *The Devil's Dictionary*, "Success is the one unpardonable sin against one's fellows." Thus the anticipation of success contains the seeds of a fear of retaliation by people who covet that success—either real people in the present or (at an unconscious, symbolic level) shadows from the past. Neurotic impostors can't rid themselves of the subliminal feeling that guilt and retribution are the inevitable consequences of success. As a result of that ambivalence, executives who believe that they're impostors may subtly engage in self-sabotage through procrastination, perfectionism (including a refusal to delegate), and ineffective use of their time. In such executives, feeling imposturous serves a useful purpose: by allowing them to keep their achievements out of conscious awareness, it enables them to deal with their ambivalence about being successful.

Performance anxieties typically increase as an executive reaches the higher regions of an organization. Thus executives who suffer from the fear of success may do very well in middle management, where it's easier to "hide." When they reach a top position, however, their dread of being exposed is heightened, because there's so much more at stake. Having reached their desired goal—being CEO or chair of the board, for example—neurotic impostors often become extremely anxious, deprecate their accomplishments, and engage in self-defeating behavior, thereby "snatching defeat out of the jaws of victory." They live under the faulty belief that because they're impostors, they can't continue to be successful; failure is inevitable. Unfortunately, this often becomes a self-fulfilling prophecy.

Consider a person I'll call Robin Klein, a senior executive at Hermes Software, an information technology company. At an exceptionally young age he was accepted into an Ivy League school—a "lucky break" that he assumed must have been the result of an admission error. The tendency to underestimate himself in relation to others remained a major theme in his personality as he moved into the business world—in spite of strong evidence to the contrary. After graduation, he decided to take an MBA at one of the better-known business schools, where he graduated in the top five per cent of his class. After a short stint as a consultant at McKinsey, he accepted an offer from one of his clients, where he had a stellar career before joining his present firm.

At Hermes, Robin was extremely successful at turning around one of the company's global divisions. As a result, when the CEO neared retirement, Robin was asked if he would like to be considered for the job. After painful consideration (and many sleepless nights), Robin decided to throw his hat into the ring. He was somewhat surprised when, following half a year of candidate reviews and interviews, he was offered the CEO position. He accepted the offer, but by the time he took the reins, he was feeling ill at ease—a feeling that didn't go away with the passing months. Rather, he became increasingly preoccupied with the question of whether he could pass muster. Would he be able to bring the company to its next level? Could he live up to his mandate? At times he fantasized about stepping off the treadmill, moving off the fast track, yet he felt that success offered him no option: a person who achieved success, it seemed to him, had no choice but to continue going up that tough slope.

The nights were worst for Robin. When sleep eluded him (as it often did), he would sit by his bedroom window, tormenting himself with questions. Had the big decision he made the previous day been sound? Would he be able to continue to execute his responsibilities properly? Would his subordinates accept his leadership? Would he satisfy the investment analysts and the financial press, stakeholders that kept after him to reach new highs? Even worse, when he finally fell asleep he was often haunted by nightmares. He dreamed of flying and crashing, of being followed by shadowy monsters, of failing a major exam. To relax, he started to have a drink (or two or more) in the evening, a practice that turned—without his acknowledgment—into a full-fledged drinking problem. Further handicapping himself, he engaged in a number of what became very public affairs with several women. Within the year he was divorced from his wife and estranged from his three children. At work, he found it increasingly difficult to concentrate and make decisions. He worried—and now for very good reason—about how many of his problems at work were noticed by his non-executive board members. When were they going to see that he was an impostor? When would they realize that they had made a mistake, that the other final candidate for the CEO position would have been a much better choice?

The kinds of thoughts that preoccupied Robin are typical. I've encountered many highflying executives who function extremely well as long as they aren't in the number-one position. The moment they're put into that position, however, their effectiveness diminishes and their tendency to succumb to the temptation of self-destructive behavior increases. Being at the top seems to bring imposturous feelings to a head. True enough, being in the alpha role is quite different from holding other positions in the organization. After all, organizations aren't democracies. Relations with others are seen in another light when one is CEO. It becomes much harder to talk freely and openly to people, and harder to find support and encouragement. Only when Robin was at the top of the heap did he realize how important having a mentor had been in helping him maintain his delicate mental equilibrium. Such support was extremely helpful in counteracting his feeling of fraudulence. Now, in the number-one position, he found it much harder to ask for advice and to let other people in. Furthermore, he felt (and was) more exposed. It was now much harder to hide behind someone else. As President Truman used to say, "The buck stops here." The president—whoever he or she is in whatever the organization—has to make the crucial decisions. He can't pass the buck to anybody else; no one else can do the deciding for him. He's the person who is ultimately responsible, and in that extremely visible role he's vulnerable.

THE DREAD OF NOT LIVING UP TO EXPECTATIONS

Another characteristic common among people who suffer from the impostor syndrome is the constant dread of not living up to expectations. The behavior of many self-labeled impostors is driven by, and also evaluated against, perfectionism. Many neurotic impostors hold such high standards for self-evaluation, and are so self-critical, that they're intolerant of any shortcoming, no matter how minor. Perfectionism has two sides to it, of course. In its positive manifestation, it provides the driving energy that leads to great accomplishments. What we might call "benign" perfectionists—those who are middle-of-the-road—derive pleasure from their achievements and don't obsess over failures. "Absolute" perfectionists, on the other hand, set excessively high, unrealistic goals and then experience self-defeating thoughts and behaviors when they can't reach those goals. Thus, although a perfectionist outlook is desirable (and even necessary) for success, in its absolute form it becomes dangerously counterproductive. As the actress Bette Davis said in the film *The Lonely Life*, "I am doomed to an eternity of compulsive work. No set goal achieved satisfies. Success only breeds a new goal. The golden apple devoured has seeds. It is endless." The thought processes that accompany this kind of behavior have a moral masochism about them; they reflect a tendency to subject oneself to unpleasant or trying experiences.

Consider Mitch Larson, a vice-president in a biotechnology firm. Growing up the oldest in a family of overachievers—his father ran a chain of restaurants and his mother was a dentist—he was always a star performer at school. College followed, leading to entry into one of the country's top medical schools. During his medical studies, his professors encouraged this highly talented, organized, considerate, and conscientious individual, lauding his creativity and insight. But the picture of success that Mitch portrayed to the outer world, wearing a mask of positive self-esteem and self-confidence, wasn't what he saw when he looked in the mirror. His inner world didn't match outer appearances. Although he pretended to be pleased about his accomplishments, he was always afraid that someone would see the real him, and that the hidden but true self wouldn't live up to others' expectations. To Mitch, making errors wasn't an option, a state of mind that created great anxiety. And yet, paradoxically, even when he was "good" he felt bad. He was chronically haunted by "shoulds" and ideals. On the rare occasions when he had an insight into why he was so troubled, he realized that his inner world was permeated by concerns about parental expectations and perceived parental criticisms. Far too often, he engaged in an internal dialogue where an inner voice shouted, "Impostor, impostor!"

As a youth, Mitch was the kind of student who set demanding goals that didn't allow for failure of any kind. But even when successful, he was unable to enjoy his success. Praise from others (including the rare praise from his parents) didn't help, because that praise reinforced a belief that unrelenting perfectionism was the price he had to pay to be noticed. This need to succeed drove him to push himself harder and harder, because he felt that until he achieved what others expected, he wouldn't be safe from his inner demons of inadequacy. And yet even when he graduated from medical school with top honors, the feeling of being a fraud didn't leave him. He never felt that he was doing things well enough.

Years later, after a brilliant academic career as a researcher in medicine (and after garnering quite a few patents), Mitch was given a very attractive financial offer to take a research position at GeoLabs, a worldwide company specializing in over-the-counter drugs. He accepted; and not long thereafter he was asked to become a member of the executive board and help direct the research activities of the corporation worldwide. He hesitated to take on this responsibility, because it would imply a major change from his previous mode of functioning. Having worked in the past with a small group of people in the lab, he would have to shift in this new position to directing a large department and being a people manager. After considerable thought, he decided to take the job, seeing it as a way to hone his people skills.

Mitch started his new mandate by spelling out a set of wildly ambitious goals for R & D. For example, he declared that he was going to make the lab a world-class operation within the coming four years. Wonderful as that would be for the firm, it was such a lofty aspiration that it had a hollow ring. The way he set about achieving his new objectives didn't win him any popularity contests, either. He was seen as a very difficult boss, because he was as hard on others as he was on himself. Unwilling to accept imperfections in himself or his subordinates, Mitch drove himself mad, along with the people who worked for or with him. When others were asked to describe him, labels such as "maniacal perfectionist" came to mind—and they were never offered with affection. Ironically, Mitch's perfectionist orientation was actually dampening the team's productivity and creativity.

As Mitch and his colleagues worked to achieve the department's new goals, meetings led to endless discussions, which led to new meetings and discussions. Many of the people who worked for him saw these meetings as a total waste of their time. They realized that Mitch's search for the perfect solution often led him (and them) to just the opposite: a flawed hodge-podge. Although Mitch also earned the label "slave driver," he found it hard to delegate work: his fear of making mistakes, his negative thinking, meant that no one could live up to his standards. In fact, he often angrily chided his subordinates for not working hard enough and for failing to meet his (impossible) standards—a blow to workplace morale. In addition, his obsessive need for perfection and control led him to focus on the wrong things and to shy away from acceptable risks, slowing down the research process. In light of these developments, other members of the executive board began asking themselves whether they had made a mistake in putting Mitch in the leadership role.

While Mitch realized that he was digging a hole for himself, it was difficult for him to ask for help. Deep down, he feared that by doing so, he would be giving his colleagues proof of what they surely expected: that he was an impostor, a fraud. To avoid being "found out," he worked even harder (but unfortunately not smarter). As time went on, he began to lose focus. He withdrew more and more into himself, haunted by his inner demons. He agonized over what his colleagues thought about him, worried about not living up to their expectations, and waffled over every decision. The result was considerable anxiety and many a sleepless night. Eventually he began to wonder whether he was suffering from burnout.

Unfortunately, as the case of Mitch illustrates, people who suffer from the kind of perfectionism associated with neurotic imposture often enter into a vicious cycle. This cycle starts with the self-professed impostor setting impossible, unreachable goals. He or she fails to reach these goals, of course—they're targets that no one could reach—and tortures him- or herself about the failure. This orgy of self-blame does little to improve effectiveness, unfortunately; rather, it incites further self-flagellation and nurtures imposturous feelings. And then the entire cycle begins again. Perfectly capable executives with this mindset handicap themselves, bringing about their own demise by asking the impossible of themselves. Feeling like an undeserving person can be dangerously self-fulfilling.

Executives who suffer from the impostor syndrome often engage in all-or-nothing thinking. Living in a world of extremes, they're unable to see their situation in perspective. If they don't accomplish all their goals—in fact, if they have a single failure—they over generalize that shortcoming and feel like a total failure. In other words, their self-esteem is tightly intertwined with their accomplishments. They fear that if they aren't perfect, others will reject them. But the resulting fear of making mistakes (like that which we saw in Mitch) leads to an unwillingness to experiment, learn, and develop. Furthermore, neurotic impostors live with the misconception that they're the only ones who fail and who are plagued by self-doubt, and thus they feel quite isolated.

While some people respond to the fear of making mistakes with decision paralysis and procrastination, others become workaholics. Executives in the latter category, dependent on constant, tangible results for the maintenance of their sense of self-esteem, have difficulty saying no and thus tend to over commit themselves. Both hyper-compensating habits—procrastination and workaholism—interfere with an executive's ability to learn. As we saw in the case of Mitch, the pendulum between workaholic behavior and procrastination swings quite easily. While one group of people tries to do too much, forgetting how productive they are while doing it, another group, paralyzed by the fear of not living up to their own and others' expectations, can never manage to get anything done.

The pendulum for most people who suffer from neurotic imposture stays pointed toward workaholism, however. Because they work too many hours a week, they're often viewed as ideal employees, always ready to make the extra effort. Given their work habits, they're taken advantage of by their superiors. I'm reminded of a cartoon of a CEO who is seen handing over a dossier to his subordinate. "Take your time," he says. "I'm not in a hurry. Take the whole weekend if necessary." Neurotic impostors, whether superiors or subordinates, often enter into sadomasochistic collusions of this sort.

Are You a Neurotic Impostor?

To test your disposition toward the impostor syndrome, ask yourself the following four questions:

1. Do you feel that every day at work is a test you have to wing your way through?
2. Do you think that you've fooled others into believing you're smarter or more capable than you really are?
3. Do you believe that you're going to be unmasked eventually, revealed to be incompetent and fake?
4. Do you think, whenever you're successful: I fooled them this time, but my luck isn't going to last?

If you answered these four questions in the affirmative, welcome to the club of self-professed impostors. Be happy in the knowledge that you're in good company. Many of the most successful people (whether in business, politics, or the arts) have similar doubts; they're just as confused and troubled by their perceived talent as you are. In fact, the majority of executives I've interviewed suffered, to one degree or another, from this syndrome. Deep down, many of them believed that they had been lucky to slip through their various jobs without being unmasked as frauds.

If the above questions left you in any doubt, consider the following symptoms of neurotic imposture: low self-esteem, due to one's inability to meet self-imposed excessive standards of achievement; panic attacks; social anxiety, due to a preoccupation with what other people think and a desperate need to gain approval and recognition; depression, with its associated symptoms, such as loss of energy and activity level, reduced concentration, loss of appetite, weight loss, lack of interest in sexual activity, slowness of thought, inability to respond to the mood of the occasion, insomnia, suicidal thoughts, and feelings of fatigue—in short, a diminished zest for life. Unfortunately, these symptoms hurt not just the neurotic impostor but his or her colleagues as well. An executive's fearful, cautious leadership is contagious, spreading throughout an organization.

INFECTING THE ORGANIZATION

Neurotic impostors can, and do, damage the organizations they try so hard to please. Their work ethic can be contagious, but because they're so eager to succeed, their impatience can also lead to abrasive behavior. Being extremely hard on themselves, neurotic impostors aren't predisposed to spare others. They drive their people too hard, creating a gulag-like atmosphere in the organization, which inevitably translates into high employee turnover rates, absenteeism, and other issues that can affect the bottom line. Moreover, given their intensity, neurotic impostors are poor at people development. They don't have what it takes to be an effective leadership coach and thus they aren't the kind of executives who are good at leadership development and succession planning.

More dangerous, however, is the effect of neurotic imposture on the quality of decision-making. Executives who feel like impostors can make disastrous decisions for their organizations, because they're afraid to trust their own judgment—after all, who would trust an impostor? An executive's fearful, overly cautious leadership can easily spread across the company, with dire consequences for the organization. For instance, a CEO who doesn't trust his instincts is very likely to suppress his subordinate's entrepreneurial capabilities and thus hamper necessary innovation company-wide.

CEOS who are neurotic impostors are also likely to become addicted to consulting companies. The reassurance provided by the "impartial outsiders" provides compensation for their feelings of insecurity. Of course, outside advice is often no bad thing, but imposturous CEOs all too easily turn into puppets whose strings are manipulated by the outsiders.

Consider Andrew Patterson, the CEO of a global engineering firm who took one of my seminars. During one session he explained that he hadn't really chosen engineering; his father had chosen it for him. Andrew had conceded to his father's wishes and entered the business world, but he never felt comfortable in his corporate role. When he reached more senior positions, he began to rely on consultants, some of whom took advantage of his insecurity at a very high price. Not only did they charge the engineering firm substantial fees for their services, but the consultants' predatory behavior increased Andrew's feelings of insecurity, perpetuating his state of anxiety and dependency.

This inefficient behavior of companies led by neurotic impostors is exacerbated when the organization is one that punishes failure. If the company culture tolerates no mistakes, the leader's level of anxiety increases, making neurotic behavior all the more likely. This is paralyzing for the perfectionist, whose fear of failure then has an even more negative impact on the organization.

Let's look at a senior executive I'll call Anne Holton. She had a successful career at a consulting firm before accepting an offer from a prominent media company. In her previous job as a consultant, Anne had functioned extremely effectively. But this changed when she accepted a senior management role in the new enterprise. Her assignment was to run the firm's European operation.

Although she was an outstanding source of good ideas, Anne's fear of failure led her to manage in ways that came to be seen as countercultural. In an organization that had always been decentralized, for example, she decided to centralize many of the functions in her part of the business. But what really grated on many people was that Anne wanted to make most of the decisions herself. Her perfectionist attitude and her need for immediate results (both rooted in her performance anxiety) made real delegation an anathema to her, thus dampening the team's productivity and creativity.

As time passed, Anne's co-workers started to worry about the abrasiveness that had crept into her manner. Her prickliness about real or perceived criticism was becoming an irritant to a growing number of her colleagues. Not much was needed to put her on the defensive. She reacted in a hostile manner to questions and comments having to do with any of her proposals, reports, or decisions. Furthermore, she now took ages to prepare for meetings. Anxious not to be found wanting, she tried to anticipate every conceivable question that could be asked. Such precautions extended her already lengthy work week into the weekends, and she expected others to show the same commitment.

Anne's sense of neurotic imposture deeply affected the organization. As time went on, many of Anne's team asked for a transfer to other parts of the organization. Others (without her knowledge) were in discussions with headhunters. The ones that remained took a passive-aggressive attitude toward her. Since they felt it wasn't worth the effort to reason with her, they let her make all the decisions but undermined them in subtle ways. Given the degree of discontent in her part of the organization, the European division was increasingly seen as a liability, though it had once been the flagship operation. The year's-end result showed that profitability for Anne's division had fallen into a deep slump, confirming the company's growing belief that she was incompetent. In the end the division was sold to a competitor. Anne's neurosis had ruined not only her career but a perfectly respectable business as well.

A SEARCH FOR ORIGINS

Perceived parental expectations, perceived parental criticisms, and concern over past mistakes are among the salient factors that contribute to the impostor syndrome. Many self-professed neurotic impostors are ashamed, even in adulthood, for having failed to live up to their parents' standards of perfection and achievement. Having had parents who took their children's successes for granted and didn't acknowledge them, they're preoccupied in adulthood with their failures.

Clinical, in-depth interviews suggest that certain types of family constellations enhance feelings of imposture. When parents or other important caretakers are demanding critics, future impostors learn early to internalize their dictates. They learn that the only way to shore up a fragile sense of self-esteem is through other people's approval. Even when other, less demanding adults—teachers, neighbors, the parents of friends—become important to these youngsters, they assume that those others are equally demanding. With all that pressure from without—first real and then perceived—they're incapable of internalizing and appreciating their own accomplishments. Of course, the demanding parents of some neurotic impostors are in fact proud of them, both as children and as adults. However, the typical family of the self-professed impostor is conflict-ridden and not very supportive, offering only limited opportunities to express emotions such as pride or joy. The fathers of women impostors are often perceived as distant and even rejecting, while their mothers are perceived as controlling.

Birth order and academic acceleration also influence the development of neurotic imposture. In families with multiple children, firstborns are often expected to assume greater responsibility and leadership. Young people who are expected to behave in a prematurely grownup manner feel tremendous pressure to live up to parental expectations and to perform. Children who skip a grade because of their talents likewise feel tremendous pressure to excel, to be "worthy" of their promotion. Those with special talents often have difficulty fitting in, precisely because of their giftedness. As they progress at school and university, they're labeled oddballs, adding to their feelings of insecurity. Because they perform so well with little effort and advance so quickly, they doubt their true abilities, thereby widening the gap between how others see them and how they see themselves.

Some families of future neurotic impostors attempt to dissuade their growing child from pursuing his or her educational or career aspirations because those aspirations conflict with (or aren't the norm for) gender role, race, status, or other expectations of the family. When young people pursue those aspirations anyway, the family disapproval climbs the career ladder with them. Thus even when they succeed, their sense of self-esteem is vulnerable to the opinions and criticisms of others. In such people, the feeling of imposture is often associated (at least unconsciously) with doing better than their parents. When they're successful, they feel that they have crossed socio-cultural boundaries. But this external success has a high price tag: the loss or distancing of close personal relationships, along with crises of identity and self-esteem [12]–[14].

Women who have goals that put them outside their family's way of thinking about gender roles suffer especially hard from this mindset. Female gender socialization makes women compare themselves, consciously or unconsciously, with the role their more traditional mother may have played. Nothing could be more different than a fast-track career businesswoman and a suburban housewife. The contrast is exacerbated by the fact that career women have to function in a business world dominated by male norms. When they're successful, they're not the only ones who suspect imposture: many of their prideful male colleagues likewise assume it was chance. It's generally only the women, though, who worry that their "luck" may not last. Many of these women play dumb as a tactic for dealing with their recurring feelings of self-doubt. In some instances, gifted women even deliberately select mediocre and gender-stereotypic jobs.

THE LIGHT AT THE END OF THE TUNNEL

Fortunately, much can be done to counteract the self-handicapping of neurotic imposture. No one has to accept feeling like a fraud as part of the human condition. Of course, the best thing that can be done is to identify and deal with the factors that lead to this phenomenon very early in life so that the dysfunctional effects never come to the fore. Parents and teachers can help growing children when they recognize warning signs such as fear of failure, procrastination, and/or perfectionism. Early efforts—the earlier the better—to encourage small successes, foster moderation regarding success and accomplishments, and teach self-acceptance, go a long way toward helping at-risk young people avoid some of the misery associated with this syndrome.

In the workplace, executives should be on the lookout for signs of neurotic imposture in their colleagues and subordinates. Bosses must remain alert for the symptoms of neurotic imposture in their employees: fear of failure, fear of success, perfectionism, procrastination, and workaholism. Of course, recognition is one thing, and changing deeply rooted beliefs and behavior patterns is another. Nevertheless, in performance reviews bosses should signal (uncritically) any danger signs to their direct reports. They should complement this by explaining how anxiety about performance can take on a self-destructive quality, and they should emphasize the value of life-work balance, pointing out that strength, overdone, can easily become weakness.

Above all, bosses need to make sure that a subordinate suffering from neurotic imposture understands that criticism goes with responsibility. This means teaching, by word and example, that criticism is an opportunity for new learning and not a total, unrecoverable catastrophe. They must point out that everyone in a responsible job feels smaller than the job at times. At these moments, especially in a new position, the worst thing a neurotic impostor can do is to compare his or her abilities with those of seasoned executives. This is guaranteed to be an exercise in self-flagellation. Neurotic impostors need to be convinced that everyone needs time to adjust and learn the ropes.

At the same time, leaders must strengthen the perceived link between positive achievement and effort. They can be extremely helpful by giving all subordinates, but especially those with neurotic imposturous tendencies, constructive feedback when appropriate, and encouraging them for work well done. Positive experiences that highlight employees' abilities and increase their confidence gradually convince neurotic impostors that they're talented and can be the masters of their own fate.

Senior executives need to offer their subordinates not only praise when it's due, but also the perspective that making mistakes (though not repeating them) is part of any successful corporate culture. The philosophy of the wise organization shouldn't be to punish smart mistakes. To "fail forward" needs to be part of an organization's implicit cultural values. As the saying goes, people who don't make any mistakes aren't doing anything! Mistakes can offer great opportunities for learning and personal growth, and leaders need to help neurotic impostors understand that their fear of failure is part of the human condition.

In many instances, getting such a change process into motion requires outside help. This is especially true for top executives, who typically have fewer colleagues with whom they feel comfortable sharing personal concerns. The specific situation a self-professed impostor finds him- or herself in determines what kind of mentoring professional would be the most suitable choice. Clinical experience has shown that cognitive and dynamic interventions can be very effective in helping a person change distorted self-perceptions. (Part Two of this book describes successful intervention techniques.) Sharing inner feelings with a caring other (such as a leadership coach or a psychotherapist) can be a great catalyst to recovery. Both leadership coaching and psychotherapy can help executives remove self-limiting assumptions and beliefs, encourage them to perceive themselves more accurately, and remind them that defeat harbors great opportunities for learning and personal growth.

Group coaching experiences are another very successful form of intervention for neurotic impostors. Because group experiences are based on personal narration—telling one's own story—they're journeys of self-discovery and offer validation of personal experiences. If done in a safe environment, telling stories about significant events and situations that made an individual the way he or she is helps that individual work through internal conflicts and crises and arrive at meaningful, personal life integration. The acceptance and support given by the other members of the group help instill a sense of hope for change and for the future. Furthermore, listening to the stories of others, and seeing their

dysfunctional patterns, helps participants recognize their own dysfunctional patterns (and hear how unreasonable those patterns are).
This form of vicarious learning in a safe, nurturing, and "playful"
space paves the way for cognitive and emotional restructuring.

In the end, however, it's the neurotic impostor him- or herself
who has to bring about change. Impostors seeking "recovery" need
to challenge both their own expectations and the expectations of
others regarding success. They need to see success in a broader
context than positive figures on a balance sheet, redirect attention
to the process of succeeding rather than considering only the end
products of success, and learn to accept that other people care about
them as individuals as well as "producers."

Consider the following example of a successful intervention:
Joanne Stemler was a regional vice-president of a global consumer
products company, responsible for their European operations.
Despite her stellar academic success—she graduated with high
marks from a well-respected engineering school—and her steady
and speedy progression through the office ranks, she was a typical
case of the neurotic impostor syndrome. While appearing extremely
successful, she experienced intense feelings of imposture in achievement situations. Though she had far exceeded the expectations of
her parents at school and in her career, she never felt satisfied with
her accomplishments. Her good family life and her success in business were tainted by constant feelings of guilt at having pulled the
wool over everyone's eyes. She couldn't rid herself of the idea that
she wasn't really competent at anything. She had just ridden the
wave of affirmative action, which had found her in the right place
at the right time. Occasionally, when the pain was most acute, she
even went so far as to hide her considerable abilities, playing the
role of the dumb blonde. Eventually, because of various stress
symptoms, she decided to enter a top management leadership
program that focused on personal and organizational dynamics to
learn more about herself and to become more effective in dealing
with her problems, both privately and in her business life.

The program was an eye-opener for her. As the group of senior executives shared personal stories, expressing their own fears, doubts, and concerns, she realized that she wasn't alone in feeling imposturous. This helped build up her fragile sense of self-confidence. The presentations of the other participants encouraged her to talk, in that relatively safe environment, about her own feelings of guilt and inadequacy. Encouraged by this progress, she decided to work on herself at a greater depth than the group experience could provide. She supplemented the group program with the individual support of a leadership coach, who helped her understand that it was perfectly normal to feel somewhat inadequate when stretched beyond one's comfort zone. He assured her that many executives in responsible jobs occasionally felt insecure and in over their head. At the same time, he helped her see the value of her many and considerable successes.

Joanne came to realize that one of the contributing factors to her sense of inadequacy and guilt was that she had been unconsciously comparing herself to her own mother, a typical housewife. Her mother and father had not encouraged her to pursue her studies, suggesting instead that she stick to typical "feminine" jobs such as nursing or secretarial work. That she had chosen not to stay at home but rather to pursue a career, a situation so different from what she had experienced while growing up, made Joanne feel like a "bad" mother to her own daughter and a "bad" wife to her husband.

As these reflections about her background gradually helped Joanne to see things from a different perspective, she learned to be nicer to herself. She began to allow herself not to be perfect, realizing that every person, no matter how successful, has shortcomings. (There are, after all, very few superwomen in this world—or supermen either, for that matter.) She learned to accept the fact that she didn't need a perfect batting average to be appreciated in the company. Given her outstanding track record, less would certainly do. Furthermore, she came to accept that stretching outside of one's natural comfort zone would be uncomfortable for anybody. Lots of people she admired appeared "perfect," but (like anybody) they had hidden problems of their own.

The acid test of her new way of thinking came when she accepted a more senior position that her company offered her. This time, with the benefit of insights gained through her leadership program and coaching, she gave herself time to adjust to her new responsibilities; she accepted that it would take a while before she would become familiar with what was expected of her. Honoring that period of learning, she didn't commit herself to excessive goals. As she got to know other executives in her new field of expertise, she curbed her instinct to compare herself against them. More realistic now about human frailties, she understood that they had their share of hiccups too, especially while learning. This improved perspective helped prevent her usual orgy of self-flagellation. She realized that she should aim for success, but not necessarily for perfection—two concepts that she had formerly equated. Now, whenever she made a mistake, she tried to learn from it, but not to dwell on it and make herself miserable. Because of her greater understanding of some of her driving forces, her self-criticism diminished and her social anxiety abated. She started to become more confident both at work and in the world at large. Less troubled by doubt about her abilities, she was less needy of applause and therefore easier to be around.

Joanne had learned two crucial things about success:

- Failure is a better teacher than success. People have to pass failure on the way to success—in fact, mistakes are the major building blocks of success, offering lessons in wisdom. No mistakes, no experience; no experience, no insight.
- Success, as measured by dollars earned and promotions granted, is no guarantee of happiness. True success, the kind that does bring happiness, has less to do with performance on specific tasks than with meaningful, rich relationships with others.

As time passed and these lessons sank in, Joanne began to live life on her own terms, becoming much less dependent on what others thought. She acquired greater faith in her own achievements and accepted that she was talented. Most important, she became kinder to herself.

Joanne learned that success is a journey, not a destination. The doing is often more important than the outcome. In fact, the arrival may be only a sideshow. People who suffer from the impostor syndrome would do well to realize that, as the above story suggests, the road to success usually veers off the beaten path. Success lies not in a list of achievements, but in the way we experience the journey, the way we deal with obstacles, the way we appreciate our experiences. And we need not—indeed, must not—be discouraged by failure. As suggested, failure can be a positive experience (though it rarely feels that way when it occurs). Paradoxically, failure is the royal road to success.

All of us need to realize that we take two journeys, one external and one internal. The way we experience the internal journey determines how we conduct and perceive the external journey. No matter how hard we work for success, if our thoughts are saturated with the fear of failure (and of success), that negative thinking will kill whatever we attempt, making success impossible. When we know how to read and understand what happens inside us, when we recognize what we stand for, we don't have to depend so heavily on the reactions of others. If constructive thoughts are planted and cultivated in our inner theaters, positive outcomes will result.

To acquire inner peace, to become more in touch with our true selves and oust our imposturous selves, we need to take a journey into ourselves. We have to learn to feel good in our skin, not assume the skin of others. Only by doing so are we able to live life in our own way rather than the way we think others want us to. To come full circle: if we hope to manage and overcome the impostor syndrome, we need to realize that success and achievement imply liking ourselves, liking what we do, and liking how we do it. We also need, like Joanne, to learn that success isn't the key to happiness. On the contrary, happiness is the key to success!

REFERENCES

1. Kets de Vries, M. F. R. (2003). *Leaders, Fools and Impostors*. New York, iUniverse, Inc.
2. Clance, P. R. (1985). *The Impostor Phenomenon: Overcoming the Fear that Haunts Your Success*. Atlanta, GA, Peachtree.
3. Clance, P. R. and S. A. Imes (1978). "The impostor phenomenon in high-achieving women: Dynamics and therapeutic intervention." *Psychotherapy: Theory, Research & Practice* 15: 241–247.
4. Deutsch, H. (1965). *Neuroses and Character Types*. Madison, Conn., International Universities Press.
5. Fried-Buchalter, S. (1992). "Fear of success, fear of failure, and the imposter phenomenon: A factor analytic approach to convergent and discriminant validity." *Journal of Personality Assessment* 58: 368–379.
6. Greenacre, P. (1971). *The Impostor. Emotional Growth, Vol 1*. P. Greenacre. Madison, Conn., International Universities Press.
7. Greenacre, P. (1971). *The Relation of the Impostor to the Artist. Emotional Growth, Vol 2*. Ed P. Greenacre. Madison, Conn., International Universities Press.
8. Kolligian, J., Jr. and R. J. Sternberg (1991). "Perceived fraudulence in young adults: Is there an "impostor syndrome?" *Journal of Personality Assessment* 56: 308–326.
9. Lester, D. and T. Moderski (1995). "The imposter phenomenon in adolescents." *Psychological Reports* 76: 466.
10. Topping, M. E. and E. B. Kimmel (1985). "The impostor phenomenon: Feeling phony." *Academic Psychology Bulletin* 7: 213–226.
11. Freud, S. (1953). *Some Character-Types Met within Psycho-Analytic Work. The Standard Edition of the Complete Psychological Works of Sigmund Freud, Vol 14*. J. Stratchey (editor and translator). London, Hogarth Press and Institute of Psychoanalysis.

12. Cozzarelli, C. and B. Major (1990). "Exploring the validity of the impostor phenomenon." *Journal of Social and Clinical Psychology* 9: 401–417.

13. King, J. E. and E. L. Cooley (1995). "Achievement orientation and the impostor phenomenon among college students." *Contemporary Educational Psychology* 200: 304–312.

14. Langford, J. and P. R. Clance (1993). "The impostor phenomenon: Recent research findings regarding dynamics, personality and family patterns and their implications for treatment." *Psychotherapy* 30: 495–501.

PART TWO

CHANGING MINDSETS

CHAPTER 8

CAN LEADERS CHANGE? YES, BUT ONLY IF THEY WANT TO

Look upon that last day always. Count no mortal happy till he has passed the final limit of his life secure from pain.

—Sophocles

He who can no longer pause to wonder and stand rapt in awe is as good as dead; his eyes are closed.

—Albert Einstein

We are all of us balloons dancing in a world of pins.

—Anthony Montague Browne

As long as you seek for something, you will get the shadow of reality and not reality itself.

—Zen proverb

There's a Zen tale of a lion who was completely convinced of his dominance of the animal kingdom. One day he decided to check whether all the other animals knew that he was the king of the jungle. He was so confident about his position that he decided not to talk to the smaller creatures. Instead, he went straight to the bear. "Who is the king of the jungle?" asked the lion. The bear replied, "Of course, no one else but you, sir." The lion gave a great roar of approval.

He continued his journey and met the tiger. He asked the striped creature, "Who is the king of the jungle?" The tiger quickly responded, "All of us know that you are the king." The lion gave another roar of pleasure.

Next on his list was the elephant. He caught up with the great beast at the edge of a river and asked him the same question: "Who is the king of the jungle?" The elephant trumpeted with raised trunk, grabbed the lion, threw him in the air, and smashed him into a tree. After a moment he fished him out of the tree and pounded him on the ground, then lifted him up once more and dumped him into the river. With the big cat gasping for air, the elephant pulled him out, dragged him through the mud, and finally left him draped over some bushes. Dirty, beaten, bruised, and battered, the lion struggled to his feet. He looked the elephant sadly in the eyes and said, "Look, just because you don't know the answer, that's no reason for you to be so mean-spirited about it."

As most of the examples in Part One of this book illustrate, many leaders are like the lion. Listening and careful observation aren't something they're good at. Reality-testing isn't their forte. Instead, driven by the forces of narcissism, they create their own reality, seeing only what they want to see. Furthermore, they're not very open to change. As the jungle tale suggests, change isn't a simple process, nor is it a comfortable one. The unlearning of habitual patterns can be decidedly anxiety-provoking. Like the lion, many executives hold on to their own personal logic, illogical as that logic may appear to others. Instead of making an effort to change, they stick with the status quo, even if they end up dragged through the mud and miserable.

Unfortunately, they rarely go down alone. When executives cling tenaciously to the status quo even when it isn't working, the mud-spatters are far-reaching. And the more senior the executive, the more devastating the potential consequences. Given the power that leaders wield, their personal dysfunctions often become organizational dysfunctions. The results, some of which we've looked at in previous chapters, include collusive interactions, unrealistic organizational ideals, toxic corporate cultures, neurotic organizations, faulty patterns of decision-making, motivational problems, organizational alienation, and a high rate of employee turnover [1]–[5].

Part of what makes change hard for executives is the very thing that makes it so necessary: organizational leaders are always "on stage" at work. Every move they make is carefully observed, analysed, and discussed by colleagues and subordinates. Given that scrutiny, apparently innocuous actions can have dramatic consequences. As a participant in one of my senior executive workshops said, "Every day when I go into the office I have the ability to make the lives of my ten thousand employees either miserable or positive. It doesn't take very much to go either way. That's an awesome responsibility. I need to keep reminding myself daily of the role I play." To fill that role successfully, executives need to put the interest of the organization before their self-interest; speak to the collective imagination of the organization, so motivating people that they give their best and more; face reality as it is, not as they would like it to be; and be confident enough of their own abilities that they're not afraid to encourage and develop the next generation of leaders.

WHY RIDE A DEAD HORSE?

Many executives genuinely want to fit the above description, but they keep getting derailed by their human foibles—those dispositions discussed in earlier chapters. They want to keep an eye on the competition but verge into paranoia; they want to benefit from the wisdom of others but become swamped in dependence; and so on and on. They keep doing and saying the same destructive things over and over again. Apparently they're not familiar with the old Sioux Indian saying: "When you discover that you're riding a dead horse, the best strategy is to dismount." They seem to believe that they can resuscitate the horse.

But even many executives who claim to believe in the value of change undertake it only half-heartedly. Although they give lip service to change, they'd rather see others change than change themselves. And some executives don't so much resist change as misunderstand it; they have the will but not the skill to change. They need help to navigate the change process. John Maynard Keynes had a point when he said, "The greatest difficulty in the world is not for people to accept new ideas, but to make them forget their old ideas." Far too many people are frightened of new ideas, though it's often the old ideas they should worry about.

How, then, can corporate leaders master the change process? What can they do to make themselves receptive to change so that they can better motivate and support their employees? How can they make their organizations better places to work? In short, how can executives become better leaders?

Greater self-awareness is the first step toward becoming more effective as a leader. If leaders want to reinvent or renew themselves, they have to look within; they have to explore their inner theater. As Socrates said, "The unexamined life is not worth living." Thus the intention to change implies a willingness to engage in self-exploration.

But that willingness is just the beginning. Let's take a look at the change process and see what it entails.

CHANGE AND THE TRIANGLE OF MENTAL LIFE

In our effort to understand the complex process of change, it helps to look at human behavior as being made up of a triangle of forces: cognition, emotion, and behavior. This triangular force field determines the script that's acted out in our inner theater. That script involves all three elements of the triangle of mental life and, as was discussed in Chapter 1, is written in response to the motivational need systems on which choice is grounded.

Taking this basic triangle of mental life—with its linking of cognition, emotion, and behavior—as our point of departure, we can see that for any change effort to be successful, the individual seeking change has to be swayed both cognitively and emotionally; in other words, a person has to be affected in both the head and the heart if behavior is to change. Affect and cognition go hand

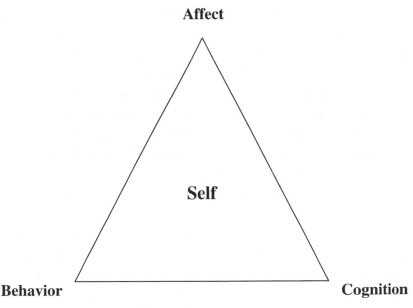

Figure 8.1   Triangle of mental life

in hand; they're inseparable in all things, including the determination of behavior. Although someone seeking change needs to see intellectually the advantages that a change effort will bring, cognition alone isn't enough; that person also needs to be touched emotionally. The three legs of this triangle of mental life are closely interwoven. Architects of leadership change programs, take note!

HITTING YOUR HEAD AGAINST THE WALL

Initially, in my role as an educator and consultant, when I addressed the subject of changing people and organizations I quite naively used what we might call the lecture method. I composed long harangues, explaining to executives where and why they were making faulty decisions, why their organizations were malfunctioning, and what and how they had to change. I used every kind of logic I knew to explain why they couldn't continue doing things the same way they'd been doing them. Although intellectually I may have been quite correct, I soon discovered that my interventions didn't make an iota of difference. Most of the executives I dealt with paid lip service to my exhortations but merrily kept on with their old ways. Eventually, as I kept hitting my head against the wall, I realized that I needed to find a different angle. I was using a filibuster of logic when logic alone wasn't good enough. I had to reach these people in a different way to help them change themselves, and their organizations with them.

It was a participant in one of my intensive leadership workshops who helped me see a new way. This executive, Chet Parker, had received a considerable amount of feedback from the other participants and faculty about his tendency to remain emotionally aloof in difficult situations, using distancing as a defensive mechanism. We had noticed that, when stressed, Chet withdrew and didn't react, a pattern that would surely have negative effects on the decision-making processes in his organization. The problem was so pronounced that I'm sure he must have heard comments about it before. In other words, cognitively he must have been aware of the problem. But knowing the problem in his head was apparently not good enough. He had to experience whatever was going on in his "gut" as well. It was obvious that additional "ammunition" would be needed to make him change his ways interpersonally, to make him more effective in executing decisions. The question was, What could be done to get a "hook" into him? What could I, as a workshop facilitator, do that would make a real difference? How could I understand and overcome his resistance?

To find the hook I needed, I decided to consult with the people who were most important to Chet. With his permission, I contacted not only co-workers but also his close friends, his wife, his children, and other family members, asking them via e-mail to describe how they perceived him and to suggest what he needed to change about his behavior. When I presented this information during the second week of the workshop, I could see that the feedback was beginning to stick. One response—a very emotional statement from his nineteen-year-old daughter—really shook him up. With teary eyes (very unusual for an otherwise always-composed banker) he shared the e-mailed response from his daughter expressing her sadness about his inapproachability. She wrote about her long-frustrated wish to be closer to him—to have a real relationship with him. She referred to all the efforts she had made in the past to create such a relationship.

This note was the turning point for Chet. From that moment on the other participants noticed a change in his behavior. He became truly emotionally involved in the discussions that took place at the workshop and finally heard the insights provided by the other participants. The other presentations began to touch him emotionally. Most importantly, however, he began to experiment with other ways of behaving when in stressful situations outside the workshop. That isn't to say that there were no lapses. But what kept him on course were the comments made by the other participants reminding him of the feedback from his daughter any time he fell back into his old behavior patterns. The other participants functioned as a "learning community" to reinforce desired behavior. Gradually, over the course of half a year, Chet's new, more expressive behavior became second nature to him.

The transformation that I saw in Chet helped me to look at the personal change process in a different manner. It confirmed for me the importance of the triangle of mental health, and it illustrated the power that various constituencies can have in encouraging change. As people from home, the office, and the newly established learning community—people whose opinions Chet valued—were drawn in, all these parties acquired a stake in the change effort, and they all reinforced Chet's experimentation with new relational approaches. This strategy helped to create the "tipping point," that point at which Chet realized that the cost of staying with the status quo was much higher than that of experimenting with new options, and he was able to begin lowering and working through his resistances.

THE CEO "RECYCLING" SEMINAR

Once a year I run a workshop at INSEAD called "The Challenge of Leadership: Creating Reflective Leaders," a workshop shaped by my work with Chet and others like him. Approximately twenty very senior applicants (many of them CEOs) are invited to participate. These executives apply to the program for a variety of reasons. They might, for example, be dealing with a seemingly insoluble dilemma, negative feelings about themselves, or perceptions of the world and others that tend to make fulfillment seem impossible. Typically, these dilemmas aren't clearly articulated in the applicants' minds when they apply to the program.

To be accepted into the program each potential participant has to complete a complex application form. The information provided helps me to make an initial assessment about the suitability of the candidates for the program. Is their psychological makeup sufficiently robust to withstand the rigors of the program? Will their presence add to the program? The application includes a series of short essays that can be seen as psychological preparation for what the program will have in store for them. It makes future participants aware that this isn't yet another typically run executive program. In addition, all future participants, wherever they're located, are interviewed by me, either face-to-face or over the phone, to help me ascertain whether they have what it takes to go through this kind of workshop. During the interview I explain to them that, in contrast to other programs, the "life" case study will be the main source of interpretive material. I ask them if they think they can handle such an approach. Although many of them say that talking about themselves in an intimate way is no problem, my experience tells me just how anxious and defensive it will probably make them. Still, if the interview reveals traces of psychological-mindedness—that is, the capacity to be open and responsive, and a serious interest in understanding themselves—I know I've got a good candidate.

The workshop consists of three five-day sessions with breaks of approximately seven weeks in between, followed by a three-day session half a year later. The expectation is that the participants will learn more about themselves each week we're together, agree on a "contract" specifying what they'll work on while on the job and at home, and return to the workshop for the next session to deepen their understanding. I assign "homework" particular to each individual, to be tackled between the modules and monitored by the other participants. (Mutual coaching is part of the design of the program.)

I run the program with the help of a colleague. Having a second person in the workshop allows for a more complete view of what happens in the group and serves to protect both faculty members from major blind spots. In addition, having two faculty members gives each of us the opportunity to move in and out of active and passive observational modes. The interchange between the two workshop leaders also provides a model for the participants of ways of relating to each other and handling conflict, and provides the participants with a richer way of understanding complex human phenomena.

Although the basic material of the workshop is the "life" case study, as noted earlier, the first week of the program is fairly structured. Part of the time is spent on a number of interactive lectures/discussions concerning high-performance organizations, organizational culture, leadership (exemplary and dysfunctional), communication, the career life cycle, cross-cultural management, organizational stress, and other organizational dilemmas. Built on this structure, the workshop's central model of psychological activity and organization is the personal case history. At some point during the multiweek process, each participant sits in what some have described as the "hot seat." Although this is voluntary, eventually everyone does it, realizing its importance. The presentation of one's life story is a process of self-discovery, giving a framework to previously puzzling experiences and actions. As listeners compare their own stories, the narration also helps the other participants better understand problems in their public or private lives. Puzzling and disturbing as some of these presentations can be, the emerging material helps participants become better at the process of making sense of the human experience. As Henry Thoreau once said, "Not until we are lost do we begin to understand ourselves."

During the second week of the workshop some time is devoted to the processing of a number of multi-party feedback instruments and a personality test, providing the person not only with rich feedback from the organizational world but also from family members and friends. This information serves as the basis for a more refined action plan in the period between the second and third workshop components. The main focus of the third week is the consolidation of the acquired insights, the internalization of change, and future action plans. This process of consolidation is then further reinforced by the short workshop half a year later.

Apart from the plenary sessions, participants spend considerable time in small groups in and outside the classroom. These interactions are extremely valuable because they serve to consolidate and internalize newly discovered behavior patterns. Eventually, the twenty people form an intense learning community, with each participant constructively giving feedback to anyone who falls back into a behavior pattern that he or she is trying to unlearn. It wouldn't be an exaggeration to say that by the third week, many of the participants know each other better than many of their family members do. Because by that point they feel safe with each other and have become more emotionally intelligent, the interchange in the plenary sessions is free-flowing and information-rich, with much less intervention needed by the faculty. Most important, by the third session the members of this self-analysing group have begun to take important steps toward change both at the office and at home.

Many of the groups, after concluding with their half-year follow-up, choose to hold follow-up sessions year after year. This offers the participants a chance to renew good friendships and reinforce new behaviors, and it gives the faculty an opportunity to assess the degree to which new behavior patterns have become truly internalized, and thus whether the change efforts have truly held.

LOOKING IN ON "THE CHALLENGE OF LEADERSHIP"

Let's look in as a new group of participants gather for their first "Challenge of Leadership" meeting:

Getting Started

The cocktail party that launches "The Challenge of Leadership" workshop has the familiar artificial quality found on many such occasions. There's the usual nervous laughter, the clinking of glasses, the jockeying for positions. People mill around, trying to make contact and start up a conversation. Quite a few of the people present are ill at ease, unsure what to talk about and how to relate to each other. Topics of conversation range from recent political events, to travel, to cross-cultural anecdotes.

Though this looks like an ordinary cocktail party, with a random group of executives engaged in meaningless activity, it isn't. The party has been carefully choreographed. There's a purpose behind the social ritual. It's an awkward but necessary step to get the leadership workshop on its way—a deliberate effort to prepare a group of individuals for change.

From all over the globe, the participants arrived earlier at their destination. Now they're trying to feel their way around. Specialists on group behavior would call what happens at this initial gathering of participants the "being polite" group phase. During this time, the members of the group struggle with questions of inclusion and exclusion: Who else has been selected into the program? What's the background of the other participants? What will they be like to work with? The tentative behavior of the partygoers is a snapshot in time, reflecting both their excitement and their anxiety.

A spectator from Mars would be amused to see this gathering of captains of industry, because in this context they look like fish out of water. For once, they aren't in control. For once, they don't know exactly what to expect. For once, they aren't the ones pulling the strings. For once, they're not masters of the universe. Instead, they're anxiously testing the waters. They introduce themselves to each other. They engage in polite talk. Some maneuver awkwardly to position themselves among their peers. Some of them talk too much: that's their way of coping with an uncomfortable situation. Others try to numb their anxiety by drinking too much. At a subliminal level they're aware, however, that it will be harder to hide behind a public self here than it is at the office. It won't be as easy to keep a mask on or to skate by with formulaic responses. Participants are well aware that they're caught up in a totally unknown situation, and each one fosters specific fantasies and defensive reactions. Many thoughts race through their minds: Why didn't I stay at the office? Why did I leave familiar ground? There must be a better way to spend my time. What am I going to get out of all this? What if this is just a waste of time? What am I doing here?

Although over the years word-of-mouth has been the most powerful driver behind executive applications, for a number of the participants gathered here the journey started when their VP of Human Resources or another colleague gave them a brochure about the program and it lit a spark of interest. Something in the description of the program piqued their curiosity or stimulated their fantasy. Some prospective participants see the workshop as an opportunity to do something different—to take a break from the routine of office life. Others see in the workshop a source of answers to the existential questions they've been asking themselves lately—questions about how to regain the former excitement of work, play, and marriage; questions about how to get out of their rut and restore the sense of discovery that used to make work a joy.

Among the prospective participants who read the brochure at their desk back home, there were a few who dropped out of the process when they saw how complex the admission form was. It asked far too many questions, for one thing. Such forms were good for students, sure—but at their level? Some of these questions were downright puzzling—quite different from the standard questions posed by journalists or investment analysts—and most of them were terribly personal. Who wants to write about things he or she is not good at? Who knows how to respond when asked about risks taken (and possibly lost)? While the questions asked on the admission form caused some irritation and anxiety, they clearly indicated that this wasn't going to be a traditional executive program.

And then there was the telephone interview. Out of the blue, a stranger—the workshop leader—called to ask even more questions, equally personal (or worse!). He asked what complaints the spouse had about the prospective participant, for example. And what kind of things made the participant angry, sad, frustrated. He even asked questions about wild fantasies. Whose business was that? they wondered. What did any of that have to do with becoming more effective as a leader? Strangely enough, though, when asked at the end of that phone call if they still wanted a place in the program, everyone in attendance at the cocktail party had given an affirmative response.

After the cocktail party, there was a short introduction describing the daily workshop schedule, followed by a tour of the campus and a nice dinner. As the participants chatted politely during the meal, they sensed that they were enjoying the calm before the storm.

The Workshop Proper

The next day the seminar started in earnest. At the announced opening time the anxiety ran high; people appeared quite apprehensive, and they looked expectantly at the workshop leader for reassurance. He gave a short lecture on emotional intelligence and irrational behavior in organizations and then reiterated the basic premise of the workshop: that it was fueled by the "life" case study (meaning that case presentations from participants would be the main learning tool). He mentioned that each life case study would offer a unique situation that would contribute to the learning process and cautioned that there could be "no interpretation without association." (In other words, each participant would get as much out of the workshop as he or she put into it.) He reminded the group that he had spoken to all the participants beforehand and that all had accepted the ground rules and had committed to work on a number of significant problems that needed resolution. He also stressed the need for confidentiality regarding what happened in the classroom.

From then on the workshop was on its way. How the various participants would handle the emerging anxiety would depend on their personality structure, their historic defense mechanisms, and the specific dynamics that evolved in the group. The immediate behavioral data that would emerge in the group would be used as clues in the exploration of conscious and unconscious material, and of defensive operations.

THEORETICAL UNDERPINNINGS

Though, as I noted earlier, I had an epiphany about the need to involve all aspects of the mental health triangle in any change effort, it took me years of struggling and experimentation to settle on the format for "The Challenge of Leadership." The end result truly does foster the change process—but why? To understand how and why it works, let's look at some of the "science" of personal change.

Developmental psychologists have estimated that at the age of thirty, two-thirds to three-fifths of an individual's personality is formed [6]. But the fact that people have a greater plasticity early in life doesn't rule out their ability to change at a later life stage, if they know how to go about it. To jumpstart a change effort, certain conditions need to be met; specific steps have to be taken. Does this mean undergoing lengthy therapeutic procedures? Rarely.

As a psychoanalyst and psychotherapist (roles for which I've been formally trained, just as I've been trained in business and economics), I'm steeped in traditional methods of creating personality change. More traditional psychoanalytic thinking dictates that the main route to insight and lasting change occurs through a lengthy treatment procedure involving anywhere from two to five sessions a week. Needless to say, the prospect of such a monumental undertaking isn't very attractive to senior executives who have neither the time nor the patience for such an activity. Furthermore, executives tend to think they're the center of the universe. That meant I had to find a more time-effective way of reaching them. I needed to find a procedure to get the attention of a group of highly self-centered people, and to get that attention fast.

My task, then, was to develop a method of intervention that would accelerate and condense the more traditional therapeutic process while remaining true to basic clinical principles. I had to find a less traditional way to overcome resistances to change and to confront problems that were often out of awareness—problems of a preconscious and unconscious nature. I had to mobilize in an effective way unconscious mental processes to achieve therapeutic results. In addition, I had to make sure that any changes in behavior patterns that resulted wouldn't turn out to be "flights into health"—transient "highs"—as is so often the case with the miraculous "cures" offered by psychological snake-oil salesmen.

As I weighed my options, I saw considerable promise for accelerating the process of change in short-term dynamic psychotherapy [7]–[26]. This therapeutic approach offered a different avenue than long-term psychotherapy to help people acquire insight into the life events and ongoing experiences that contributed to their problems. Therapists using this approach discovered that focused interventions of a more direct nature, combined with a solid dose of empathy and psychological support, frequently resulted in remarkable improvement. They also found that clarification of defensive reactions, which allowed the presenting problem to be brought into sharper focus, appeared to contribute to behavior change. These techniques made the client's problem more explicit and gave the client a greater awareness of the psychological forces affecting his or her behavior.

After experimenting with short-term dynamic psychotherapy in one-on-one encounters with executives who came to me wanting to increase their effectiveness at work, I realized that, though in most cases we achieved progress, more was needed to create lasting change in their behavior patterns. Simple one-on-one coaching, valuable as it was, generally had only limited results [27]. Given the limited time available, I needed to increase the discomfort zone of the participants. I discovered that if I could create a situation of high intensity and total involvement through the creation of a learning community—whereby each member had a stake in creating a "corrective emotional experience" for others—there was the possibility that the change process could be further accelerated [28].

After a great deal of trial and error, I conceived that I could create an intense learning community by combining some of the methods used in short-term dynamic psychotherapy with the interventions derived from group dynamics while adding concepts taken from organizational and leadership theory [29]–[37]. In using the most effective principles of the first two I was able to set the stage for a more intensified change effort.

Because minds are like umbrellas, in that they function only when they're open, I had to prepare the executives I was dealing with to be willing to open up. That meant I needed to create a transitional space—that is, a space in which participants, protected from the reality of the outside world, could safely experiment with new forms of interacting [38]–[40]. This is a crucial element in any developmental or change process.

The pediatrician and psychoanalyst Donald Winnicott, whose emphasis was children's play and learning, described how so-called transitional objects help children develop self-reliance, independence, and the ability to separate themselves from their caregivers so that they can differentiate themselves from the world around them [39]–[40]. His writings talk of an everyday world, with all its demands, and an intrapsychic world—a world of inner reality where drives, wishes, needs, and fantasies thrive. In addition, however, he speaks of a third world, an illusionary place between reality and fantasy where connections are drawn between the inner and outer worlds. This world is occupied by "transitional objects." A child who is initially totally dependent on the mother or father (or other caregiver) uses these transitional objects, such as a teddy-bear or a blanket, as a surrogate protective figure when the mother or father isn't readily available for help or support. Thus transitional objects help the child overcome the anxiety of becoming independent and self-relying; these objects serve as enablers of intellectual and emotional development through a guided "letting go" of a former, more dependent relationship.

In its original form, this transitional world, with its transitional objects, is part of the process of resolving the developmental challenges of childhood to arrive at adulthood and maturity. A place of play and imagination, transitional space is an incubator for creative thought. This is the place where such processes as symbolization, make-believe, illusion, daydreaming, playfulness, curiosity, imagination, and wonder start. Though transitional space is essential to healthy development in childhood, there's no such a thing as definitive closure. At maturity, people don't give up their transitional world. They continue to reenter it regularly when they need to find unorthodox ideas and solutions.

Thus providing transitional space in the workplace, in the psychologist's office, or in the context of "The Challenge of Leadership" is a productive way to encourage innovation, experimentation, and learning. This space can't be forced into existing forms and structures, because it needs to be fluid, able to change form in response to the interests, desires, wishes, and memories of the people involved. The main requirement is that it simultaneously provide the assurance of safety and the degree of frustration needed to foster new learning.

Because "The Challenge of Leadership" offers transitional space, it becomes an "identity laboratory," a forum in which people can tolerate feedback (even when it's negative) and are willing to experiment with new ways of doing things [41]. The transitional space offered by the workshop is a place where people can let go of their resistances and enjoy the freedom to create and enjoy illusions. It's a place where they can discover and rediscover aspects of themselves, where missing experiences come back into mental consciousness. It's a place where they can abandon their false selves and experiment with living according who and what they are, not according to what others ask them to be. It's a place where people are encouraged to do new things rather than merely repeat what they've done in the past.

Playing in a transitional space—being part of such an "identity laboratory"—encourages workshop participants to break out of established patterns in order to look at things in a different way. It enables them to take a hard look at their propensity toward self-deception. It helps them deepen their intimate relationships. It helps them connect the unconnected. It encourages them to explore feelings they thought they had forgotten and to enjoy moments of wonder. Most of all, it fosters the creative process. As Ralph Waldo Emerson once said: "There are no days in life so memorable as those which vibrated to some stroke of the imagination."

REFERENCES

1. Hamel, G. and C. K. Prahalad (1989). "Strategic Intent." *Harvard Business Review* (May-June): 63–76.
2. Kets de Vries, M. F. R. and D. Miller (1984). *The Neurotic Organization*. San Francisco, Jossey-Bass.
3. Kets de Vries, M. F. R. and D. Miller (1988). *Unstable at the Top*. New York, New American Library.

4. Morgan, G. (1986). *Images of Organization*. London, Sage.

5. Pfeffer, J. (1998). *The Human Equation: Building Profits by Putting People First*. Boston, MA., Harvard Business School Press.

6. McCrae, R. R. and P. T. Costa (1990). *Personality in Adulthood*. New York, Guilford Press.

7. Balint, M., P. H. Ornstein and E. Balint (1972). *Focal Psychotherapy*. London, Tavistock.

8. Breuer, J. and S. Freud (1895). *Studies on Hysteria. The Standard Edition of the Complete Psychological Works of Sigmund Freud*. Ed J. Strachey. London, Hogarth Press and the Institute of Psychoanalysis. 2: 3–311.

9. Crits-Christoph, P. and J. P. Barber, Eds (1991). *Handbook of Short-Term Dynamic Psychotherapy*. New York, Basic Books.

10. Davanloo, H., Ed (1994). *Basic Principles and Techniques in Short-Term Dynamic Psychotherapy*. London, Jason Aronson.

11. Davanloo, H. (2000). *Intensive Short-Term Dynamic Psychotherapy*. New York, John Wiley & Sons, Inc.

12. Freud, S. (1893–95). *Standard Edition of the Complete Psychological Work of Sigmund Freud, Vol 2*. J. Strachey (editor and translator). London, Hogarth Press. 125–134.

13. Groves, J. E., Ed (1996). *Essential Papers on Short-Term Dynamic Therapy*. New York, New York University Press.

14. Gustavson, J. P. (1986). *The Complex Secret of Brief Psychotherapy*. New York, Norton.

15. Horowitz, M. J., C. Marmor, J. Krupnick, N. Wilner, N. Kaltreider and R. Wallerstein (1984). *Personality Styles and Brief Psychotherapy*. New York, Basic Books.

16. Luborsky, L. and P. Crits-Cristoph (1998). *Understanding Transference: The Core Conflictual Relationship Theme Method*. Washington, American Psychological Organization.

17. Malan, D. and F. Osimo (1992). *Psychodynamics, Training, and Outcome in Brief Psychotherapy*. Oxford, Butterworth Heinemann.

18. Malan, D. H. (1976). *The Frontier of Brief Psychotherapy*. New York, Plenum.

19. Mann, J. (1973). *Time Limited Psychotherapy*. Cambridge, Mass, Harvard University Press.

20. Mann, J. and R. Goldman (1982). *A Casebook in Time-Limited Psychotherapy*. New York, McGraw-Hill.

21. McCullough Vaillant, L. (1997). *Changing Character*. New York, Basic Books.

22. Molnos, A. (1995). *A Question of Time: Essentials of Brief Psychotherapy.* London, Karnac Books.
23. Rawson, P. (2002). *Short-Term Psychodynamic Psychotherapy: An Analysis of the Key Principles.* London, Karnac Books.
24. Sifneos, P. E. (1979). *Short-Term Dynamic Psychotherapy.* Cambridge, Mass, Harvard University Press.
25. Strupp, H. H. and J. L. Binder (1984). *Psychotherapy in a New Key: A Guide to Time-Limited Dynamic Psychotherapy.* New York, Basic Books.
26. Winnicott, D. W. (1972). "Basis for Self in Body." *International Journal of Child Psychotherapy* 1: 7–16.
27. Balint, M. (1957). *The Doctor, his Patient and the Illness.* New York, International Universities Press.
28. Alexander, F. and T. M. French (1946). *Psychoanalytic Therapy.* New York, Ronald Press.
29. Foulkes, S. H. (1975). *Group Analytic Psychotherapy: Methods and Principles.* London, Gordon & Breach.
30. Freud, S. (1921). *Group Psychology and the Analysis of the Ego. The Standard Edition of the Complete Psychological Works of Sigmund Freud, Vol 7.* J. Strachey (editor and translator). London, The Hogarth Press and the Institute of Psychoanalysis.
31. Harwood, I. N. H. and M. Pines, Eds (1998). *Self Experiences in Groups: Intersubjective and Self Psychological Pathways to Human Understanding.* London, Kingsley.
32. Kaplan, H. I. and B. J. Sadock, Eds (1993). *Comprehensive Group Psychotherapy.* Baltimore, Williams and Wilkins.
33. Klein, R. H., H. S. Bernard and D. L. Singer, Eds (1992). *Handbook of Contemporary Group Psychotherapy: Contributions from Object Relations, Self Psychology, and Social Systems Theories.* Madison, CT, International Universities Press.
34. Rosenbaum, M. (1983). *Handbook of Short-Term Therapy Groups.* New York, McGraw-Hill.
35. Scheidlinger, S. (1982). *Focus on Group Psychotherapy*: Clinical Essays. Madison, CT, International Universities Press.
36. Scott Rutan, J. and W. N. Stone (2001). *Psychodynamic Group Psychotherapy.* New York, The Guilford Press.
37. Yalom, I. D. (1985). *The Theory and Practice of Group Psychotherapy.* New York, Basic Books.
38. Bion, W. R. (1962). *Learning from Experience.* London, Heinemann.

39. Winnicott, D. W. (1951). *Transitional Objects and Transitional Phenomena. Collected Papers: Through Paediatrics to Psycho-analysis.* London, Tavistock Publications.

40. Winnicott, D. W. (1971). *Playing and Reality.* New York, Basic Books.

41. Korotov, K. (2005). *Identity Laboratories: Experiencing Transitional Space.* INSEAD Doctoral Dissertation. Fontainebleau, France.

CHAPTER 9

TAKING THE ROAD
LESS TRAVELED

By three methods we may learn wisdom: first, by reflection, which is the noblest; second, by imitation, which is the easiest; and third, by experience, which is the bitterest.

—Confucius

Where is the Life we have lost in living?

—T. S. Eliot

But a lifetime of happiness! No man alive could bear it: it would be hell on earth.

—George Bernard Shaw

The most important point is to accept yourself and stand on your own two feet.

—Zen proverb

A Zen story tells of a man who heard that somewhere far away there was a valley carpeted in beautiful flowers. According to all

211

accounts, it was a place of wonder and delight. Determined to see this valley, he set off in search of it. As he walked and walked, and walked some more, he became increasingly unhappy at not reaching his destination. Eventually, quite distraught after many months of travel and many hardships, the man found himself exhausted at the edge of a forest. To his delight, he saw in the distance an old man sitting on a bench in front of a tree. He said, "Old man, somewhere there exists a valley full of beautiful flowers. I've walked for many months on end to find this valley. I'm worn out and at my wit's end. Please, can you tell me where that valley is?" The old man answered, "Behind you!"

OWNING YOUR OWN LIFE

This Zen story is a reminder of St Augustine's statement: "People travel and wonder at the heights of mountains, at the huge waves of the seas, at the long course of rivers, at the vast compass of the oceans, at the circular motion of the stars, and they pass themselves without even wondering." Too many of us do nothing but run, never allowing ourselves to reflect on where we're running to or what we're running for. Too many executives, especially, are like the rat in the proverbial maze, not only running endlessly but running in circles. And yet we all benefit from stopping occasionally to reflect and to change direction. Life goes on no matter what we do, but personal growth and development happen only if we choose wisely.

What can executives expect when they open their lives to change? How can they begin to "own" their own lives? What's that particular journey all about? In the previous chapter I described the initial steps needed to undertake the journey of transformation. In this chapter, I'll further explore this process, continuing to use "The Challenge of Leadership" workshop as an example of a successful change effort. (Please note, though, that different permutations of this workshop design are possible, as we'll see in Chapter 11.)

CHALLENGE 1: PREPARING FOR THE JOURNEY

As I noted earlier, the major precondition for change is a willingness to change. Certain other conditions also have to be met, however, before a person can successfully undertake the rigorous journey executives share in "The Challenge of Leadership." As mentioned in Chapter 8, careful selection is crucial. Only comparatively healthy people—here I'm speaking of mental health—have the psychological strength to participate in this intensive change seminar. And the relatively public forum of "The Challenge of Leadership" isn't the intervention of choice for everyone; some people prefer a more individualized approach.

The criteria by which we assess potential candidates for inclusion in the leadership workshop reflect the psychological nature of the endeavor.

Level of motivation. Are potential participants prepared to take a hard look at themselves? Are they willing to do serious work, or are they looking for a quick fix—a magic pill that will take care of all their problems?

Capacity to be open and responsive. Are potential participants not only willing but also able to open up to others? Can they establish relationships without years of groundwork?

Interpersonal connectedness. Are potential participants willing and able to engage in meaningful emotional interaction? Having the capacity to talk about very personal thoughts and feelings makes the change process a lot easier. Experience has shown that people who have a history of give-and-take with a number of significant people in their lives are more likely to change. (Hermits, please don't apply!)

Emotional management skills. Can potential participants tolerate the anxiety that comes with putting themselves in a vulnerable position? Is their emotional life passionate, or are their emotional experiences rather flat? Can they relate when another person talks about life's ups and downs? Do they ever get tears in their eyes during emotional movie scenes?

Degree of psychological-mindedness. Are potential participants curious about their inner life? Would they like to learn more about themselves? Would they like to understand better why they behave the way they do? Can they sometimes look beneath the surface and grasp the emotional meaning of maladaptive behaviors? Can they verbalize their thoughts, feelings, fantasies, and inner life?

Capacity for introspection. Do potential participants have the ability to recognize how contemporary psychological processes are integrated and related to past experiences? (As Kierkegaard noted, "The tragedy of life is that you understand it only backward but you have to live it forward.")

Responses to observations of others. Are potential participants receptive to interpretations of their actions and attitudes by others, or do they become defensive? Do they generally understand what other people are trying to tell them?

Flexibility. Do potential participants react constructively and appropriately to stressful interventions, or do they seek refuge in indirect defensive behaviors?

CASE STUDY

Perhaps the best way to illustrate preparedness for the journey of change is by presenting a sample case study of a participant. The case study is introduced here and then referred to and fleshed out as I discuss the remaining five challenges of change.

One CEO participating in "The Challenge of Leadership"—a woman named Carole—started her presentation by declaring that she was an unwanted child, an "accident." This made a number of the other executives very uncomfortable: the workshop had only just started, and they were expecting to hear about knotty business problems, not open emotional wounds. Carole mentioned that she was a latecomer, an unexpected arrival after her parents already had four daughters. Taking care of yet another daughter was the last thing they had in mind. All during Carole's childhood, her mother had made quite clear her disappointment about the girl's unexpected arrival. If she had planned for another child, the mother had said often, she would have liked it to be a boy. Carole expressed her sadness about her mother's comments and explained how her mother's attitude had shaped her life. The theme of being unwanted had always haunted her.

Carole also mentioned her father, who wasn't very present during her childhood, either physically or emotionally. He had worked long hours as an internist at a local hospital. And when he was around, he remained distant; it was always difficult to get his attention. Furthermore, he took his wife's side whenever Carole had a fight with her mother about some behavior that her mother found inappropriate (and there were many behaviors which fell into that category). Rarely could Carole count on his support. As a youngster, she had felt that she needed to compete for her father's attention. Looking back, she thought that it had been the youngest of her sisters who'd had to bear the brunt of her competitiveness. She told the workshop a funny story about the way she had succeeded in shifting to this sister the blame for a dent that she herself had put in the family car. She mentioned to the group, almost as an aside, that she had always been good at shifting responsibility, at making others take the blame.

Carole realized, she told her workshop colleagues, that a major theme in her life was proving that she was worth having around, that she counted for something. To get her parents' attention, she had excelled in school and at sports. But she emphasized that she hadn't been just a teacher's pet. There was another side to her—a rebellious streak that she had generally kept hidden. She noted that this rebellious streak had often showed itself in the number of boys she went out with as a teenager (and beyond), and in their disreputable nature.

After graduation from high school, Carole had chosen engineering as her field of study, to impress her father. Programming was her undergraduate specialty, so after obtaining her engineering degree, she had taken a job in the computer industry. Fairly soon thereafter, she had married for the first time, and the young couple had had a daughter. After an uphill struggle at work and in her personal life—including several career setbacks, a divorce, and a second marriage and breakup—she had eventually become the president of a very successful software company. While that business victory gave her pleasure, the price she had paid for her success—the two failed marriages, a difficult relationship with her only daughter, and a long list of stress symptoms—was terribly high.

When commenting to the members of the workshop on her leadership style, Carole noted that she had always had quite a temper. As she mentioned jokingly, "Speak when you're angry, and you'll deliver the best speech you'll ever regret." According to her, people in her company either loved her or hated her. Because she set extremely high standards for herself, she could be a harsh taskmaster with others. Unfortunately, she had lost a number of very capable executives as a result. The latest departure (a high-potential woman who had been liked and admired) had irritated the company's non-executive chairman, who had strongly suggested that Carole needed to work on her leadership style. She had heard his comment but let it be.

What had gotten Carole started really thinking about her life and her relationships was the discovery of a lump in one of her breasts. Though after a biopsy the lump proved to be benign, it had given her a real scare, one close family member having recently died of breast cancer. Her decision to apply for the leadership workshop had been a response to the convergence of these two things—the cancer scare and the comment from the chairman about her leadership style.

Carole's frankness as she talked about her life loosened up the group early in the workshop. Many of the participants were touched by the intensity with which she described her feelings and experiences. Because of the strength of her presentation, she made it easy for others to visualize (and empathize with) what she had gone through. Furthermore, many of the themes she touched upon echoed themes in the lives of the others, evoking for many a host of memories and associations.

Carole's presentation made it clear that she was a woman who was highly motivated to do something about her present situation. She realized that her personal life was a mess and that she had to work on her leadership style. As she talked about her problems, she expressed considerable emotion, on several occasions wiping tears from her eyes. That meant that human connectedness wasn't likely to be an issue for her as she attempted to change. In spite of her being a harsh taskmaster at the office, she related well to the other group members and, from what she told us, to her colleagues at work. Psychological-mindedness wasn't likely to be an issue either: she was clearly interested in understanding herself better. Furthermore, her responses to questions from the group made it clear that she was able to make connections between her present behavior and her past experiences. She seemed to be ready to take the plunge, to try to change some of her destructive behavior patterns.

CATALYSTS FOR CHANGE

We've looked at how to assess preparedness for the journey of change. Now the question is, Where does that preparedness—that motivation to change—come from? If the human tendency is to resist change, how does the process of change ever get underway? Why does a person's resistance start to weaken? When is someone really ready to explore the implications for change, and to play with the ambivalence of doing or not doing? When does the tipping point occur?

As we saw in the case of Carole, above, disrupting the relative stability of personality to get the process of change into motion requires a strong inducement in the form of pain or distress—discomfort that outweighs the secondary gains that hanging on to the present situation offers. (You may remember from Chapter 4 that secondary gains are positive benefits such as sympathy, attention, or other advantages that result from a negative situation.) When is enough, enough? People must experience a sense of concern about their present situation, whether the trigger be family tensions, health problems, negative social sanctions, an accident, feelings of isolation leading to a sense of helplessness and insecurity, problem behavior at work, distressing incidents happening to someone close, or basic daily hassles and frustrations [1]. They have to go beyond "I don't see a problem" or "I have a problem but I don't really want to do something about it" to "I want to do something about my problem," which may lead to "I'm actively working on my problem." Clearly, Carole had the motivation to do something about her life. She recognized that her current path might well lead to loneliness at home and a pink slip at work.

Surveys of people who have undergone major internal change confirm that a high level of unpleasant emotion (anxiety, anger, sadness, or frustration, for example) exists in the period just prior to change, generally precipitated by a stressor such as one of those listed above. This negative emotion, which brings to awareness the serious negative consequences that can be expected if dysfunctional behavior patterns continue, makes the status quo (in spite of the elusive advantages) increasingly difficult to maintain.

When people realize that bad days are turning into a bad year—in other words, that the isolated occurrence of occasional discontent has become a steady pattern of unhappiness—it becomes harder to deny that something needs to be done about the situation. From this point on, every new disturbance is recognized as part of the general pattern of dissatisfaction. Complaints coalesce into a coherent entity. Many people have an "aha!" experience at this stage, a moment when they're finally able to interpret decisively what's happening to them. They see clearly that neither the passage of time nor minor changes in behavior will improve the situation—indeed, the situation is likely to become even worse if nothing drastic is done about it.

Even the insight that drastic measures are required doesn't automatically compel a person to take action. However, playing with the ambivalence—with the pros and cons of change—typically sets into motion a mental process whereby people allow themselves to consider alternatives to the adverse situation. It's an essential process that tips the status quo. Everyone has a wish (both conscious and unconscious) for redress of personal grievances. This wish turns into one of the engines of change if it helps people realize that they need to do something about their present situation. Having made the transition from denying to admitting that all is not well, people are able to undertake a reappraisal process. Although initially every alternative to the troubling situation appears more frightening than the status quo, gradually a preferable alternative to the stalemate begins to emerge. The hurdles may still seem insurmountable, but at least a goal is in sight [1]; [2]–[5].

Accepting the need for change is a necessary first step—I can't stress that enough—but on its own it's no guarantee of action. People need a push, in the form of something that can later be described as a "focal event"—a crisis, if you will. Although we typically think of a crisis as something so acute that it's obvious, the focal event that triggers change is sometimes only retrospectively interpreted as a milestone.

The metaphor of the last straw is very appropriate here, because it indicates that if a person is prepared—if not actually ready—to take a decisive step, the triggering event can be minor: the final additional element (one among many) that puts matters into focus. Experience suggests that while major events certainly can be focal, the focal event often turns out to be a minor occurrence that's seen as focal simply because it enables a discontented person to take that long-delayed first step. Thus it's the catalyst in the change process, whether it's perceived as major or minor to an outside observer. A focal event often involves someone important to the distressed person. In the case of Carole, it was the conjunction of problems with her daughter, a cancer scare, and problems at work (including a cautionary word from the chairman of the board) that called her to reevaluate her lifestyle.

CHALLENGE 2: IDENTIFYING THE PROBLEM

To be able to change, we have to know what it is we want to change. Thus we have to identify our focal problem and formulate explicit, tractable improvement goals. When we tell our history to others, we often see a thin red line that began in our past and continues over time into our present. The challenge we face is to identify this thin red line—to clarify what it's all about. That means carefully listening to our own story to discover the focal problem.

More often than not the stories we tell about ourselves have to do with seemingly insoluble dilemmas grounded in a negative self-concept and a misguided perception of the world and of others—dilemmas that often cause unhappiness, a lack of fulfill-ment, and problems at work [6]–[10]. Though these dilemmas have the potential to wreak disaster, they aren't ordinarily clearly conceptualized in our mind; they're often preconscious and thus only vaguely experienced. What we feel more keenly is various mixtures of helplessness and hopelessness. So how can we arrive at greater specificity? With the help of others.

At "The Challenge of Leadership" change workshop, the people in the "hot seat" and the "audience" hearing their case presentation talk through issues such as self-esteem, and they iden-tify together, in each presenter, specific present-day dilemmas that have grown out of underlying problems of esteem and worth—dilemmas that can be remedied by addressing those problems. These specific dilemmas are then the basis for "contracts" between each presenter and the rest of the participants.

MAJOR THEMES FOR EXECUTIVES

Looking back at the hundreds of CEOs and board members who have gone through my change workshops, I can identify a number of common themes or change-triggers. Among them are loss, anxiety, interpersonal conflict, symptomatology that reflects inner turmoil (for example, habit disorders, sexual dysfunction, and insomnia), developmental imbalance, life imbalance, and questions about meaning. Let's look at each in turn:

Loss. The broad theme of loss, which can encompass events and situations that are past, present, and pending, is one of the most difficult things humans have to deal with [11]–[16]. The most dramatic example of loss is the death of an important figure in one's life, or the loss of a spouse through separation or divorce. Such a loss can have enormous repercussions, as can the loss of one's own health and well-being through illness. Regardless of the form that loss takes, its consequences may linger for months or even years in the form of depressive reactions as the person grieves about the poor hand of cards he or she was dealt, about what could have been if the cards had been better [17].

Loss is a frequent guest in the world of work as well. The loss of a job (and of one's community of colleagues) can be devastating. Career setbacks can likewise be experienced as a form of loss, as can retirement. Many executives feel a deep loss when they compare their career expectations with their actual achievement. They fear that their original hopes for career success won't ever be fulfilled. A midlevel manager may realize that she'll never become the chairman of the company, while a corporate VP may watch in dismay as a colleague is handed the coveted board chairmanship. The consequences of such losses may linger in the form of panic or depressive reactions. How will they be able to manage their disappointment? The challenge is to break out of this depressive cycle, reframe the situation, recognize and appreciate new alternatives and opportunities, and arrive at a more hopeful outlook on life.

Anxiety. Another concern that often arises among executives has to do with the anxiety of being or becoming number one in an organization. Many executives who are new to (or close to) that position wonder if they'll be able to hack it. Will they be able to talk effectively to the press? How will they come across at large meetings? Will they be sufficiently astute in dealing with the investment community? Will their colleagues accept their newly increased authority? Some executives who deal with this sort of anxiety have difficulty making decisions; they're so afraid that their actions will show them to be impostors (see Chapter 7) that they succumb to decision paralysis.

Interpersonal conflict. Another area of difficulty that can be a catalyst for enrolling in "The Challenge of Leadership" is an intensification of an interpersonal conflict, whether with family members, friends, or work colleagues. In one example, an executive described how stressed out he was due to an ongoing battle with one of the non-executive members of his board. He enlisted the help of his fellow workshop participants to find a constructive solution to his impasse. Another senior executive enrolled in the seminar hoping to figure out how to resolve a long-lasting feud with one of his brothers over the future direction of their family firm. A CEO caught up in a merger process hoped that participation in the workshop might give him some ideas for solving an organizational culture (and cross-cultural) incompatibility problem.

In the case of strictly personal relationships that executives are involved in, disputes frequently develop when the two partners (whether spouses, parents and children, or good friends) have nonreciprocal expectations about their interaction and relationship. A lack of interpersonal competencies often lies at the core of such problems. Some executives just don't have the skills needed to initiate and sustain meaningful interpersonal relationships [18]. Others have the skills to start a relationship but can't maintain it when such a relationship requires true commitment, intimacy, and expectations of fidelity and loyalty.

Symptomatology. At times, the thin red line that determines a problem area is of a more symptomatic nature, which makes identification of the problem easier. Although some of the symptoms are brought up during the plenary sessions of "The Leadership Challenge," they're more likely to come out in small-group discussion. The range of potential symptoms—all troubling—is enormous, ranging from habit disorders, to sexual dysfunction, to alcohol or drug problems, to insomnia, to phobias such as a fear of flying or of public speaking. The origin of such symptoms varies. Many of them, however, are triggered by long-ago frightening experiences that have long since been forgotten by the conscious mind. Whatever the origin, these symptoms can become so severe that they interfere with everyday functioning and thus are a significant source of distress.

Developmental Imbalance. Another issue that regularly emerges among the CEOs who participate in the leadership workshop is developmental imbalance, which is the label given when certain expectations about life remain unfulfilled [19]–[26]. Developmental imbalance occurs when a person moves from one social role to another and struggles to adjust to the new role. Consider, for example, the man who one day, realizing to his dismay that everybody his age is married, fears that he's doomed to bachelorhood—a sorry fate made even worse by his longing to have children. Consider the woman who faces a demotion, the loss of a much-loved job, or retirement before she's ready. People who fail to cope adequately with these transitions and develop symptoms often experience role transition as a loss that can contribute to depressive reactions. The workshop may help them discover that one way of coping is through establishing new connections, exploring new relationships.

The issue of developmental imbalance was pointed out to one executive during a leadership workshop. This executive—let's call him Peter—repeatedly referred to the terrific relationship he had with his girlfriend. He went to great lengths to explain what a good time they had together. After some questioning from fellow participants after Peter's presentation, it became clear that this relationship had been going on for more than seven years and that the girlfriend was becoming increasingly exasperated by his lack of commitment. A previous girlfriend, Peter finally confessed, had eventually given up on him after a similar delay. During the ensuing discussion, the problems Peter experienced with commit-ment became increasingly clear. The marriage of his parents had ended in a painful divorce, and he suspected that that experience played a role in his unwillingness to take the next step with his girlfriend. He spoke of wanting to have children someday, however, and he described his pleasure in playing with the children of his brother, commenting with pride that he was their favorite uncle. Peter's lack of commitment spilled over from his private life into his life at the office. Making decisions didn't come easily to Peter, who was a great procrastinator. Others had to push him to decide on closure. Although he was now running the show at the office, this pattern of behaving and acting had delayed his career progression.

Life imbalance. The theme of life imbalance shows up in most of the presentations made by senior executives in "The Challenge of Leadership" [22]–[23]; [27]. As life passes and children grow up, many executives feel increasingly that they're leading a mortgaged life. Finding time for the family becomes more and more of an uphill struggle. Executives clinging to the career ladder feel that they're missing out on quality time with their children, missing out on soccer games and teacher conferences and ballet perfor-mances. And as the children grow older, these executives find themselves increasingly estranged from them.

Though executives experiencing a life out of balance regret missing the family time, they often don't know how to regain it. They feel like prisoners of their own ambitions: they like being on the fast track, but they feel guilty about what it means for the family. One executive told me that the turning point for him—the event that brought his life imbalance clearly to the forefront of his consciousness—was when he found himself alone with his seven-year-old daughter and discovered that he had nothing to say. He felt uncomfortable with the little stranger beside him. That was his wake-up call.

Questions about meaning. Finally, last but not least, many of the executives in the leadership workshop raise questions about meaning [28]–[30]. Though they bear outward signs of worldly success, they wonder what they could do to give their life more meaning. Increasingly bored on the job, they sometimes engage in crazy ventures—unlikely mergers and acquisitions, for example—just to break the boredom. Often belatedly, they realize the importance of the words of Carl Jung: "The least of things with meaning is worth more in life than the greatest of things without it." Most people want to belong to something greater than themselves, they want to make a contribution to society, and it's the wise leader who pays attention to this need.

For some executives, the search for meaning may have been a theme all through their career. For others, it has developed only with the passing years. Both groups, having been successful, feel a strong urge to give something back. They're concerned about how to do this. Can it be achieved within the context of work, or do outlets outside work such as religion have to be found for this kind of gratification? How can they have the biggest impact? What can they do that's most suitable, given their personality makeup?

THE TRIANGLE OF CONFLICT

To understand conceptually the reasons behind the emergence of a focal problem or central theme in a person's life, we need to look at the "triangle of conflict." Like the earlier described "triangle of mental life," it's part and parcel of the human condition [31]–[33]. The triangle of conflict clarifies that an individual experiences a conflict (perceived as anxiety) due to unacceptable feelings or desires that create anxiety and lead to defensive reactions. Because the three components of the desire-anxiety-defense triangle affect (and are affected by) one another, we describe the triangle as psychodynamic.

Though the mental triangle appears on these pages as a visible, identifiable entity, the psychodynamic process of the triangle of conflict generally stirs in the person only a vague awareness about what he or she is defending against; the exact nature of the unacceptable thoughts and wishes may not always reach consciousness. Nevertheless, they evoke anxiety. Defensive behavior serves as a means of avoiding the awareness or experience of those unpleasant thoughts or feelings. If the person quickly changes the subject when a certain issue is brought up, or denies a problem that's obvious to others, or concedes a problem but then ignores it, those are good signs that defensive behavior is being employed. If you're a board member concerned about a CEO, or a leadership coach working to resolve a problem in the workplace, your role now is that of a psychological detective: you must find out what the person is defending against. What are the underlying fantasies that drive the person's actions?

The challenge for participants in "The Challenge of Leadership" is to identify their own triangle of conflict—identify their

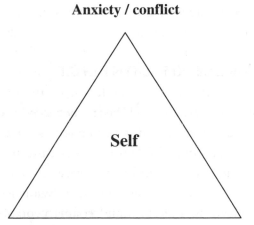

Figure 9.1   Triangle of conflict
Adapted from Malan (1963)

greatest source of anxiety and then track down the feelings that inspired it and the defensive behaviors it spawned; in other words, they have to identify their focal issue. Confrontation and clarification by the workshop leaders and the members of the group help in that process, leading to greater specificity of the problem [4]; [34]–[35]. During the questioning that follows a "hot seat" presentation, workshop participants try to get the presenter to be more explicit about issues and events so that he or she can gain a better grasp of the situation. In the case of Carole, for example, the other participants asked her to talk about her interactions with other women. Did she, they asked, have the same problems managing both women and men? Were her demands toward women different than from those toward men? The need for clarifying answers prompted her to talk about her daughter and their relationship.

This process of confrontation and clarification—the so-called critical-incident method—is generally very enlightening. It helps organize the person's comments, giving the presentation a sharper focus; helps sort out cause-and-effect relationships; identifies multiple meanings; and helps foster an appreciation of the connections between past and current patterns. All these things set the stage for associations made by the members of the group, which they offer following each "hot seat" presentation. These associations, and the focal-issue-identification process that preceded them, lay the groundwork as the presenter undertakes a thoughtful, detailed reappraisal of goals (goes beyond the status quo position), and then formulates and experiments with alternatives to defensive ways of living. The destination of this sometimes-painful inner journey is increased self-knowledge, insight and a new beginning.

The whole process by which the focal issue is identified—the presentation of personal feelings and concerns, followed by confrontation and clarification, followed by associations—is probably unlike anything the presenter has ever experienced. Public self-recognition changes a person, especially when it follows a lifetime of running to avoid coming face to face with oneself. There are chapters in everybody's life which are seldom read—and certainly not aloud. When these chapters are read aloud, in a caring environment, the experience and the support the person receives may be an eye-opener. The presenter typically feels deeply understood in reference not only to current difficulties but also to the way he or she has always felt. Reflective, respectful listening and expressions of deep empathy prompt a deeply emotional experience. When that experience occurs, the self-explorer is encouraged to become the explorer of everything else.

That the group can understand what seems like so much in such a short time gives the person a feeling of being truly supported. That support, along with validation and encouragement from other members of the group, is crucial while this inner journey is taking place. It not only helps the presenter acquire greater insight about his or her problem change, but makes it possible for him or her to discuss the ambivalence that accompanies any effort at change—ambivalence that follows the ebb and flow of his or her resistances.

The feeling that other people care isn't just a warm and fuzzy byproduct; it makes a real difference when a person is addressing major issues [36]–[39]. It's important that the workshop leaders be empathetic too, but it's the role of the group that's critical. The presenter needs to feel as if the group is sharing the "hot seat"; that they aren't frightened, depressed, or even disgusted by what they see; that they accept the presenter with all his or her frailties; that they're optimistic about the future. Because of the attitude of the group, the presenter feels a deep gratitude and trust reminiscent of the trust he or she had in earlier caregivers.

As we look back at Carole through the lens of the triangle of conflict, we see that an important issue for her had to do with her anger toward her mother. At times Carole felt like she could "just kill her." Of course, to express that thought as a small child would have caused great internal conflict, given her very real dependence on her mother. The thought alone would have caused enormous anxiety. Thus Carole repressed her angry thoughts and took them out of conscious awareness. She was also angry with her father for rarely standing up for her. She denied that anger as well, pretending that everything was all right. To defend against her anxiety over her anger at her parents, she unconsciously employed a couple of defense mechanisms: repression and displacement. In the latter, she redirected her angry feelings toward people who were less "dangerous" than her mother and father: sisters, girlfriends, and later husbands and people at work. She also suffered from conversion symptoms (implying that psychic conflicts transformed into somatic symptoms) in the form of migraine headaches.

CHALLENGE 3: UNHOOKING "FALSE CONNECTIONS"

The interpretive process is complicated by yet another triangle, the "triangle of relationships." This triangle addresses the issue of transference, discussed in Chapter 2 and elsewhere. As you may remember from that earlier discussion, in every situation there are two kinds of relationships. First, there's the "real" relationship between the person and the other—a relationship between two colleagues at work, for example, or between an employer and an employee. This real relationship becomes the context for another, more elusive relationship grounded in the past—what psychologists call the "transference relationship" [35]; [40]–[41].

The concept of transference suggests that no relationship is a new relationship; all relationships are colored by previous relationships. And obviously the relationships that have the most lasting potency, coloring almost every subsequent encounter, are those that we had with our earliest caregivers. Our behavior today has its roots in those primary early relationships. As we relive our earlier relationships again and again, behavior patterns emerge by which we act toward people in the present as if they were people in the past: we behave toward them as children behave toward their parents, for example, forgetting that we're now adults. In other words, without even being aware of it, we're often confused as to person, time, and place. Like it or not, our past relationships have solidified into organizing themes in our personality structure. In our everyday present, we experience attitudes, thoughts, and emotional responses that, though appropriate to the interpersonal processes governing our earlier years, are maladaptive now.

Because transference is largely an unconscious process, in "The Challenge of Leadership" we use the triangle of relationships—with its three prongs of self, present-other, and past-other—to bring it to the surface. Thinking consciously about the triangle of relationships helps participants clarify those intolerable feelings that originally were experienced toward family members in the distant past, are repeated in relation to people in the person's current life, and during the course of the workshop become directed to the other participants and the workshop leaders. This triangle, highlighting the similarity of past relationships to what happens in the present, provides a conceptual structure for assessing patterns of response [32]; [42]–[44].

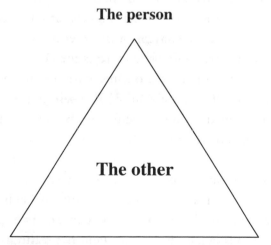

Figure 9.2 Triangle of relationships

LINKING THE PAST WITH THE PRESENT

In my work with executives I've discovered (as many psychothera-pists have done before me) that (apart from creating a supportive environment) transferential interpretation is a crucial tool in the change toolbox. When the link between present relationships and the distant past is made meaningful—in other words, when a person understands old patterns of interaction and then learns to recognize those patterns in current relationships—the process of change is more likely to be successful. An understanding of trans-ference allows a person to change how he or she superimposes long-standing and maladaptive past patterns onto current relationships.

For example, returning once more to Carole, the other work-shop participants pointed out similarities between her relationship with her mother and her relationship with other female executives at the office, a comparison that made sense to her. They helped her see the underlying theme for her angry lashing out: it was as if she were saying, "You're a bad mother; you really don't care how I feel." Another transferential theme that emerged, echoing a memory of her father's behavior, was "Men are weak. Why don't you stand up for me when I've been wronged?" Both these themes, carried over by the executive from her childhood, were apparent to the participants after they'd heard her description of her past. When Carole snapped at one of the female executives in the work-shop for no apparent reason at all, this point became even more explicit. When others pointed out the connection, she realized the dysfunctional behavior pattern she had gotten stuck in. The group's discussions helped her see that what was survival behavior when she was small was no longer functional in her role as an adult. These observations helped her understand her feelings of ambiva-lence about changing and highlighted the costs and benefits of doing so.

The recognition of transference is a crucial point in the change process, because it signals a weakening in defensive resistance. Once Carole could see how her emotional energy had been "transferred"—held over from concerns of the past to aspects of the present and the future—she was mentally ready to tackle a more constructive future. She dealt with her ambivalent feelings and was prepared to take action.

Perhaps another example would be helpful in illustrating what transference is all about. A CEO in another leadership workshop (let's call him Steven) had a father who was rather autocratic, always wanting to have his way. Steven discovered, in childhood, that the best way of dealing with his father wasn't to confront him—that only led to violent arguments—but to comply. Knowing this background, we could predict with a higher than average probability that the adult Steven, in a difficult situation with a rather assertive person, would avoid conflict. And that's in fact what he reported. He described to the group how irritated he got at himself when he let certain people have their way against his better judgment. At times, he said, he let people walk all over him, and he just couldn't understand why (since transferential reactions happen at an unconscious level). "I don't know what happened," he said of one interaction with the chairman of his board. "I knew that the organization was making a wrong decision, but I let this man have his way. Do you know how much money we wasted by my agreeing to his insane decision?"

As we talked about transference in the workshop and looked for its footprints in this executive's behavior, he came to understand the transferential nature of his relationship with the chairman. Seeing the extent to which his past behavior influenced his present behavior, he could also see that he had a choice: he could continue on automatic pilot and do more of the same, or he could stop the process and say, "There must be a better way of handling this situation."

CHALLENGE 4: CREATING A HOLDING ENVIRONMENT

Change is so difficult that, even with the best of intentions, people can rarely manage it single-handedly. Thus the next step in the change process is getting other people involved. In "The Challenge of Leadership," participants can involve others in bringing about change only if they feel that it's safe to experiment in the group setting. As was described in Chapter 8, a transitional, safe space—a holding environment—needs to be created, a confidential place permeated by trust where secrets can be contained. Only in such a safe space will it be possible to fantasize about new possibilities, to play and experiment [38]; [45]–[46].

One of the chief functions of a holding environment is to be a forum for a public commitment to change. Making a public commitment is an important step because it doubles momentum: it not only influences the person making the announcement (cementing his or her willingness to confront a difficult situation), but it also enlists the support of others, thus working as a strong reinforcement for change. If, for example, a person states the wish and intent to become more assertive, the members of the group that approve of that decision are likely to remind him or her of conflict-avoidant behavior when they see it happening. Furthermore, by taking a public stance, people give themselves an ultimatum: go through with the change, or lose face. In the case of Carole, her public commitment in the workshop centered on finding better ways of dealing with her temper. Success would be indicated by better relationships with the people at work, improved contact with her daughter, and the ability to establish a new meaningful relationship with a significant other.

To create a holding environment that allows people to talk about their feelings, anxieties, and concerns, I use various supportive techniques in "The Challenge of Leadership." These include positive reframing, encouragement, and anticipation or rehearsal of dealing with difficult situations [47]–[50]. Reframing is a cognitive technique used to assist the person in defusing or sidestepping painful situations, thus enhancing self-esteem. Encouragement, which is a sibling of reframing, encompasses reassurance, praise (which, to be meaningful, must affirm something that the recipient considers praiseworthy), and empathic comments such as, "That must have been very hard for you," "I guess you must have been pretty scared," or "It sounds like you handled that situation quite well." Anticipation allows a person to move through new situations hypothetically and to weigh different ways of responding. By permitting someone to become better acquainted with a situation, it reduces anticipatory anxiety. Rehearsal permits a person to actually practice more appropriate ways of engaging in future events, expanding his or her adaptive repertoire.

All these therapeutic interventions were used with Carole to help her deal with her personal and workplace problems. It was particularly interesting to see how, with her newfound self-awareness, she suggested dealing with a hypothetical messy situation. One of the CEOs in the workshop presented a dilemma he was facing with one of his subordinates and asked Carole how she would deal with it. Although she admitted that her old self would have lashed out at the person who was responsible for the screw-up, she suggested that the CEO go to his office and work with the subordinate on a solution.

CHALLENGE 5: ACTIVELY WORKING ON THE PROBLEM

I can't stress enough that therapeutic learning is experiential learning; it takes effort and practice. People change as they work through emotionally painful and ingrained interpersonal scenarios and as the interaction with supportive others gives rise to outcomes different from those feared.

Far-reaching personality changes can be achieved; old dogs can learn new tricks. Such changes demand systematic challenges to one's defenses, conscious manipulation of one's transferential reactions, and respect for the complex interconnections of the cognitive and emotional dimensions of the problem. They also require careful timing. Contrary to the usual saying, people striving for personal change must "strike when the iron is cold." Interpretations can't be heard by, let alone become effective in, a person in the middle of an emotional crisis. When emotion impairs cognition too much, lasting change will be difficult.

In "The Challenge of Leadership," with its two faculty members, most of the teaching is done indirectly, by the participants, who offer continuous feedback about behavior and character to their colleagues. Participants work as a team to develop their capacity to examine their feelings and behavior, to understand conflicts and areas of vulnerability, and to develop more varied and flexible defensive systems that protect them from anxiety [51]. Although interpretations by workshop leaders have an impact on participants, in a group setting executives often have less resistance to learning about themselves from peers than they have to input from people in positions of authority. Consequently, one of the challenges for the workshop leaders is to resist the impulse to make an interpretation and wait for group members to suggest and develop solutions [52]. As the saying goes, there are two parts to wisdom: having a great deal to say, and not saying it!

The collaborative learning that comes out of group discussion and feedback helps the participants do the following:

- See discrepancies between self-perception about capabilities and actual achievements.
- Recognize (and accept reinforcement for) what they're really good at.

- Arrive at more appropriate styles of thinking and acting in both a business and a personal context.
- Realize the extent to which they engage in catastrophizing—that is, assuming that every error will be followed by catastrophe.
- Overcome the so-called helpless fallacy, the faulty belief that they have no control over their lives.
- Recognize a tendency to engage in "filtering"—that is, emphasizing the negative and ignoring the positive regarding their skills and circumstances.
- Scrap their "should" list, that long list of rules that outline how they believe others think they should act.

Much of the work that the participants do, in themselves and for each other, is unconscious. In the safety of the holding environment offered by "The Challenge of Leadership," each presenter does something to the other participants (and vice versa), evoking in the other members subtle unconscious reactions known as "countertransference reactions." These countertransference reactions then shape the observations of each member [40]; [53] [54]. The emotional responses of the group members to any given presentation reveal members' sensitivities and offer evidence of the presenter's attempts (both conscious and unconscious) to evoke certain emotional reactions in others.

This process of subtly transferring feelings and thoughts can also be conceptualized under the heading "projective identification," a concept introduced in Chapter 6 [55]–[56]. As you may recall, through this primitive form of communication—also labeled "countertransference"—part of what a person experiences is "expelled" and "deposited" in other people. In other words, the speaker gets the audience to experience a set of feelings similar to his or her own. Led by memories and imagination, the listeners respond with empathy.

The conjunction of countertransference and empathy allows participants to put themselves in the presenter's place and

experience whatever he or she thinks and desires. Sensitive participants can penetrate, by thought and feeling, the inner life of
the presenter, though they retain enough objectivity to create
hypotheses and theories about that inner life. The information
provided as group members talk about the feelings and fantasies
that came up in response to a presentation helps the presenter better
understand what his or her key issues are. In fact, these emotional
responses to presentations represent one of the most important
tools as participants strive to change.

The spectrum of countertransference reactions ranges from
subtle responses such as vague feelings of anxiety, sleepiness,
boredom, futility, helplessness, or disdain; to more blatant responses
such as becoming angry, feeling intimidated, experiencing sexual
arousal, or not listening; to dramatic forms of acting out such as
blowing up at a fellow member, leaving the room in a huff, or
being paralyzed by the fear of losing control and causing harm.
Over time, participants become increasingly proficient at translating these subtle (and not so subtle) signals into imagery that has
meaning, and they learn to notice not only what is expressed
verbally and nonverbally, but also what is avoided.

For example, in the case of Carole, every time the harsher side
of her personality came to the fore, another group member brought
it to her attention, whether it took place in a plenary session, a
small group, or a social occasion. Thus for Carole (and every other
presenter in turn), every act both within the seminar and in related
social settings became a learning opportunity. Each encounter
with another participant offered an occasion to gain new understanding, attempt new behavior, and work through chronic personality problems.

The task of the group is huge indeed. In the complex interpersonal encounter of the workshop, past and present experiences
intertwine. Participants have to try to unravel the resulting knots
of past life situations, current life situations, and transferential patterns, bringing to awareness hidden feelings and wishes, defensive

reactions, and underlying causes of anxiety. They have to integrate in their minds and feelings what was, what is, and what will be. What was consists of memories of people and events of importance to each individual, and the feelings attached to those people and events. As participants recall their affect-laden memories, reviewing and picking up the threads of their past, present, and future, they grow in knowledge about themselves, expanding their awareness of what was, what is, and what will be. Succinctly put, by facing up to the past, they acquire mastery of the present and learn to shape the future.

RESTRUCTURING THE INNER THEATER

The transformational process that's the goal of "The Challenge of Leadership"—a process that, as we've seen, interweaves participants' past and current life situations (and the anxieties, defenses, and hidden feelings underlying each) via transferential patterns exhibited in group members' relationships with fellow members and with workshop leaders—results in a restructuring of the participants' inner theater. This complex process involves incremental changes on a number of different fronts: defense restructuring, affect restructuring, and self-perception restructuring [44]; [57]. When successful, this process helps participants manipulate the forces that make up the core of their personality: their defensive structures, their affect (or feelings), and their image of self and others.

Defense restructuring. Giving up inappropriate or excessive defensive behavior patterns is a crucial challenge for anyone who wants to change. The initial step in defense restructuring, and perhaps the hardest one, is the recognition of the kind of defenses used by the individual. A person who senses the need for change, along with his or her champions within the holding environment, needs to watch for patterns of defensive behavior, determine the intensity and duration of those patterns, and formulate hypotheses that explain them. Then it's time for "resistance judo" as a person's defenses are rarely successfully tackled head-on. Collaborators need to move with the person; otherwise, he or she may dig in and become resistant to any further help.

As you may recall from our case study, it didn't take Carole and her fellow workshop participants long to identify her use of specific defenses. She had a tendency to deny responsibility for her actions, "forget" unpleasant things she was supposed to do, redirect angry feelings toward others, and develop conversion symptoms (such as migraines) when under stress. With the group's help, Carole came to see that these maladaptive defensive reactions, like most others, were usefully adaptive in the situation in which they were first learned and applied. Denial of responsibility, for example, was a successful survival mechanism in the CEO's family; already feeling worthless, the young girl sensibly avoided anything that would put her in an even worse light with her parents. Migraine headaches and other physical problems worked well as a way of getting some attention from her father, the doctor. Unfortunately, these antiquated solutions—and the parallel solutions that each one of us carries over from childhood into adulthood—are no longer good enough. Rather than fixing problems, these learned patterns now cause them. While in the short run these defenses were quite useful, they can have catastrophic results in the long run.

The first component of defense restructuring is recognizing defensive behavior and understanding its origin; the next is building better coping mechanisms. After weighing the costs and benefits of using certain defenses, we need to consider our alternatives. What would it mean to give up certain defenses, and what would we gain by adopting other, more present-focused approaches?

To illustrate, when Carole described an incident where she publicly humiliated a subordinate and took no responsibility for the consequences, her colleagues in the group asked questions such as, "Looking back, do you think that this was a constructive way of handling the situation?" "Have you found that not thinking about the incident makes you feel better, or is it festering anyway?" "Do you now think that you should have apologized?" "What do you think would have happened if you had apologized?" "How else might you have handled the situation?" In the search for alternatives to defensive behavior, open-ended questions are essential, because they allow the person seeking change room to express him- or herself.

Affect restructuring. The second aspect of personality change concerns how a person experiences emotions. Anyone interested in fundamentally changing has to evaluate the way he or she expresses emotions and look for emotional patterns that seem unhealthy. People who have little experience expressing emotions interpersonally—and there are a lot of them in top management—struggle with this step. They can jump-start their evaluation by asking questions such as: What kind of emotions do certain situations evoke in me? Do certain types of emotional reactions lead to conflict? How do I physically feel when expressing this emotion or that?

Once people get a handle on current patterns of emotional experience and expression, they can begin to look at alternatives. In a group such as "The Challenge of Leadership," some of those alternatives will come from fellow participants, who can draw on their own emotional history. Fantasy is also a useful tool: people can role-play different ways to respond to conflict-laden situations and see how the alternatives sit with them.

When Carole told her group about her anger, they encouraged her to consider whether it had the desired results. Although at first she said, "That's the way I am. I can't act differently," she eventually saw that there were more constructive ways of handling her feelings. After reflecting on the repercussions of her anger on the morale of the other people in the company, she realized that it was acceptable to express anger, but only if it was properly channeled and respectfully expressed. Greater awareness of the effect of her emotional outbursts on others was an important step in her change process. Carole also realized the effect that her outbursts had on her: she gradually learned that when she got a tense feeling in her chest, she was about to burst. With that warning sign, she could control her hair-trigger temper by asking the person to whom her anger was directed lots of questions.

Self-perception restructuring. The third area of change concerns the restructuring of perceptions about the self, especially as the self relates to others. As I explained in discussing the concept of Core Conflictual Relationship Themes in Chapter 1, in early childhood we develop habitual patterns by which we process information on how we expect others to respond to us. These patterns of expectation are likely to be self-confirming; in other words, they're likely to determine our future interactions with others. The child who is treated with empathic respect and understanding is likely to grow up into an adult who likes him- or herself, enjoys human interaction, and has no difficulty establishing supportive relationships. In contrast, the mistreated child, growing into adulthood, understands relationships in unhelpful ways and acts so as to prove people's negative expectations. Put another way, the way we construct reality tends to create the reality that we confront.

Having a negative sense of how others perceive us and how we perceive ourselves can lead to serious interpersonal problems. To correct this dysfunctional perception, we have to identify adaptive and maladaptive inner representations and find the origins of the latter. Then we need to initiate a self-affirmation process, rebuilding our perception of ourselves by allowing ourselves to see and acknowledge our strong points [1]; [36]–[37]; [46]; [50]; [58]–[61].

Creating a more positive and realistic perception of ourselves requires the help of others. These others can help support self-efficacy, encouraging our belief that change is possible. In "The Challenge of Leadership," discussion of adaptive and maladaptive self-representations is a natural outgrowth of the "hot seat" presentation. As group members come to know a particular presenter, their support and caring is an essential boost to self-esteem. In the case of Carole, the group suggested to her that in her relationship with men she was engaging in a self-fulfilling prophecy. Because she perceived herself as not being likable—after all, she was an unwanted child—she created situations that made her unlikable. Her two failed marriages were living proof. She readily admitted that while married, she would pick fights with her two husbands, testing their attachment to her. When (sure enough!) they left her, she felt that she had proved her theory of unlovability. In order to change, Carole first had to recognize that she not only perceived herself as unlovable but also tended to make herself unlovable. The next step was to trust other people's view—expressed often and with conviction by group members—that she was a great person when she let her true self shine through.

KEEPING ON TRACK

As people learn new skills in an effort to bring about change in their defenses, feelings, and self-perceptions, they need to keep on track by repeatedly asking themselves where they are in regard to the interwoven elements of personal change. Questions such as the following can keep them from going astray:

- What habitual defenses do I use to deal with stressful situations? Are there certain patterns that I can recognize? What can/should be changed about these defenses?
- How do I experience and express emotions? How could I express emotions more appropriately?

- How do I perceive myself? Do I feel secure about who I am? What do I think others think about me? Do I see myself in a one-down position? Am I capable of honest self-appraisal?

As indicated, these questions are difficult to answer alone. Only with investigative and affirmative behavior from others can we reach valid answers. And only with the help of others can we begin to relinquish defenses, express emotions honestly, and perceive self and others in ways that accord with reality.

CHALLENGE 6: CONSOLIDATING THE CHANGE

Once executives in "The Challenge of Leadership" have identified problems and practiced alternate approaches to them, they face the critical task of maintaining acquired gains. Gradually, over time, they need to revise the script of their inner theater, all but rewriting the entire thing. But that kind of serious inner transformation can take place only once a new way of looking at things has been internalized.

Internalization is a gradual process by which external interactions between self and others are taken in and replaced by internal representations of these interactions. In the leadership workshop, telling (and retelling) one's own story and listening to the stories of others—and recognizing similarities among them all—consolidates this process of internalization. Once participants leave the group, they have to try to hold on to the insights they acquired through the internalization process, even though the group is no longer there to provide external reinforcement [62].

After this process of internalization has taken place, do people feel changed? Is there a palpable difference? Yes and no. When I talk with people at their follow-up session a year after the workshop, they often say something like, "I'm basically the same." And yet they often talk of evidence of change. The following quote from a "graduate" illuminates that summary.

> I feel about the same, although I'm more certain about what I can and can't do. I have more confidence in my abilities. I always used to feel like an impostor in my management role. It was as if I were acting in a role that wasn't me. Now, though, I enjoy what I'm doing. Also, I have a more positive outlook on life. I'm much clearer about what my priorities are. My wife tells me that I've changed too, so I guess something must have happened. I play much more with my children; I'm no longer so opinionated; I find it easier to open up to others. But have I changed? I really don't know.

Most participants are able to hold on to the gains they've made, although many mention that some erosion occurs over time. Interestingly enough, with greater clarity about the issues they need to deal with, a significant number of them decide to see a coach, counselor, or therapist on a regular or intermittent basis after the workshop, to keep them on target. They've learned to enjoy having sparring partners who don't tiptoe around them.

Many successful participants speak of improved quality of life, as assessed in terms of an increase in self-esteem and adaptive functioning, a decrease in anxiety, and a rebirth of the ability to play. They note that better feelings about who they are allow for a broader vision of their relationships with others and facilitate different and better ways of responding. They reveal, in behavior if not words, that the automatic defense mechanisms with which they used to cope (albeit ineffectively) with life have been replaced by the awareness of choice.

MAKING THE BEST OF A POOR HAND OF CARDS

The aim of most forms of personal growth and development is the achievement of self-direction and autonomy. Paradoxically, total autonomy leads to chaos; total control leads to suffocation. Wisdom can't be taught. On the contrary, as I've tried to demonstrate in this discussion, the acquisition of wisdom is an experiential journey. That journey brings us to the realization that we can't have it both ways: we can't be both impulsive and conformist. The challenge we face is to feel free in a gentle harness, to subordinate our impulsive strivings to controls from the outside until our personal responses unfold into self-control. From the start our goal is to create a wider area of choice. That's what mental health is all about.

The journey taken in INSEAD's leadership workshop is to educate for optimal personal freedom while taking into account the demands of reality and society. The challenge for all of us, as individuals, is to modify our inner script. We have to make it our script, not a script written by others. We have to own our own lives, recognizing and taking responsibility for our own our impulses and actions.

In the leadership workshop, the executives participating learn that in order to develop a strong sense of what they're all about they have to trust their feelings. They also have to trust others. This trust, of both self and others, fuels self-disclosure and learning. The trusted others that participants come to know in the workshop become their guides on their inner journey. Helped by those guides, participants gain a better perspective on their past, their present, their future, their wishes and desires. They discover new patterns of behavior more suited to present-day reality than their self-defeating patterns of behavior and thought were, gaining perspective on these patterns by seeing their feelings and behaviors in context. As a result of these changes, they develop a more flexible, self-directive, and mature way of dealing with others.

One of the lessons I've learned from listening to senior executives over the years is that all outward success, if it's to be truly appreciated, must be matched by inward success. If we're to attain that inner success, we need faith and confidence in our own powers. We have to realize that living a full life isn't the result of having been dealt a lucky hand of cards. On the contrary, a full life grows out of our ability to make the best of even a very poor hand.

The recipe for living life to the fullest—if such a recipe exists—is to laugh heartily and often, play with abandon, appreciate beautiful things, build and maintain deep friendships, take pleasure in family, and enjoy the task at hand. It's the journey of life that counts, not the destination. How we cope with the obstacles that we inevitably encounter on that journey determines the richness of our life. Participants in "The Challenge of Leadership" learn, through their extensive self-exploration, a lesson that can help all of us: most of our obstacles are self-made. If we want to, we can remove or restructure them. We can learn from experience.

REFERENCES

1. Miller, W. R. and S. Rollick (2002). *Motivational Interviewing.* New York, The Guilford Press.
2. Bandura, A. (1989). "Perceived Self-Efficacy in the Exercise of Personal Agency." *The Psychologist: Bulletin of British Psychological Society* 10: 411–424.
3. Fisch, R., J. H. Weakland and L. Segal (1982). *The Tactics of Change: Doing Therapy Briefly.* San Francisco, Jossey-Bass.
4. Kets de Vries, M. F. R. and D. Miller (1984). *The Neurotic Organization.* San Francisco, Jossey-Bass.
5. McCrae, R. R. and P. T. Costa (1990). *Personality in Adulthood.* New York, Guilford Press.
6. Denning, S. (2001). *The Springboard: How Storytelling Ignites Action in Knowledge-Era Organizations.* Boston, Butterworth Heinemann.
7. McAdams, D. P. (1993). *Stories we Live by: Personal Myths and the Making of the Self.* New York, William Morrow and Company.
8. McLeod, J. (1997). *Narrative and Psychotherapy.* London, Sage.
9. Rennie, D. L. (1994). "Storytelling in psychotherapy: the client's subjective experience." *Psychotherapy* 31: 234–243.

10. Spence, D. P. (1982). *Narrative Truth and Historical Truth.* New York, Norton.

11. Bowlby, J. (1969). *Attachment and Loss, Vol 1.* New York, Basic Books.

12. Bowlby, J. (1973). *Attachment and Loss, Vol 2.* New York, Basic Books.

13. Bowlby, J. (1980). *Attachment and Loss, Vol 3.* New York, Basic Books.

14. Dietrich, D. R. and P. Shabad, Eds (1993). *Problem of Loss and Mourning: Psychoanalytic Perspectives.* New York, International Universities Press.

15. Marris, P. (1974). *Loss and Change.* London, Routledge & Kegan Paul.

16. Parkes, C. M. (1972). *Bereavement: Studies of Grief in Adult Life.* New York, International Universities Press.

17. Solomon, A. (2001). *The Noonday Demon: An Atlas of Depression.* New York, Simon & Schuster.

18. Sullivan, H. S. (1953). *The Interpersonal Theory of Psychiatry.* New York, Norton.

19. Erikson, E. H. (1963). *Childhood and Society.* New York, W.W. Norton & Society.

20. Levinson, D. (1978). *The Seasons of Man's Life.* New York, Knopf.

21. Millon, T. and G. S. Everly (1985). *Personality and its Disorders.* New York, John Wiley & Sons.

22. Sheehy, G. (1995). *New Passages.* New York, Ballantine Books.

23. Sheehy, G. (1998). *Understanding Men's Passages: Discovering the New Map of Men's Lives.* New York, Random House.

24. Stassen Berger, K. (1998). *The Developing Person through the Life Span.* New York, Worth Publishers.

25. Vaillant, G. E. (1977). *Adaptation to Life.* Boston, Little Brown.

26. White, R. (1966). *Lives in Progress.* New York, Holt, Rinehart and Winston.

27. Hochschild, A. R. and A. Machung (2003). *Second Shift.* New York, Penguin.

28. Frankl, V. (1962). *Man's Search for Meaning: An Introduction to Logotherapy.* Boston, Beacon Press.

29. Frankl, V. E. (1967). *Psychotherapy and Existentialism: Selected Papers on Logotherapy.* New York, Washington Square Press.

30. Kets de Vries, M. F. R. (2002). *The Happiness Equation*. London, Random House.

31. Freud, S. (1933). *New Introductory Lectures. The Standard Edition of the Complete Psychological Works of Sigmund Freud, Vol 22*. J. Strachey (editor and translator). London, The Hogarth Press and the Institute of Psychoanalysis.

32. Malan, D. and F. Osimo (1992). *Psychodynamics, Training, and Outcome in Brief Psychotherapy*. Oxford, Butterworth Heinemann.

33. Menninger, C. (1958). *Theory of Psychoanalytic Technique*. New York, Harper.

34. Balint, M., P. H. Ornstein and E. Balint (1972). *Focal Psychotherapy*. London, Tavistock.

35. Greenson, R. R. (1967). *The Technique and Practice of Psychoanalysis*. New York, International University Press.

36. Kohut, H. (1971). *The Analysis of the Self*. New York, International Universities Press.

37. Kohut, H. and E. S. Wolf (1978). "The Disorders of the Self and their Treatment: an Outline." *International Journal of Psychoanalysis* (59): 413–426.

38. Rogers, C. R. (1951). *Client-centered Therapy*. Boston, Houghton-Mifflin.

39. Rogers, C. R. (1961). *On Becoming a Person*. Boston, Houghton-Mifflin.

40. Etchegoyen, R. H. (1991). *The Fundamentals of Psychoanalytic Technique*. London, Karnac Books.

41. Freud, S. (1905). *Fragment of an Analysis of a Case of Hysteria. The Standard Edition of the Complete Psychological Works of Sigmund Freud, Vol 7*. J. Strachey (editor and translator). London, The Hogarth Press and The Institute of Psychoanalysis.

42. Luborsky, L., P. Crits-Cristoph, J. Mintz and A. Auerbach (1988). *Who Will Benefit from Psychotherapy?* New York, Basic Books.

43. Malan, D. H. (1963). *A Study of Brief Psychotherapy*. New York, Plenum.

44. McCullough Vaillant, L. (1997). *Changing Character*. New York, Basic Books.

45. Amado, G. and A. Ambrose, Eds (2001). *The Transitional Approach to Change*. London, Karnac Books.

46. Winnicott, D. W. (1951). *Transitional Objects and Transitional Phenomena. Collected Papers: Through Paediatrics to Psycho-analysis.* London, Tavistock Publications.

47. Seltzery, L. F. (1986). *Paradoxical Strategies in Psychotherapy: A Comprehensive Overview and Guidebook.* New York, John Wiley & Sons, Inc.

48. Watzlawick, P., J. Weakland and R. Fisch (1974). *Change: Principles of Problem Formation and Problem Resolution.* New York, W. W. Norton.

49. Weeks, G. R. and L. L'Abate (1982). *Paradoxical Psychotherapy: Theory and Practice with Individuals, Couples, and Families.* New York, Brunner/Mazel.

50. Winnicott, D. W. (1975). *Through Paediatrics to Psycho-Analysis.* New York, Basic Books.

51. Scott Rutan, J. and W. N. Stone (2001). *Psychodynamic Group Psychotherapy.* New York, The Guilford Press.

52. Reik, T. (1949). *The Inner Experience of a Psychoanalyst.* London, Allen & Unwin.

53. Heimann, P. (1950). "On Countertransference." *International Journal of Psychoanalysis* 31: 81–84.

54. Racker, H. (1968). *Transference and Countertransference.* New York, International Universities Press.

55. Ogden, T. H. (1982). *Projective Identification and Psychotherapeutic Technique.* New York, Jason Aronson.

56. Thoma, H. and H. Kachele (1987). *Psychoanalytic Practice: 1. Principles.* Berlin, Springer Verlag.

57. Wachtel, P., Ed (1982). *Resistance: Psychodynamic and Behavioral Approaches.* New York, Plenum Press.

58. Bandura, A. (1997). *Self-Efficacy: The Exercise of Control.* New York, Freeman.

59. Basch, M. F. (1988). *Understanding Psychotherapy.* New York, Basic Books.

60. Basch, M. F. (1995). *Doing Brief Psychotherapy.* New York, Basic Books.

61. Kohut, H. (1977). *The Restoration of the Self.* Madison, Conn., International Universities Press.

62. Pine, E. (1985). *Developmental Theory and Clinical Process.* New Haven, CT, Yale University Press.

CHAPTER 10

COACH OR COUCH,
ANYBODY?

All of us, at certain moments of our lives, need to take advice and to receive help from other people.

—Alexis Carrel

It was a high counsel that I once heard given to a young person, "Always do what you are afraid to do."

—Ralph Waldo Emerson

Hell is other people.

—Jean-Paul Sartre

The quieter you become, the more you can hear.

—Zen proverb

Zen monks are given a "koan"—an apparently impossible puzzle— to contemplate. One monk went to a Zen master for coaching and was asked to explain the sound of one hand clapping. The Zen monk concentrated upon what the sound of one hand clapping could be. But as much as he tried, he couldn't find the solution. At one point the Zen master told him, "You are not working hard enough. You are too attached to food, wealth, and worldly things. It would be better if you died. That would solve the problem."

The next time the monk appeared before the Zen master he was again asked what he knew about the sound of one hand clapping. As a response to the question, the monk fell over as if he were dead. "You are dead all right," observed the Zen master, "But how about that sound?" The monk responded, "I haven't solved that koan yet." The Zen master looked at him and said, "Dead men do not talk. Go away!" It was only then, that the monk realized the sound of one hand.

As I noted previously, Zen has as its fundamental purpose the awakening of the mind on its path toward spiritual enlightenment. Zen teachers are concerned with self-help and helping others, with wisdom and compassion. That outlook makes them the forerunners of leadership coaches. Like Zen teachers, leadership coaches provide learning opportunities by giving their clients—usually executives needing professional assistance with particular aspects of their job performance—constructive and balanced feedback. They serve as sparring partners, helping their clients reflect on and, where necessary, change their behavior. As a way of clarifying and enhancing consciousness, leadership coaching has become the Zen of executives. In recent years the coaching market has ballooned into a multi-billion-dollar enterprise. Originally as the purview of one-person shops, leadership coaching has become a major activity for many large consulting firms.

Why this growing interest in leadership coaching? Why does every self-respecting executive now demand a leadership coach? There are various reasons:

• The pace of change in our world today is frenetic. Business strategies that were effective five years ago aren't necessarily valid today. Competencies that were effective in the past may now be outdated. There's great pressure on executives to transform their way of thinking to accommodate present-day realities so as to improve bottom-line results. Motivated by this pressure, achievement-oriented executives are eager for opportunities for learning and renewal.

- Coaching and commitment cultures have replaced the command, control, and compartmentalization orientations of the past. Flatter organizations, networking structures, boundaryless organizations, and virtual organizations put much higher demands on the emotional intelligence and interpersonal skills of executives.

- Organizational leaders have come to realize that talent and human capital are what differentiates mediocre from high-performing organizations. Under the traditional psychological contract between employer and employee, people knew that good work would be rewarded with lifetime employment and financial security. That contract has been shattered through endless downsizing and reengineering, so new ways have to be found to retain and inspire talented people. The war for talent is a never-ending reality, and new weapons—such as leadership coaching—are welcome.

- People are being promoted to senior executive positions at an ever-younger age. Being at the top of the heap often engenders enormous feelings of insecurity and loneliness. For executives, the claim of having "nobody to talk to" isn't just an empty statement. The higher someone is in the organization, the more difficult it is to talk to others about personal issues and concerns. New ways need to be found to help reinvent and revitalize highly stressed executives and prevent looming burnout.

- Top executives' legal and corporate governance responsibilities are increasing daily, as regulations multiply and litigiousness abounds. That means more stress and a need for new strategies to deal with it.

No wonder coaching has become one of the most powerful strategic and tactical weapons in the executive repertoire: it has the potential to establish, fine-tune, or rebuild the many and varied competencies executives need to remain effective in the workplace.

WHO ARE THE CLIENTS?

Leadership coaching is a highly effective way to get additional performance out of senior people. In most leadership coaching situations, the objective is to help successful people become even better. Effective coaches go to great lengths to emphasize and develop the unique potential of the people they work with, thereby maximizing their performance. They question and challenge their clients in order to help them modify their behavior. They encourage their clients to be more open to change. They help their clients gain confidence and validation. They foster entrepreneurship, team behavior, accountability, and commitment. They help their clients become more responsible corporate citizens. Given these strengths, it's not surprising that leadership coaching improves the bottom line.

Though coaching has always been an asset, the image of coaching has changed. Having an executive coach used to be a professional embarrassment—an indication that something was wrong with the executive—but now the coach is a highly coveted status symbol. Every self-respecting executive wants to have a suitable leadership coach. Receiving coaching has become one of the indicators that top management thinks a person is worth investing in, is worth putting on the fast track. Because the basic intent of most coaching is to make highly effective people even more effective, not to help weak executives get out of a hole, it no longer carries any stigma. ("Last chance" coaching does happen occasionally, but it tends not to be very effective, largely because it's usually recommended by a conflict-avoidant senior executive attempting to avoid dealing personally with a struggling subordinate.) With its new and well-deserved cachet, coaching is now perceived as an excellent strategy to help individuals, teams, and organizations become more productive. Although leadership coaching can be useful at all levels of the organization, it's particularly beneficial for high performers at senior levels of the organization, where maximum leverage can be achieved [1]–[8].

As noted above, the image of leadership coaching has changed dramatically. In the past, senior executives were reluctant to acknowledge the need for outside assistance in polishing their rough edges. Bringing a leadership coach into play conflicted with cherished self-images of self-sufficiency, autonomy, and independence. I listed earlier some of the reasons that people's perceptions of coaching have changed. The roles that leadership coaches fill are as many and as varied as those earlier reasons. Leadership coaches are used, for example, to help create more effective teams, to assist key players in organizations as they set priorities, and to help executives balance work/private life concerns. While an executive may still become (or feel like) a laughing stock if people learn that he or she is visiting a psychoanalyst, psychiatrist, or psychotherapist, visiting a coach has become highly fashionable. In fact, coaching is today's most acceptable way of doing psychotherapy.

As the perceptions of coaching have changed, so has the nature of coaching itself. Originally coaching was directed toward executives who showed great promise but had one area (or even a few areas) in their behavior that hampered their career advancement. Such people were told that their "fatal flaw"—perhaps abrasive behavior, conflict avoidance, a lack of follow-up, or a tendency toward micro-management—could sidetrack their career progression. The message given to such clients was quite clear: if they didn't shape up, there would be serious consequences. Often that "fatal flaw" was a trait that showed up when someone with technical expertise was promoted into management. A common problem indeed! Who among us hasn't encountered technical and financial wizards who rose rapidly in their careers, only to hit the corporate ceiling due to a lack of emotional intelligence? Who among us hasn't dealt with executives who had difficulty progressing beyond the technical expertise of their job? The skills that served those men and women well in the early stages of their career are typically not the right skills at the summit of the organization. Coaching, in its early days, was intended to put the career of such leaders back on track by bringing their emotional quotient—that is, their ability to handle interpersonal relationships, teambuilding, and change management—into balance with their technical expertise.

Although such "fatal flaw" clients are still around, leadership coaches now have as their main clients another group of executives: individuals who are quite effective in their roles but believe that there are ways to improve their leadership skills. These achievement-oriented people seek help not because they've been given an ultimatum but because they want to be and do their absolute best, and they're willing to work hard to achieve that goal. They recognize their weaknesses but don't know what to do about them. In addition, they may be looking for someone outside their organization's political system to help them brainstorm critical decisions. Through a reflective interchange with a leadership coach, they hope to improve their decision-making, acquire greater ownership of any problems that are unearthed, and maximize their potential. In short, they hope that leadership coaching will help them achieve an even more outstanding performance.

WHAT IS LEADERSHIP COACHING?

So what is coaching? Though definitions vary, I view coaching as a one-on-one or group service to executives designed to create more effective, healthier organizations. This definition assumes that when executives (especially senior executives) improve their performance, such benefits spread throughout the organization. This contagion happens in part because exposing senior executives to successful coaching contributes to a coaching culture in the organization. As people responsive to coaching apply their newfound skills to other people in the organization, improved interaction cascades down the organization. Thus coaching can also be viewed as passing on a set of skills used by executives in the organization on a day-to-day basis that enhance the performance of their people [9]–[10].

As the above discussion suggests, the focus of coaching can be quite broad. Leadership coaching concerns itself not only with the individual but also with the team and the overall organizational performance. I have found leadership coaching to be especially helpful in transitional situations, such as when someone is promoted to the position of CEO or becomes a member of the executive board. Coaches can be very effective at helping people work through such transitions. Working as a third party, they become closely involved with executives and their organization to manage for better results. They serve as "insultants," challenging executives' preconceived notions about how to become more effective. Committed listeners, they play the role of the "wise fool."

To see what coaching is, first rule out what it *isn't*. It isn't mere technical guidance, though coaches have strong technical expertise. It isn't career counseling, though coaches can often help a client find the right job. Nor is it consulting, though there are quite a few similarities (and at times the boundaries between coaching and consulting are vague). While consultants typically play the role of the specialist, having the answer to any question, coaches prefer to *ask* questions. They don't pretend to have all the answers; instead, they help people think, encouraging clients to come up with their own ideas and answers [11]–[12].

Likewise, coaching isn't mentoring [13]–[14]. An executive coach is typically someone from outside the organization who is hired to improve the performance of an executive (or his or her team), while a mentor fulfills a similar function from *within* the organization, offering a form of watered-down in-house coaching. Many large companies have mentoring schemes whereby each junior executive who wants to move up in the organization is assigned or asked to select a mentor—a senior person who provides professional and organizational know-how, career support, and assistance if a junior executive runs afoul of the political system of the organization. While such sponsorship by a senior executive can have a career-enhancing effect, the neutrality of the mentor is threatened when his or her interests conflict with those of the junior executive. Coaches, on the other hand, are more assuredly neutral. Unaffected by the reality of the company culture, they're able to raise issues that mentors are reluctant to bring up—the so-called undiscussables. Furthermore, coaches often have broader work experience than the typical mentor, and they're specifically trained in such matters as how to give constructive feedback.

And finally, leadership coaching isn't training. By definition, a simple training perspective is far removed from any form of reflection and introspection. Most trainers don't have the psychological expertise to recognize the often deeply rooted nature of specific problems. For example, someone who hasn't been exposed to the basics of psychotherapy would most likely not recognize the presence of a mental disorder if one lay at the bottom of a complaint about leadership style. Furthermore, a trainer without a clinical background would probably not recognize transference reactions when they occurred (as they inevitably would) between executive and colleagues and between executive and trainer. And yet to ignore such reactions, or to abuse them—for example, by putting the client in an inappropriate dependency situation—could be outright dangerous for both client and organization. Furthermore, a failure to understand transferential issues could lead the trainer to overstep the boundaries of the coaching relationship or to engage in unethical behavior.

SHORT-TERM PSYCHOTHERAPY VERSUS LEADERSHIP COACHING

Although, as noted earlier, there's still a stigma attached to psychotherapy in the business world, some executives choose that route. There's considerable overlap between leadership coaching and short-term psychotherapy, but there are significant differences as well. Both the differences and the similarities warrant mention here.

Though psychotherapy was unregulated in its earlier years, the field is now subject to much regulation. It's no longer a simple matter of putting up a shingle and calling oneself a psychotherapist. In contrast, the coaching field, still in its infancy, remains relatively unregulated and fragmented. At the moment, just about anybody can call him- or herself a coach. As the field is maturing, however, certification systems are being put into place [15]–[16].

The most effective leadership coaches draw heavily on psychotherapeutic frameworks and skills. After all, both leadership coaching and psychotherapy deal with behavior, emotion, and cognition. Depending on the psychological background and orientation of the coach, leadership coaching can take on many different forms, some of which look very much like short-term psychotherapy. Many coaches go beyond mere confrontation (helping the client recognize that there's a problem) to clarification (helping the client gain a new understanding of the problem) to interpretation (mutually examining unconscious conflicts and wishes) to insight and working through (whereby the client acquires an increased capacity for self-understanding. In leadership coaching, as in psychotherapy, there may be a discussion (depending on how deep the leadership coach and the client are willing to go) of blind spots, defensive reactions, distorted thinking, and irrational thoughts. Not surprisingly, then, there are—or can be—rather fuzzy boundaries between short-term psychotherapy and leadership coaching. Regardless of the depth to which the leadership coach is willing to go, he or she must be able to recognize danger signs that can derail the coaching process and know how to respond to them promptly [17].

Generally speaking, though, leadership coaches have a broader perspective than do psychotherapists. Most psychotherapists have not supplemented their clinical experience with the training necessary to diagnose problems of executive leadership, dysfunctional team behavior, social defenses, corporate culture, neurotic organizations, and faulty organizational decision-making. Effective leadership coaches, on the other hand, are expected to know not only the essentials of psychotherapy, but also the requirements of organizational management. A deep understanding of the specific organizational context, and of organizations in general, is crucial to helping coached clients [18]–[22]. Because the organizational context is so important, leadership coaches take a holistic, not a reductionist, approach to framing problems; they favor a systemic over a piecemeal approach. For example, while in most forms of therapy, information is principally taken from the client, leadership coaches gather information not only from the client but also from other people who have dealings with the client.

Furthermore, psychotherapy—particularly its more psychodynamic orientations—tends to be *past*, present, and future oriented, while most leadership coaching has a present and future orientation, despite its attention to transference [23]–[25]. (Psychodynamically informed therapies emphasize the importance of early development, unconscious aspects of behavior, the therapeutic relationship between therapist and client, defensive reactions, and the presence of repetitive behavior.) As a result, in leadership coaching we find a more active goal-and-action orientation, while in psychotherapy the interaction is more passive and reflective. Finally, in leadership coaching the focus is on personal growth and skill development, while in therapy the question of symptom reduction and character problems is the primary area of interest.

In the case of psychotherapy, help to the client stands central, and there's no confusion about who the client is. In the case of leadership coaching, on the other hand, the identity of the client isn't as self-evident. When successful, leadership coaching helps *both* client and organization. Well, then, is the client the person the leadership coach works with, or is it the executive in the human resources department who organized the coach's intervention? Alternatively, is it the CEO? Or is it perhaps even an abstract "ideal," such as contributing to the good of the organization? These are important questions, because the answers have serious ramifications. For example, while in the case of psychotherapy confidentiality is absolute, that rule doesn't always apply to leadership coaching, given the potential confusion about who the leadership coach is working for. (In spite of this confusion, it's advisable for leadership coaches to be, like psychotherapists, quite rigorous about client confidentiality.)

The setting is much more flexible in leadership coaching than in psychotherapy. While leadership coaching can take place in many different environments—face-to-face meetings, e-mail exchanges, telephone conversations, or group meetings—psychotherapeutic boundaries in most instances restrict interactions to the therapist's office. The duration is likewise defined in therapy, which usually takes the form of regular 45- to 50-minute sessions. Leadership coaching sessions, on the other hand, are often as long as two or even more hours. Interpersonal boundaries differ as well: while therapists generally avoid having a social relationship with a patient, not wanting to "contaminate" future sessions, coaches may interact with a client at various company events outside of coaching sessions. These occasions give leadership coaches a great opportunity to observe the client from another perspective.

The overlap between short-term psychotherapy and leadership coaching highlights the depth of expertise that's needed to bring success in many executives' change efforts. What starts as a simple leadership coaching job targeting a few desired changes in specific cognitive skills may quickly turn into something far more complicated. In fact, it's common that the issues executives present require more than simple, surface interventions [17]. People tend to hope for easy, quick-fix answers, but few psychological problems invite that sort of response. On the bright side, though, the array of problems that respond well to careful, thoughtful leadership coaching, in conjunction with committed work on the part of the client, is vast.

THE COACHING PARADE

What are the various forms of coaching? What kinds of distinctions can be made between them? First, there are both external and internal coaches, each having advantages and disadvantages [26]. Although an outside coach may not have the kind of intimate knowledge of the business that an inside coach has, he or she offers a greater assurance of confidentiality. Typically, clients find it much easier to open up to external than to internal coaches. If the internal coach is also a member of the human resources group, confidentiality is especially iffy, given that sensitive information may be forwarded to top management. With external coaches, clients have less reason to be concerned about the potential spread of confidential information. Furthermore, external coaches tend to be more objective, less likely to judge the client. In general, they have a broader range of business experience and are more prepared to discuss issues that are otherwise undiscussable in the organization.

We should also distinguish between one-on-one coaching— the most prevalent form—and group coaching [27]–[28]. One-on-one coaching can take a variety of forms. In *shadow coaching*, a one-on-one variant, the coach follows the client when engaged at work and gives him or her feedback about what's observed. In *assimilation coaching*, the coach helps the client adjust to a new job. In *career-transition coaching*, the coach helps the client explore new career possibilities, redefining direction and assessing strengths, weaknesses, and personal values. In *life coaching*, the most general form of one-on-one intervention, the coach doesn't limit him- or herself to the work part of the client's life but also pays close attention to personal dimensions, blurring the distinction between psychotherapy and coaching.

Another way of differentiating coaching is by looking at the degree of psychological depth attempted by the coach. Leadership coaches more comfortable with staying on the surface focus on coaching that contributes to very specific cognitive-, task-, and skill-oriented learning. This so-called *competency coaching* encompasses simple how-to techniques and skill development. This type of coaching most closely resembles the work of sports trainers. Coaches trained to work at a somewhat deeper level do what's referred to as *performance coaching*, where the goal is to transform the business by transforming the person. These coaches help the client attain a determined set of stretch goals. Coaches who excavate farther still, working at the deepest level, encourage experiential, reflective learning through their *developmental coaching*. They help the client improve his or her emotional intelligence and strive for a more effective leadership style. The emphasis is on creating a personalized plan to help the client find answers to existential dilemmas. In this case coaching really involves the whole person. The deeper coaches go into the iceberg of the mind, penetrating elusive (even unconscious) processes, the blurrier become the boundaries between coaching and psychotherapy. This differentia tion by depth illustrates a major problem with much leadership coaching: coaches may have an idea how to start the process but not know where their efforts will lead them. Those who are prepared for (and have adequate training regarding) the obstacles to be found on the way have a distinct advantage.

THE FUNDAMENTALS OF COACHING: WHY AND HOW

Why Hire a Coach?

There are various reasons why people or organizations ask for executive coaching, as suggested earlier. Generally, people hire coaches to help them do one (or several) of the following things:

- become better at handling difficult relationships
- engage in more effective career management
- expedite goal- and priority-setting
- develop a more effective leadership style
- speed up personal development
- improve self-understanding of motivation in order to facilitate decision-making
- hone teamwork skills
- learn conflict-management skills
- manage superiors effectively
- strengthen personal self-confidence, assertiveness, and/or well-being
- make systemic gains, such as greater employee retention, enhanced customer satisfaction, and better overall results for the organization

How to Get Started: Contracting for Success

Whatever the specific agenda may be, it's important (for both coach and client) that a realistic coaching plan be put into place. Such a plan demands that the client articulate what needs changing and conceive a design for that change, a process that allows the coach to assess whether the client is truly committed to take on tough goals. It's important that the client include in that plan a number of small wins that mark progress toward the end goals. A timeframe for completion of the goals is also essential.

In such a plan—a contract, if you will—expectations need to be clarified by both parties, and ground rules need to be set. As in many other types of contracts, specific reference points are required, to provide clear markers in terms of both parties' mutual responsibilities. Success factors for the executive's current and future roles need to be established as well. These success criteria need to be conceptualized in such a way that they can be measured, so that *both* parties will know when they are (or are not) met.

Sometimes additional opinions are helpful. Having the client ask close associates (e.g., colleagues, subordinates, superiors, family members, and/or friends) how they think he or she is doing in regard to the success criteria facilitates the change process (and the meeting of goals). Such people are often more tuned in to changes in behavior than the actual client. In addition, their input makes them a key part of the coaching process and gives them a stake in the desired changes. That stake will encourage them to nudge the client toward the desired changes.

Among the ground rules that need to be established are such details as the scheduling of appointments, the handling of cancellations, and the amount of time that coach and client will spend together. The coaching contract should also include specific information about who the client is (the executive or the organization, a distinction that impacts confidentiality, as we saw earlier) and what the financial terms are. Finally, and perhaps most important, the contract should clarify confidentiality boundaries. Although coaches always need to keep the welfare of the organization in mind, their first priority, if they hope to facilitate meaningful change, is to respect the confidentiality of the client. Making arrangements about confidentiality up front reassures the client and lets the organization know the limits of its intrusion. If any of these conditions remain unresolved in the coaching contract, subsequent problems are all but guaranteed.

WHAT MAKES FOR COACHING SUCCESS?

The main precondition for effective coaching is a relationship of mutual trust and respect between coach and client. Trust and respect are the foundation of what psychologists call the *working alliance*. Research has shown that, as in the case of therapy, the most important factor in making coaching successful is the quality of the coach–client working alliance [29].

Certain psychological factors are also essential in clients if leadership coaching is to succeed. These are similar to those needed for INSEAD's "The Challenge of Leadership" seminar for senior executives (see Chapters 8 and 9). Clients must have a capacity for self-reflection, along with curiosity about the way their actions are perceived and about what motivates the actions of others. A degree of psychological-mindedness—that is, the ability to look beneath the surface of words and actions to underlying motives and emotions—is also helpful, as are empathy, an appreciation for people's differences, interpersonal connectedness, emotional intelligence, and the ability to deal well with frustration.

Motivation is another key factor. Is the client ready to listen? Is the client really open to change? Is the client prepared to make changes to his or her life and schedule? Leadership coaches are often asked to work with clients who don't realize the seriousness of their problems and have no interest in changing. The lack of insight that such clients manifest often comes across as arrogance: obstinately denying that any help is needed, they offer a logical rebuttal to any suggestion of change, an indicator of the strength of their resistances. To such people, disturbing the status quo is just too threatening. As a result, they're often unwilling to do the "assignments." In another group of clients, motivation exists but is no longer linked to reality. These clients have completely unrealistic expectations about their capabilities. Having risen to their level of incompetence, they simply can't rise any farther, despite their lofty expectations and their coach's hearty efforts.

Another problem population, when it comes to leadership coaching, is people who are too defensive to deal with challenging feedback. For coaching to progress, clients need to be willing to open up and talk honestly about themselves [25]; [30]–[32]. Working with extremely rigid people—that is, people unwilling to try anything new or frightening—is also difficult. In order to be responsive to coaching, people need to be willing to subject themselves to demanding interventions, accept the consequences for their actions, and be willing to take risks and experiment with new ways of doing things.

Likewise, leadership coaching rarely goes well with clients who have complex psychological problems. This group includes people with serious sociopathic tendencies; people who engage in so-called ethical trespassing; people who have psychotic or borderline reactions, including severe depression or mood swings; people who suffer from pervasive feelings of emptiness, meaninglessness, and boredom; people who act out via self-harming behaviors, including alcohol and drug abuse; people who have a low level of frustration tolerance; people who depend excessively on primitive defenses (such as splitting, denial, and projection); people who have difficulty with reality-testing; and people who suffer from identity diffusion and confusion and have a strong need to merge with others. Generally, all such people are far too needy to benefit from a leadership coaching relationship.

It must be said, however, that stagnation in leadership coaching isn't always the client's fault. The problem can also lie on the coach's side. For example, the client may have a kind of personality for which the coach has very limited empathy, meaning that the coach has too many negative reactions to facilitate progress effectively. Similarly, the coach may feel a lack of interpersonal connectedness—perhaps as a result of a cultural or social barrier between client and coach. Generally, when interpersonal chemistry is missing, the coach shouldn't take on the coaching assignment.

Some leadership coaches diminish their own effectiveness by being too opinionated. Unwilling to set aside their knowledge and perspective, they fail to truly *listen* to the client and thus cannot connect. Paradoxically, the coach must be prepared *not* to know everything that's going on. Acceptance of the fact that *not* knowing is an essential part of the process is crucial, because it liberates the coach from the need for omnipotent control. Once freed of this need, the coach will be more authentic and empathic in engaging with the client.

Other leadership coaches sabotage the coaching effort by ignoring the client's resistance. Effective change can't happen unless the coach *resists* the resistance. He or she has to acknowledge and address negative feelings immediately. Ignoring resistance, hoping that it will just go away, will almost certainly derail the coaching process. Thus any form of resistance, no matter how minor, needs to be brought out into the open and explored.

Sometimes coaches let a client down despite their best intentions. If the problems facing the client don't really fall within a coach's expertise or interest, the intervention technique chosen by the coach may be inadequate. As the saying goes, if you don't know where you're going, you may end up somewhere else! Likewise, coaches have little chance of success if the organization isn't behind them. Sometimes a company recommends coaching despite having already given up on the person to be coached, wanting the personnel record to show that all avenues have been tried. Taking on the client under such conditions is futile.

Even organizations that aren't deliberately deceptive can say they support coaching but fail to do so. For example, in organizations with a blaming culture—organizations characterized by mistrust and fear (i.e., organizations where scapegoating is the norm and the making of mistakes isn't tolerated)—effective coaching will inevitably be stymied. The same is true of organizations interested primarily in short-term results (where investments in people, such as through coaching, are an uphill struggle) and organizations that see people as disposable assets. In these toxic, neurotic organizational environments, coaches need to be careful not to be drawn into collusive relationships. They may be asked (explicitly or subtly) by top management to focus on helping their client conform to patterns of behavior acceptable to the firm, even when that runs contrary to the personal growth of the client. Coaches working in such an environment may, if they resist the pull of collusive relationships, find themselves in the awkward situation of recommending to the client that he or she quit the dysfunctional organization—despite the fact that the organization is paying for the coaching.

So how can one tell whether leadership coaching is progressing well or has succumbed to one of these many impediments? One primary indication that the coaching process is *not* going as planned is a lack of progress (or worse, regress) toward the goals set by the client in the coaching agreement. Another indication is dissatisfaction on the part of the significant others who were co-opted to take part in the change process. Another ominous sign is a stalemate during the sessions, with coach and client going through the motions but not accomplishing much. It's time to take serious notice when the client starts to discard the terms of the coaching agreement by missing sessions, not doing "homework" assignments, or not paying the bills. Finally, an even more dramatic indicator is deterioration in the client's psychological or physical health.

THE VICISSITUDES OF LEADERSHIP COACHING

To temper all the hype about leadership coaching these days, I'd like to end this discussion by presenting a number of concerns. Given the earlier discussion, it won't be surprising that my first concern is the proper training of coaches. Companies looking to hire a coach need to be selective, assessing carefully the training and experience all the candidates possess. As I've suggested, if a coach doesn't truly appreciate the problems of the client or the business, that miscalculation can prove to be extremely costly for individual and organization alike. Self-styled leadership "coaches" may have good intentions, but *real* leadership coaching is built on a solid base of psychological understanding and practice. Effective leadership coaches are acutely attuned to the unconscious life of organizations, realizing that there's more to human behavior that meets the eye.

A related concern—and a troubling one, given human nature—is that leadership coaches don't always know their limits. Leadership coaches need to realistically appraise their expertise and acknowledge which kinds of clients they can work with and which they can't. Leadership coaches who are "hungry" (in a financial sense) are the worst candidates. Wise leadership coaches know what to take on and what to refuse, and they follow the credo, Do what's best for the client. Furthermore, *any* leadership coach, even one with a great deal of experience, would do well to have regular supervision and/or an independent colleague to discuss clients with, so that an experienced "other" can give his or her opinion on difficult interventions.

Another concern I have—this one multi-pronged—relates to the ethical code of conduct for leadership coaches. First, as noted earlier, it isn't always clear whether the client is the person being coached or someone else in the organization—perhaps someone higher up the management ladder or someone in the human resources department. The hazy, potentially dual role that many leadership coaches play has the potential to create serious problems. The person being coached may fear that sensitive information will get back to top management—a realistic fear, since that's often what happens. Leadership coaches need to be clear up front, with both the person coached and anyone else they have dealings with, about how the information they receive during sessions will be used.

The issue of confidentiality extends beyond private personal data to sensitive organizational information regarding issues such as possible acquisitions or mergers, proprietary information about share price, and illegal activities. Organizations that use external leadership coaches should set confidentiality guidelines up front to ensure the client's (and organization's) privacy. Using that written agreement about how information will be shared, the leadership coach can then balance the need for privacy with a focus on improved corporate results.

Another troubling ethical issue is the question of consent. Sometimes clients participate in leadership coaching not because they believe in its value but because senior people in the organization have recommended it for career advancement. Declining such a "gift" (a word meaning *poison* in Dutch and German) isn't an option for anyone who wants to be promoted within the organization. But talk about questionable motivation! It's like the convict who enters therapy because a judge mandated it as one of the conditions of a reduced sentence. I've learned from hard experience that such scenarios don't augur well. Leadership coaches who find themselves working with clients who are under duress must exercise great vigilance in dealing quickly with resistances.

There are ethical issues around the question of money as well. If the organization finances leadership coaching, it should provide clear guidelines about the ways leadership coaches are going to be used, and for how long. Because clients who respond well to leadership coaching begin to grow and develop personally, they often want to extend the work beyond what was originally planned for. They may, for example, want what was intended to be a performance-improvement intervention to blossom into something of a very different nature. As with the work of the sorcerer's apprentice, the process can easily run out of control, becoming very expensive. Of course, it's another matter altogether if the leadership coaching is financed privately by the client.

Despite these concerns, I'm very optimistic about leadership coaching as a personal and organization change tool. Coaching, at its best, is about helping people discover, believe in, and act upon what they already know. It's about looking for the possibilities in others, rather than the limits. To quote Mark Twain, "Keep away from people who try to belittle your ambitions. Small people always do that, but the really great make you feel that you, too, can become great." It's been said that inside every successful businessperson is an even more ambitious worker trying to get out. Leadership coaching merely helps open the door. And it keeps the door from slamming shut again after something goes wrong, emphasizing that mistakes are learning opportunities, not disasters. The worst thing people can do is become paralyzed by their mistakes. If that happens, they drift into a life of suspended animation, refusing to make choices because of the fear of a repeat.

Leadership coaches have to ask themselves all the time, What's possible? They must help the people they work with stretch their imagination beyond the confines of the familiar. As the writer C. S. Lewis once said, "The task of the modern educator is not to cut down jungles but to irrigate deserts." People should never allow what they can't do to interfere what they can—or could—do. Someone who lacks confidence will always find something to trip over. On the other hand, leadership coaches must be solidly attached to reality. They should never try to teach a dog how to sing, an endeavor that wastes a lot of time and annoys the dog.

In a nutshell, what leadership coaches offer their clients is independence. True independence means being free from the domination of one's unconscious needs and desires and being courageous enough to choose one's own destiny. In this world of rules and regulations, the only discipline that lasts is self-discipline! And the only people who can create the kind of connectivity that characterizes the successful modern organization are those who are independent enough to value *inter*dependence.

REFERENCES

1. Fitzgerald, C. and J. Garvey Berger, Eds (2002). *Executive Coaching.* New York, Consulting Psychologist Press.
2. Flaherty, J. (1999). *Coaching: Evoking Excellence in Others.* Boston, Butterworth Heinemann.
3. Goldsmith, M., A. Freas, et al., Eds (2000). *Coaching for Leadership.* New York, John Wiley & Sons, Inc.
4. Hargrove, R. (2002). *Masterful Coaching.* New York, John Wiley & Sons, Inc.
5. Hudson, F. M. (1999). *The Handbook of Coaching.* San Francisco, Jossey-Bass.
6. Kilberg, R. R. (2000). *Executive Coaching.* Washington, D.C., American Psychological Association.
7. O'Neil, M. B. (2000). *Executive Coaching with Backbone and Heart.* San Francisco, Jossey-Bass.
8. Whitmore, J. (1996). *Coaching for Performance.* New York, Atrium.
9. Hunt, J. M. and J. R. Weintraub (2002). *The Coaching Manager.* London, Sage Publications.
10. Pederson, D. B. and M. D. Hicks (1995). *The Leader as Coach: Strategies for Coaching and Developing Others.* Minneapolis, Minn, Personnel Decisions.
11. Sperry, L. (1993). "Working with Executives: Consulting, Counseling and Coaching." *Individual Psychology* 49(2): 257–266.
12. Tobias, L. L. (1996). "Coaching Executives." *Consulting Psychology Journal: Practice and Research* 48(2): 87–95.
13. Judge, W. Q. and J. Cowell (1997). "The Brave New World of Executive Coaching." *Business Horizons* 40(4): 71–77.
14. Stone, F. M. (1998). *Coaching, Counseling & Mentoring.* New York, AMACOM.
15. Brotman, L. E., W. P. Liberi and K. M. Wasylyshyn (1998). "Executive Coaching: The Need for Standards of Competence." *Consulting Psychology Journal: Practice and Research* 50(1): 40–46.
16. Grant, A. M. (2002). Towards a Psychology of Coaching: The Impact of Coaching on Metacognition, Mental health and Goal Attainment, Dissertation Abstracts International.

17. Berglas, S. (2002). "The Very Real Dangers of Executive Coaching." *Harvard Business Review* 80(6): 86–92.
18. Hirschhorn, L. (1990). *The Workplace Within: Psychodynamics of Organizational Life*. Boston, MIT Press.
19. Kets de Vries, M. F. R. (2005). "Leadership Group Coaching in Action: The Zen of Creating High Performance teams." *Academy of Management Executive* 19(1): 61–76.
20. Kets de Vries, M. F. R. and D. Miller (1984). *The Neurotic Organization*. San Francisco, Jossey-Bass.
21. Levinson, H. (2002). *Organizational Assessment*. Washington, DC, American Psychological Association.
22. Zaleznik, A. (1989). *The Managerial Mystique*. New York, Harper & Row.
23. Mander, G. (2001). *A Psychodynamic Approach to Brief Therapy*. London, Sage Publications.
24. Messer, S. B. and C. S. Warren (1995). *Models of brief psychodynamic therapy*. New York, The Guilford Press.
25. Rawson, P. (2002). *Short-Term Psychodynamic Psychotherapy: An Analysis of the Key Principals*. London, Karnac Books.
26. Hall, D. T., K. L. Otazo, et al. (1999). "Behind the Closed Door: What really Happens in Executive Coaching." *Organizational Dynamics* 27(3): 39–53.
27. Peterson, D. B. (1996). "Executive Coaching at Work: The Art of One-on-One Change." *Consulting Psychology Journal: Practice and Research* 48(2): 78–86.
28. Witherspoon, R. and R. P. White (1996). "Executive Coaching: A Continuum of Roles." *Consulting Psychology Journal: Practice and Research* 48(2): 124–133.
29. Koss, M. P. and J. Shiang (1993). Research on Brief Psychotherapy. *Handbook of Psychotherapy and Behavior Change*. Eds A. E. Bergin and S. L. Garfield. New York, Wiley.
30. Gustavson, J. P. (1986). *The Complex Secret of Brief Psychotherapy*. New York, Norton.
31. Luborsky, L., P. Crits-Cristoph, J. Mintz and A. Auerbach (1988). *Who Will Benefit from Psychotherapy?* New York, Basic Books.
32. McCullough Vaillant, L. (1997). *Changing Character*. New York, Basic Books.

CHAPTER 11

GROUP LEADERSHIP
COACHING

Individual commitment to a group effort, that is what makes a team
work, a company work, a society work, a civilization work.

—Vince Lombardi

Never doubt that a small group of committed citizens can change
the world. Indeed, it is the only thing that ever has.

—Margaret Mead

If everyone is thinking alike then somebody isn't thinking.

—George Patton

Water which is too pure has no fish.

—Zen proverb

We've always known that the pressure that groups can exert in
creating behavior change can be formidable. And Zen masters have
always been well aware of the efficacy of those pressures, as the
following story illustrates.

When a famous Zen master held his regular weeks of meditation, pupils from all over Japan came to attend. During one of these gatherings, one of the pupils was caught stealing. The matter was reported to the Zen master with the request that the pupil be expelled. The Zen master ignored the request. Soon after, the same pupil was caught in a similar act, and again the master disregarded the matter. This lack of action angered the other pupils so much that they drew up a petition asking for the dismissal of the thief. If the master wouldn't agree, they threatened, they would all leave the temple.

When the Zen master had read the petition, he called everyone before him. "You're right, pupils," he told them. "You know what's right and what's not right. You may go somewhere else to study if you wish, but this poor brother of ours doesn't even know right from wrong. Who will teach him if we don't? How can we change his dysfunctional behavior? I'm going to keep him here even if all the rest of you leave."

In this response, the Zen master reframed his expectations in a positive way, and he praised the values of the other students. And the Zen master's conviction was proved right: surrounded by a group of peers on the watch for further infractions, the pupil found that his desire to steal had vanished. It's easy to imagine that this gentle lesson was of lasting benefit to all concerned. Featuring the sort of outcome all leadership coaches strive for, it's a fine example of the effect leadership coaching in groups can have.

I'd like to offer another kind of leadership coaching methodology—one that I've found to be extremely effective in helping people, teams, and organizations change. An adaptation of "The Challenge of Leadership" workshop described in Chapters 8 and 9, this change strategy has proven to be highly effective in the "Coaching and Consulting for Change" seminar at INSEAD, and in creating high-performance teams and high-performance organizations. Over the past years, this coaching methodology has been successfully applied to many different organizations and industries. An abbreviated illustration of the process follows.

A CASE IN POINT

It was obvious from the strained small talk and the jokes that the eight people in the room—seven men and one woman who were members of the top executive team of an information technology firm—were more than a little anxious. This was unusual, as these board members were typically self-confident and in control, and had a well-rehearsed script for meetings that they happily enacted as if on automatic pilot. This time things were different, however. Today's gathering was clearly not going to be business as usual. Their new CEO had asked them to participate in a high-performance teambuilding workshop facilitated by an external leadership coach. They had no idea what to expect. Worse yet (from their perspective), they had been asked to complete a number of 360-degree feedback instruments a couple of weeks earlier. Sitting together now—their faces revealing a mixture of curiosity and anxiety—they were wondering what their colleagues, subordinates, friends, and family members had to say about them.

They had reason to worry. For over half a year, a cloud had been hanging over their organization: a takeover threat from a much smaller competitor. Though well established in its industry, their firm wasn't as nimble as it should have been, and thus the threat was very real and very frightening. Future job security was at stake for many employees. Only a few months ago, the non-executive board members had finally realized that the CEO couldn't turn the company around, and they asked him to resign. Realizing that new blood was required to shake the company out of its complacency—to make it less bureaucratic, more entrepreneurial, more team-oriented, and more results-focused—they had hired a new CEO with a different profile. The board had made it clear that it was up to him to bring corporate returns to a level that matched, or bettered, the standards of the industry.

After his initial appraisal of the situation, the new CEO decided that one of his main priorities was to form a stronger and more effective top executive team. It was clear to him that the present team wasn't an exemplary decision-making body. From his first encounter with the group he observed that meetings tended to drift, priorities changed almost on a whim, accountability and follow-up were lacking, and the various executive board members had trouble arriving at closure. The new CEO sensed the presence of considerable unspoken conflict among the executive team. After a few meetings he picked up on the fact that several fiefdoms had been established, leading to block voting. Beyond those loose affiliations, the various members of the executive group didn't seem to feel accountable to each other. The resulting lack of focus was widely noticed at lower levels in the organization (as had been clearly indicated in company-wide satisfaction surveys). Not surprisingly, many of the complaints centered on the fact that the board members appeared to be sending conflicting signals.

The members of the executive team were aware of all this history and therefore were somewhat anxious not only about the prospective teambuilding exercise but also about the new CEO's plans for the future. They knew that things had to change—they agreed with the CEO about that—but how would pending changes affect their positions in the firm? These thoughts and concerns made a teambuilding exercise, with its associated feedback and self-disclosure, a much more risky and anxiety-ridden exercise for this particular group than it would have been for people at lower levels of the organization.

The new CEO had experienced similar interactions in his previous position, and he knew that mutual accountability was often more difficult to establish at the top level of an organization. There was always potential for conflict between corporate and line-of-business goals. Furthermore, he realized that the stakes tended to be much higher for people at the board level, given the executives' personal goals. He was confident, however, that the leadership group exercise in which his team was about to participate would provide results and lead to improvement.

GETTING STARTED

The leadership coach, an outsider whom the CEO knew by reputation, started the process by engaging the group in conversation centered on effective and dysfunctional leadership. He led the group into a discussion about the characteristics of high-performance teams and organizations, a topic to which they devoted considerable time. He asked the executives to contribute examples of what they viewed as good and bad leadership. Building on these examples, he asked individuals to talk about a personal "Everest experience," or feeling of "flow"—in other words, a situation when they'd felt especially good about their leadership [1]. This led to an interesting exchange among group members concerning their views about the competencies the future leaders of their organization should have, and what selection, development, and reward processes were needed to hire and retain this type of leader.

After a break, the leadership coach explained the difficulties most commonly associated with giving and receiving feedback. He pointed out that most executives tend to be "overestimators"—that is, they tend to have an exaggerated sense of their effectiveness at work. ("Present company excepted, of course," he added with a smile.) He explained the theory behind 360-degree feedback instruments and described how these instruments help executives understand their own competencies and weaknesses.

GATHERING DATA

Prior to the workshop, members of the executive board had completed such an instrument, The Global Executive Leadership Inventory (GELI), which measures leadership in twelve dimensions, including visioning, empowering, energizing, designing and aligning, rewarding and feedback, teambuilding, outside orientation, tenacity, global mindset, emotional intelligence, resilience to stress, and life balance [2]–[4]. The board members had completed the questionnaire themselves and had asked seven to ten work colleagues apiece to be their personal "observers." The observers had answered the same questions the participants did—not about themselves but about the participants. In addition, the observers had been asked to write answers to three questions: What behavior should this particular executive continue doing? What behavior should he or she develop further? What behavior should he or she eliminate? Answering these questions gave observers the opportunity to make specific recommendations about how the person being rated could be more effective. Their responses to these questions, which hadn't yet been shared, would make the eventual feedback session even more relevant for each participant.

The responses to all the questionnaires had been summarized in a report that compared the results of self-reporting with the aggregated results of their observers' questionnaires. To help the test-takers further analyse the results, the observers' ranking of the leader in each dimension were also separated into categories: superior(s), co-workers, subordinates, direct reports, and others, with no names attached. The leadership coach showed the group a sample graph to explain the different categories that people would see when they received their own, personalized feedback material. (See Figure 11.1 for an example of a sample GELI personal graph page.)

In addition, to complement the behavioral dimensions measured by the Global Executive Leadership Inventory, each

Global Executive Leadership Inventory

Programme Name

Franco Franco
July 2004

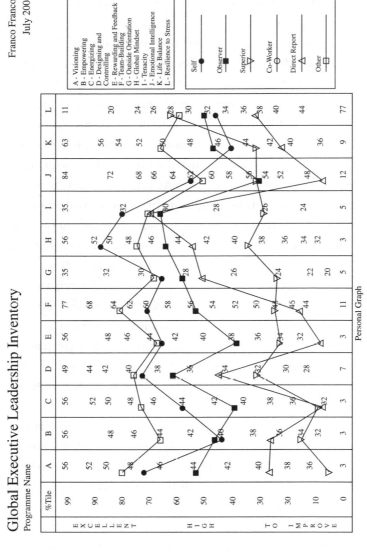

Personal Graph

A - Visioning
B - Empowering
C - Energizing
D - Designing and Controlling
E - Rewarding and Feedback
F - Team-Building
G - Outside Orientation
H - Global Mindset
I - Tenacity
J - Emotional Intelligence
K - Life Balance
L - Resilience to Stress

Self
Observer
Superior
Co-Worker
Direct Report
Other

Figure 11.1   Sample personal graph

board member had been asked to complete a questionnaire called The Personality Audit [5]. This 360-degree instrument differs from the Global Executive Leadership Inventory in that it measures personality dimensions (presented in the form of polarities) such as sense of self-esteem, conscientiousness, trust, assertiveness, extroversion, mood state, and adventurousness. For this questionnaire, the leadership coach had specified that the observers chosen should be a significant other or spouse, and two colleagues at the office who were both well acquainted with the participant (preferably one superior and one subordinate). The summarized results of this questionnaire, which were not anonymous, would offer the executives the opportunity to see the way their observers—work colleagues and personal contacts—differed in their evaluation of the leader's personality traits. This feedback would help the executives understand how they managed their public and private selves, and would illustrate the level of consistency of their presentation of self. In addition, the responses would reveal differences in how people managed upward versus downward. Once again, the leadership coach carefully explained the presentation of the Personality Feedback page to the participants. (See Figure 11.2 for an example of The Personality Audit report.)

To encourage even more personal feedback, each participant had been told to ask a number of good friends and family members to respond in writing to questions such as, "What's the first thing that comes to mind when you think about this person?" and "What should this person change about him- or herself?" Finally, the executives had been asked to complete a short biographical sketch to help the leadership coach better understand the general background of each person.

At the end of the first day of the leadership teambuilding workshop (the first phase of a three-day group coaching process), after the sample feedback graphs had been presented and all questions about the process had been answered, each member of the executive team was given an envelope containing the feedback

Personality Audit

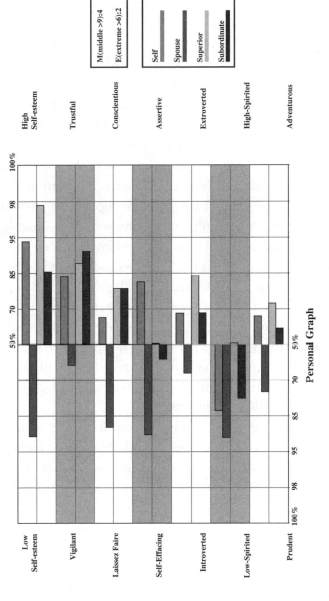

Figure 11.2 Sample Personality Audit graph

Personality Audit
Dimension 1   **Low Self-esteem**   **High Self-esteem**

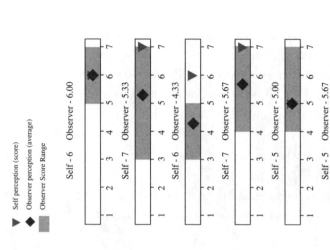

Self perception (score) ▶
Observer perception (average) ◆
Observer Score Range ▨

12. When I compare myself to other people, I feel that I have...
    very little control over events in my life
    Self - 6   Observer - 6.00
    a considerable amount of control over events in my life

13. I think other people find me...
    boring
    Self - 7   Observer - 5.33
    extremely interesting

14. When I compare myself to my peers, I feel...
    inferior
    Self - 6   Observer - 4.33
    superior

17. Looking at myself...
    I am self-critical
    Self - 7   Observer - 5.67
    I accept myself fully

20. I think other people...
    do not want to be like me
    Self - 5   Observer - 5.00
    want to be like me

38. I see myself as someone who is...
    not successful
    Self - 5   Observer - 5.67
    extremely successful

Figure 11.2   *Continued.*

information that had been assembled for him or her. The leadership coach suggested that they study this feedback carefully on their own and sleep on the results, to be prepared for the next day's program. He counseled them, tongue-in-cheek, not to go on a witch-hunt to identify or retaliate against any people who gave them a low rating on some dimension or other. "Killing the bastards who gave you unpleasant feedback," he said, "is not a productive exercise, although it might feel good!" His advice was to calmly thank everyone who had worked hard, and had the courage, to give feedback as requested. As a caveat, he reminded them that individuals—this time, "Present company included!"— are highly complex, and far too complicated to sum up via a simple questionnaire. Questionnaire results, he said, aren't an end in themselves; rather, they offer a jumping-off point for constructive discussion about future career choices and decisions. As a final quip, he mentioned that his experience with people had taught him that everyone seems normal until you get to know them better—and then everyone is revealed to be positively abnormal, flawed by interesting quirks.

Not all members of the executive team had a restful night after opening their envelopes. Although much of the feedback concerning their leadership of the company came as no great surprise to them, it was nonetheless disturbing to see it so clearly summarized in a report, negatives as well as positives. (At their level in the organization, honest feedback wasn't usually part of the deal; subordinates often said what they thought executives wanted to hear.) During the course of a late evening, while reading a mixture of praise and condemnation, the executives began to spin out rationalizations to explain any low ratings they had received.

GROUP LEADERSHIP COACHING DYNAMICS

As the morning session began on the second day, some of the executives seemed quite defensive about the feedback they'd found in their envelopes. The leadership coach understood the reason for this. He knew that a main precondition for an effective intervention is a relationship of mutual trust and respect between coach and client. These form the foundation of what clinical psychologists call the working alliance. And this group wasn't there yet. It would take some time.

The leadership coach explained the next phase: each of the executive board members in turn would be asked to share with the group the feedback he or she had received, and the other group members would give their reactions to that feedback—a two-step process that would help the individual participants formulate a personal leadership development plan. He mentioned that they needed to manage the time carefully, so that each of them would have approximately one and a half hours "in the limelight." In an effort to reduce the group's palpable anxiety, he also clarified that the purpose of the exercise was to be helpful and supportive to each other. With this short introduction, he asked who would like to start the process.

After a long moment of distinct unease, one of the executives, John, volunteered. The leadership coach confirmed with John that the executive was prepared to share the information he had received with the other members of his team. After receiving a somewhat hesitant affirmative, the leadership coach used an overhead projector to display the summary data of the Global Executive Leadership Inventory and The Personality Audit—in other words, John's personal results—on the screen.

After the other participants had had time to read and absorb the material, the leadership coach asked them how they would interpret the information summarized from the Global Executive Leadership Inventory. After a lengthy pause, one commented that John seemed to be an over-estimator (as the leadership coach had earlier suggested most executives are), rating himself higher than his observers in the organization had rated him. Soon other people joined in the discussion, offering comments about other variances between John's self-assessment and the assessment of others. To complement and focus the presentation of the data, the leadership coach shared some of the written comments that John had received from his observers. The most telling dealt with John's need for details, his problems in delegation, his inclination to take over work from weak subordinates, his occasional moodiness, and his tendency to work too hard and get stressed out.

When the discussion turned to The Personality Audit, the leadership coach pointed out that the assertiveness dimension indicated that John was something of a "tiger" in the office but a "pussycat" at home, an observation that resulted in the first comfortable laughter of the day. Although John perceived himself as somewhat extroverted, at home, according to his wife, he was rather withdrawn; her ratings indicated that he should be more adventurous in his dealings with her. The Personality Audit also showed a moderate rating on the conscientiousness dimension while being quite laissez faire at home. The supplemental personal feedback pages were revealing as well. The leadership coach asked John to read aloud some of the observations made by family and friends. Many expressed concern that he seemed to be under too much stress, that he should learn how to delegate more effectively—advice which surprised John, who had not been aware of this problem. Other comments indicated that he should be more careful about his health and that he should set clearer boundaries between his private and business life. Some commented that he was sometimes moody or hypersensitive. There were positive comments as well: for example, some observers mentioned the creative way John tackled and solved problems that other people had given up on.

During this discussion of the various forms of feedback, the leadership coach made sure that John's observed strengths were emphasized and his weaknesses reframed in a positive way to reduce defensive reactions. The coach knew that this kind of reframing was an effective way to reinforce self-esteem and make the participant more willing to engage in a change effort. He also knew that timing was critical. Hard experience had taught him that when the timing isn't right, it's better to stay silent. (Again, "Strike when the iron is cold.") In addition, he went to great lengths to present observations in the context of the experiences of others. He knew that such an approach took the sharp edges off some of the more critical behavioral observations.

After the first phase of the feedback review, the leadership coach asked John if he could mention a few things about his background as a way of helping the others understand his way of looking at the world. The leadership coach helped him structure his narrative by asking him questions such as, Can you say a few things about your personal background? Can you describe events/ situations (personal, organizational, or both) that affected your career in a significant way? Can you say something about the best/worst times in your life? What kind of people do you admire? What do you see as your greatest accomplishments? What was your greatest failure/disappointment? What makes you angry, happy, mad, or sad? What regrets do you have as you look back on your life? If you could change three things in your life, what would they be? How do you look at the future? The other participants found the responses to this information extremely helpful, because it gave them a different view of this person who had been their colleague for many years.

Following this part of the session, John was asked to be silent and just listen to what the others had to say. The leadership coach asked the others what thoughts had come to mind when they heard John talk. What kind of feelings did they have while listening to his narrative? What were their "fantasies," their associations while listening to John? To stimulate the group's creative thinking, he asked, If John were an animal, what animal did they think he would be? This particular question evoked many responses. Some mentioned a watchdog, like a German shepherd; others referred to a rat in a cage. Another person strayed from the animal motif and compared him to the mythological figure Sisyphus, endlessly pushing his rock up a hill. What stood out in the discussion were John's strong work ethic, his driven nature, and his need for control.

Next, each member of the team was asked, "as a friend," what advice he or she would give John to help him become even more effective. This question prompted an intense discussion. Two of the participants made disparaging remarks about certain members of John's management team and suggested that he should stop protecting those "incompetents" and avoid doing their work in addition to his own. He had enough work to do as it was. These respondents felt that John should take the tough step of letting some of the subordinates go. One woman suggested that he should reorganize and simplify his department's structure rather than having twelve people reporting to him. Still another participant complained about how difficult it was to approach John and the people who reported to him. This participant said that although the company claimed to aspire to be a networking, boundaryless organization, John, through his territorialism and his anger when people approached his team without his consent, had created what the participant referred to as a "silo"—that is, a part of the organization that was extremely hard to enter. This latter comment took John by surprise. He had never realized that his behavior gave this impression.

During this process the leadership coach was actively listening and trying to comprehend the key issues that John faced. He also offered tentative suggestions of other ways that John could act in certain situations, should they come up again. By reframing some of the colleagues' suggestions, he helped John to become more aware of conscious and unconscious influences on his behavior. He helped John see connections between critical life situations he had mentioned in his description of himself and the problems he was having in the workplace. Why did he have such a great need for control? What was behind his reluctance to delegate more? Why did he get moody at times? Why did he protect incompetents? During this exchange, the leadership coach used humor as a highly effective means of clarifying certain points and defusing tension.

When the discussion had reached closure after some time, John was asked how he felt, what he had distilled from everyone's feedback, and what had been most important to him during the discussion. He now had the opportunity to reply to the various observations. When he had said his piece, the leadership coach summarized the major points of the discussion (which had been jotted onto a flip chart as they came up), and these were presented as part of John's personal leadership development plan. The leadership coach explained that each person would formulate a similar personal development plan after discussing their questionnaire feedback.

This same rather intensive feedback exercise took place for each member of the executive team in turn, with each participant identifying issues to be included in their personal leadership development plan. Though the exercise was the same, the atmosphere was not: people were tense and hesitant to contribute at the outset, but they gradually became more comfortable and spontaneous. The group leadership coaching exercise created for the members of the executive team the kind of "transitional space" or "holding environment" described in earlier chapters [6].

As a result of the group dynamics of these discussions, the different roles played by the members of the executive team were clarified and the effects of the various leadership styles on the group as a whole became clearer. They recognized how they could complement each other, how they could build on each other's strengths to become more effective as a team. At that point, one executive board member remarked to another, "We've worked together now for twenty-eight years. It's sad that I learned more about you in the past two days than I had in all the previous years. But now I have a better sense of your strengths and weaknesses, and I understand what you stand for. I think we'll be able to work together more effectively now."

Before closing the workshop, the leadership coach discussed the importance of the personal development plan. He asked each member of the executive team to state out loud what he or she had learned during the past two days, and which two or three areas each of them planned to work on. (The leadership coach had learned that setting too many goals was unwise. Trying to do too many things at the same time carried the strong risk that nothing would get done.) He also asked them how they were going to deal with the people who had provided them with feedback. How would they involve those friends and colleagues in bringing about changes in behavior? He mentioned that involving the people who had given them feedback would make changes in behavior more likely—the public commitment component discussed in Chapter 9. In addition, he asked them to put down in writing a realistic, measurable action plan (with a timeline) that would be circulated among the other members of the present group. Stressing the importance of having an internal leadership coach to monitor progress, he suggested that they ask one or two people in the executive group to help them monitor and assist them to implement the desired changes. Finally, the leadership coach set a date (approximately two months later) when they would have a follow-up meeting, which he would return for, to discuss what they had done and how well they had met their set objectives. The leadership coach knew from experience that a follow-up process was essential for successful change.

CREATING HIGH-EQ TEAMS

The benefits that came out of the group leadership coaching exercise far exceeded the expectations of the CEO who had initiated it. Over time, the executives became more of a high-EQ team—that is, they had a higher "emotional quotient," or ability to understand themselves and others [7]–[9]. The members of the team also became more aware of the interpersonal roles in which, consciously or unconsciously, they had cast themselves [10]. They recognized that just as they had taken on a particular role in their own family while growing up, they now frequently occupied a parallel role in the workplace. They identified these roles in the group as task master, martyr, scapegoat, cheerleader, peacemaker, hero, and clown. They also began figuring out the complementary roles that others had been placed in, and thus saw how other members of the executive team could be used more effectively [11]. In addition, they acquired insight into maladaptive interpersonal patterns that weakened the team, discovering how such patterns, and the collusive relationships that underlay them, contributed to the team's lack of effective conflict resolution, lack of focus, and reduced productivity. After the workshop, one of the members of the team said, "In the past our meetings were get-togethers where some of us said what we really didn't think, while others didn't say what we really did think! I hope, and think, that we'll be able to change this pattern."

By participating in the intensive group leadership coaching process, the members of the team learned what it meant to coach others; the group exercise helped them add a new interpersonal tool to their repertoire. In particular, they learned how to become better listeners. They saw that listening is a precondition for any meaningful relationship, because it fosters understanding. And better relationships mean better business, because people who feel heard and understood are easier to motivate and influence.

There were many other benefits that came out of the group leadership coaching exercise. The executive board members agreed with the CEO's assessment that they had become much more of a team. Due to the teambuilding sessions, their common goals and values had become much more explicit. There was a higher level of trust and mutual respect among them. Furthermore, they noticed during subsequent meetings that team objectives were no longer being affected by an undercurrent of personal objectives [12]–[15]. Turf fights were rare. When someone strayed and resorted to behavior that the team now recognized as dysfunctional, the others stepped in to remind the person of the promises made during the leadership coaching sessions. They were no longer willing to let such behavior slip by. In addition to having better relationships with the other team members, board members were able to use their newly acquired leadership coaching skills to improve relationships with direct reports.

Communication within the executive team became more focused, less conflicted, and therefore less energy-draining. As the executive board members concentrated on what was really important to the organization, endless discussions lacking resolution and commitment became a thing of the past. Furthermore, whereas before there had been some "silent types"—executives who rarely spoke—all members of the executive team now participated. And they did so openly and honestly, engaging in constructive conflict resolution and eschewing politics. As a result, the members of the executive team felt more accountable to each other and to the organization. They took ownership and responsibility for their decisions and behaviors and followed up on their actions. Conflict between the members of the team and other members of the organization was reduced as speaking and listening took place at a deeper level.

Keeping in mind the feedback they had received, the executives attempted to unlearn specific behavior patterns that had proved to be ineffective. With the new climate of collegiality, they now found it acceptable to ask each other for help when in a difficult situation. Likewise, talking about personal matters was no longer taboo, which made the executives more willing to express concerns about their life-work balance. Becoming, in effect, a mutual support group, they experienced more satisfaction and fulfillment in their work and personal life. What this group exercise did for them was help them become a true high-performance, high-EQ team: they shared common goals and values, they respected (and built on) each other's differences, and they learned to use the complementarities in their leadership styles to create an effective executive role constellation.

In addition to personal changes that each board member initiated after the workshop, there were changes imposed from above. Encouraged by the exercise, the CEO reassigned the roles of some members of the executive group so that their duties were more in line with their real talents. For example, to help one executive come to grips with his conflict-avoidant behavior, the CEO asked him to turn around a very messy situation at a foreign subsidiary. Another executive (John, the one who favored silo formation) was given a very different portfolio in the executive team—one that was less people-intensive and more future-planning-oriented. This reassignment, the CEO felt, would prevent departmental isolation. Another executive, after reflecting for several weeks on the feedback he had received at the workshop, decided that he didn't really fit in the team. Feeling that he would be more effective in another organization, he resigned.

Looking back on the group leadership coaching process, the CEO was quite satisfied. The leadership coach had quickly created a safe transitional space for the executives, a holding environment in which they felt at ease while narrating their story. Throughout the process, the person who was being discussed engaged in a journey of self-discovery, while the other members of the group vicariously learned from his or her story and validated the experience. Thus, all the participants not only engaged in a problem-solving exercise (in the form of making action recommendations) but also learned how to practice their leadership coaching skills. This process of mutual exploration also helped ensure that the group supported the action plan of the person who was in the limelight, making behavioral change more likely. (For a summary of the process of this leadership group exercise, see Figure 11.3.)

To summarize, the group leadership coaching exercise allowed the executive team to reflect on each member's leadership style. It enabled them to deal with personal issues that had been lying dormant for a long time and to develop strong relationships based on trust and mutual respect. That foundation of trust fostered a genuine exchange of information, broke down barriers, exposed the "undiscussables," and promoted true conflict resolution. The discussions that executive board members had during the workshop, and the more open communication they practiced afterward, helped them rethink priorities, reshape the future of their organization, and improve the financial results. Since they were no longer "playing the violin while Rome burned," they developed a specific strategy that enabled them to ward off the takeover threat that had been looming over them. A follow-up session three months later

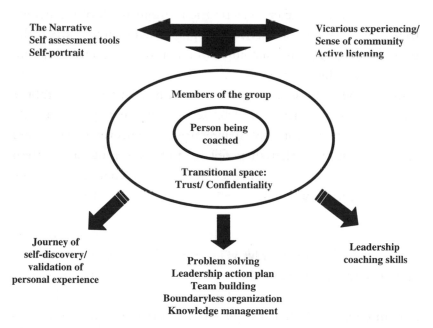

Figure 11.3 Leadership group coaching

confirmed the robustness of the group leadership coaching intervention, as did a subsequent follow-up a year later.

MAKING GROUP LEADERSHIP COACHING WORK IN EXECUTIVE TEAMS

As I described in Chapters 8 and 9, if you want to change people, merely dealing with cognition isn't enough: changing behavior requires a double-pronged approach—dealing with cognition and affect [16]–[17]. As the case study above illustrates, such a strategy really pays off when leadership coaching takes place in groups, especially "natural" working groups. That's not to say that individual leadership coaching doesn't work. On the contrary, successful leadership coaching is often the outcome of a one-on-one process. However, private coaching sessions may not have such a lasting impact, in part because they're too infrequent; and they may have a lesser impact because the reinforcement of the people from the work environment is missing. All too often, when the coached individual is back in his or her working environment, "automatic pilot" takes over and wipes out lessons learned. In addition, the business and private environments often act as "rubber fences," bouncing the client right back to the starting point despite the person's best efforts to change aspects of his or her behavior. Thus the question whether people can change must be answered in the affirmative, but whether people will change has to be answered with a maybe [18]!

THE ROLE OF COMMITMENT AND FOLLOW-UP

I've discovered that many people in search of change have a "dream." The "dream" goes something like this: "I will start exercising." "I will start dieting." "I will stop smoking." But that dream never becomes reality, because having good intentions is rarely good enough. As noted in Chapter 9, the external pressure that others exert after a public commitment can make all the difference. When a smoker says in public, "I'm going to stop smoking," that person involves others, giving them a stake in the process. After hearing such an announcement, people aren't likely to offer the person a cigarette or even to give one when asked. This public process changes the "rubber fence" into a much more robust foundation of support. What makes group leadership coaching so effective, then—whether it's a "natural" group, as described above, or a "random" group in a "Challenge of Leadership" workshop—is that participants become committed to helping each other change. The leadership coach who sets the process in motion is eventually assisted by a number of volunteer "assistant coaches," who help each other stay on the right track.

The members of the group set boundaries that become an important force in behavior change; they help each person live up to his or her promises. Because shame, guilt, and hope are powerful motivating forces (as I'm somewhat reluctant to point out), when an individual is tempted to fall back on old behavior patterns the visualization of the group's disapproval and the hope of a better future often act as effective deterrents. It's as if the group becomes internalized within each member.

THE ROLE OF STORYTELLING

The support and acceptance given by the group facilitate change because they instill in each participant a sense of hope about the future. The powerful emotional experiences that come out of group leadership coaching are also change-facilitators. As was discussed in Chapter 9, as people reveal something about themselves by telling their life stories, talking about the experiences that shaped them, and sharing the feedback they received through assessments, they undergo a journey of self-understanding. Telling personal stories is a powerful way of exploring the self [19]–[20]. It creates a readiness for interpersonal learning and insight, lays the foundation for working through internal conflicts and crises, and helps a person arrive at meaningful, personal life integration. By telling personal stories, people rediscover themselves, obtaining a better understanding of their own life. Listening to stories is a powerful learning experience as well; it allows for the vicarious instruction of role modeling and gives an empathic understanding of the questions the speaker is struggling with. Listening, not imitation, may be the sincerest form of flattery. As a form of healing, storytelling and listening to each other's stories is second to none.

THE ROLE OF TRUST

Growth can come out of the telling and hearing of stories only if trust binds all the participants in an executive team. Unfortunately, trust-building isn't easy for highly competitive people. In many organizations, trust is an extremely rare commodity. After all, relationships of trust depend on our willingness to look not only to our own interests, but also to the interests of others. For trust to exist, we need to deal with such complicated issues as openness, honesty, active listening, communication, consistency, competence, fairness, and mutual respect [21]. Trust is a delicate flower: it doesn't take much to crush it, and once destroyed, it takes a very long time to nurture it back into bloom. But if trust is honored and protected, it flourishes and bears good fruit. Trust makes for constructive conflict resolution; constructive conflict resolution makes for genuine commitment; and commitment makes for accountability—all factors that have an enormous impact on the bottom line of an organization.

The case example given earlier illustrates what can happen when leadership coaching takes place in groups. When people get to know each other better, when they understand each other's leadership styles, when they have a good sense of each other's competencies, when they understand the nature of each other's work, there's a greater likelihood that they will trust each other. In the transitional space of the coaching workshop, people open up and begin to share information, talking about the issues that preoccupy them. They stop beating around the bush, they stop playing politics, and they start to support each other.

In the cyber society of today—in the virtual teams that are becoming ever more common in the global marketplace—the building of trust is even more important, and even more of an uphill battle. To make virtual teams effective, an enormous investment in relationship-building needs to be made up front. It's impossible to e-mail a smile or a handshake (emoticons notwithstanding). Personal relationships and face-to-face communication, not electronic communication, build trust. And yet only when a significant degree of trust exists between various parties can one expect effective interaction between individuals and groups located in different parts of the world. Without the glue of trust, teams don't work well and virtual teams don't work at all.

Knowledge management can't take place in the absence of trust. If knowledge is power, why share it? Who would share information with someone he or she doesn't trust? When people trust each other, they have an incentive to share; once they open up to each other, they know what to share and how and why to do so. Thus only when there's a solid degree of trust between executives can there be true knowledge management [22]–[23]. Unfortunately, there are lots of people in the knowledge management business who haven't figured that out yet! In spite of all the hoopla, knowledge management has in many instances been a less than successful concept. That's because its advocates focus their attention on the building of data banks and don't deal with the human factor. Setting up an extensive, state-of-the-art data bank isn't knowledge management; investing heavily in electronic management systems isn't knowledge management. Vehicles for storing and categorizing knowledge do exist, but they're only tools. It's people that in the end acquire, manipulate, and manage knowledge. Thus true knowledge management means creating teams and organizations in which the participants trust each other and realize the benefits of knowledge-sharing for everybody involved. True knowledge management means the creation of social networks, of communities. True knowledge management implies paying attention to the unconscious life of organizations.

REFERENCES

1. Csikszentmihalyi, M. (1990). *Flow: The Psychology of Optimal Experience*. New York, Harper and Row.
2. Kets de Vries, M. F. R. (2004). *The Global Executive Leadership Inventory: Facilitator's Guide*. San Francisco, Pfeiffer.
3. Kets de Vries, M. F. R. (2004). *The Global Executive Leadership Inventory: Participant's Guide*. San Francisco, Pfeiffer.
4. Kets de Vries, M. F. R., P. Vrignaud, et al. (2004). "The Global Leadership Life Inventory: Development and Psychometric Properties of a 360-Degree Feedback Instrument." *Journal of Management Studies* 15(3): 475–492.
5. Kets de Vries, M. F. R. (2003). *The Personality Audit*. Fontainebleau, INSEAD.
6. Winnicott, D. W. (1951). *Transitional Objects and Transitional Phenomena. Collected Papers: Through Paediatrics to Psycho-analysis*. London, Tavistock Publications.
7. Goleman, D. (1995). *Emotional Intelligence*. London, Bloomsbury.
8. Salovey, P. and J. Mayer (1990). "Emotional Intelligence." *Imagination, Cognition, and Personality* 9: 185–211.
9. Toegel, G. and J. Conger (2003). "360-Degree Assessment: Time for Reinvention." *Academy of Management Learning & Education* 2(3): 279–296.

10. Kets de Vries, M. F. R. (2001). *The Leadership Mystique*. London, Financial Times/Prentice Hall.
11. Kets de Vries, M. F. R. (2001). *Struggling with the Demon: Essays in Individual and Organizational Irrationality*. Madison, Conn, Psychosocial Press.
12. Kets de Vries, M. F. R. (1999). "High Performance Teams: Lessons from the Pygmies." *Organizational Dynamics* 27(3): 66–77.
13. Levi, D. (2001). *Group Dynamics for Teams*. Thousand Oaks, CA, Sage.
14. Nadler, D. A. and J. L. Spencer (1998). *Executive Teams*. San Francisco, Jossey-Bass.
15. Scott Rutan, J. and W. N. Stone (2001). *Psychodynamic Group Psychotherapy*. New York, The Guilford Press.
16. Malan, D. and F. Osimo (1992). *Psychodynamics, Training, and Outcome in Brief Psychotherapy*. Oxford, Butterworth Heinemann.
17. McCullough Vaillant, L. (1997). *Changing Character*. New York, Basic Books.
18. Kilberg, R. R. (2000). *Executive Coaching*. Washington, D.C., American Psychological Association.
19. Atkinson, R. (1998). *The Life Story Interview*. Thousand Oaks, CA:, Sage.
20. McAdams, D. P. (1993). *Stories we Live by: Personal Myths and the Making of the Self*. New York, William Morrow and Company.
21. Solomon, R. C. and F. Flores (2003). *Building Trust: In Business, Politics, Relationships, and Life*. New York, Oxford University Press.
22. Morey, D., Ed (2002). *Knowledge Management: Classic and Contemporary Works*. Cambridge, MA, MIT Press.
23. Von Krogh, G., I. Nonaka and K. Ichijo (2000). *Enabling Knowledge Creation*. New York, Oxford University Press.

PART THREE

UNDERSTANDING THE PSYCHODYNAMICS OF GROUPS AND ORGANIZATIONS

CHAPTER 12

THE UNCONSCIOUS LIFE
OF GROUPS
AND ORGANIZATIONS

A team is like a baby tiger given to you at Christmas. It does a wonderful job of keeping the mice away for about 12 months, and then it starts to eat your kids.

—Anonymous

Large, centralized organizations foster alienation like stagnant ponds breed algae.

—Ricardo Semler

A manager's ability to turn meetings into a thinking environment is probably an organization's greatest asset.

—Nancy Kline

It is better to practice a little than talk a lot.

—Zen proverb

There's a Zen tale about an old man who had six sons. Though the man was kind and gentle, his sons were always fighting with each other. Their bitter rivalry didn't bode well for the future of their small family enterprise. Because the father was getting on in age, people close to him expressed concern about what would happen when he died. How would the sons deal with the inheritance? Would they be able to manage? Competitors saw the discord among the sons as an opportunity and threw oil on the fire by spreading false rumors about this son or that being favored in the old man's will.

One day, the old man asked his sons to come and see him. When they were all assembled, he gave them seven wooden sticks tightly bound together and said: "I will give one hundred gold coins to whichever one of you can break these sticks in two."

One by one, the sons tried to break the sticks but none of them was successful. They finally conceded defeat, chiding their father for giving them an impossible task. "Nobody could do it," they said. But the father responded, "Nothing is simpler." He untied the sticks and, taking them one by one, broke them in two.

The sons protested, saying, "Of course, anybody can break the sticks when they're untied." To which their father replied, "What has happened to these sticks could also happen to you one day. As long as all of you remain united, you'll be strong and nobody will be able to overcome you. But if you continue your fighting and don't find common ground, you too will be reduced to the state of the sticks you see lying on the ground."

As in this anecdote, a team or group that wants to function effectively within an organization must unite around what needs to be accomplished. Though each member of a team is important, there's no such thing as an individual that exists in isolation; everyone is part of a group. And everyone brings his or her uniqueness to the group. Thus, to understand the group, we have to understand the individuals who comprise it.

There's a curious circularity to group dynamics. Individuals become who they are in part because of the "group" they're born into: a person's early caretakers, who carry with them the influence of the social setting, influence that person's developing character [1]. In that way, and in the socializing process of school and friends, society enters the individual. In other words, social realities affect a person's intrapsychic life. But the influence goes the other way too: individuals influence group processes, from the likely democracy in which they vote, to the organization in which they work, to the biking club they establish.

Though unity is a prerequisite for group effectiveness, it's a rare commodity. The participants of a group typically have many different agendas when they first come together, and those agendas don't necessarily have anything to do with the primary task of the group. They may, in fact, be personal issues such as wanting to make peace, or needing to seek attention. Following these agendas, people take on various informal roles in additional to formal roles such as CEO or head of personnel—roles such as fool, victim, warrior, persecutor, rescuer, or provocateur. These informal roles sometimes help, but can just as easily hinder, the work that needs to be done. And to complicate the group process even further, issues such as the pressures of the environment, the nature of the task, the changes that the organization has experienced over time, and the history of the group all factor in.

As with most human behavior, the informal roles which people take on in groups are driven by needs that are more often than not unconscious; they're an intricate part of the participants' personality, so familiar and habitual that they're automatic. These informal roles are taken on to balance tensions, reduce anxieties, and gratify various emotional needs that originated in dysfunctional family dynamics. The problem is, sometimes people become trapped in the delusion that the drama of their lives, their self–scripted inner theater, constitutes their real and entire existence. This delusion makes for non–authentic identifications and emotional rigidity.

On a positive note, the taking on of informal roles can simplify communication among the members of a group. Likewise, in an organizational setting, informal roles that work well together in an executive role constellation can lead to more effective decision-making. With such a constellation, executives consciously or unconsciously take on the roles within a group that are most suitable to whatever task needs to be done. This complementarity creates a certain order in the interaction patterns. It's a division of emotional labor, if you will. Despite these potential positives, it's more likely that the adoption of informal roles in the workplace will result in rigidity and hamper creativity, because people interpret their roles as restricting them to narrowly defined parameters.

In addition to the formal and informal roles that people undertake, the group process is also colored by the history of the group. That history, over time, results in specific group "myths"—some explicit, some not—that form the basis of the group's collective "we" feelings. In every organization, there are cultural values, beliefs, norms, and behaviors that are affirmed and transmitted throughout the organization via stories. In studying life in organizations, I've noted that people are always telling stories (organizational myths) to each other that have particularly inspired or moved them—either in a positive or a negative way. Common organizational myths have to do with the founding of the company, critical leadership transition processes, the manner in which certain setbacks were dealt with, and so on. Members learn about the corporate culture and pass on its essential characteristics by telling such stories.

These organizational myths (even in the form of gossip) are an extremely powerful and often underestimated form of human communication, because they help maintain social order and determine behavior in unpredictable circumstances. But subjugation to these myths—like subjugation to a specific informal role—may come at the cost of personal responsibility and independence. Although there can certainly be positive myths about an organization that translate into guiding norms contributing to a positive team spirit and the facilitation of goal-directed behavior, there can also be myths that block the effective execution of important tasks.

When dysfunctional myths take the upper hand, the organization is particularly susceptible to the phenomenon of "groupthink," whereby members of the group attempt to conform their individual opinions to what they believe to be the consensus of the group. When groupthink prevails, decision-making suffers. Under the sway of groupthink, the members of a group don't consider all alternatives; instead, they give preference to people and programs that subscribe to the prevailing "ideology."

Groupthink gives an illusion of unanimity which creates enormous pressure on group members to conform to whatever the predominating form of thinking is assumed to be [2]. In addition to the self-censorship that forces individuals to align with the group, organizations hampered by groupthink typically harbor "mind guards"—individuals who encourage others to toe what they see as the company line, discouraging all forms of individuality. Diversity is experienced as a threat; conflict within the group is suppressed or denied. The pressure is great: participate in the prevailing outlook of the group or be excommunicated. Those who dare to deviate become scapegoats.

The work of psychiatrist and psychoanalyst Wilfred Bion is extremely helpful to an understanding of groupthink and other group phenomena that cause groups to derail. In researching the psychodynamics of human interaction, Bion identified three basic assumptions that people make, a trio that's one of the cornerstones of group theory [3]. These basic assumptions—which take place at an unconscious level—create interaction patterns that often make it hard for people to work together productively. They're regressive—that is, they lead to more primitive, not more advanced, patterns of functioning—and thus they deflect people from the principal tasks that need to be performed in the organization. According to Bion, groups subject to these regressive assumptions eventually retreat into a world of their own. The result is often delusional ideation—in other words, ideas completely detached from reality—which is fertile soil for the proliferation of dysfunctional decision-making and organizational pathology.

The Spanish surrealist filmmaker Luis Buñuel portrays the regressive potential of groups brilliantly in his film *The Exterminating Angel*. In that film, a group of socially prominent guests arrive at an elegantly appointed home for a dinner party. Once the dinner is over and the guests retire to the drawing room, they discover that the servants have gone away and that they themselves, for some mysterious reason, seem unable to leave the room. There's no explanation—there are no locked doors or barred windows preventing the guests from leaving—but they're convinced that they're stranded.

As time goes by, the film's bourgeois characters become increasingly incapable of functioning as rational human beings. They give in to fear, superstition, and irrationality as the disasters mount. Left to their own devices, they gradually degenerate into genteel savagery. The fancy tuxedos and pristine makeup dissolve into a pigpen of disgust and temper tantrums; dignified conversations segue to biting insults. Men and women search for private corners where they can indulge in activities they would never have dreamed of participating in before. They violently break a water main to quench their thirst; they kill and eat sheep in a sort of religious ritual to fill their stomachs. By the end, the household has become a portrait of total chaos. All the elaborate pretenses and facades that the wealthy guests had built up by virtue of their position in society collapse completely as people are reduced to animal behavior. In this richly symbolic and subtly allegorical tale on the nature of human behavior, Luis Buñuel strips away all social pretense and exposes the fundamentally archaic, primitive nature that signifies the human soul.

With that example of a group run amok, let's take a close look at Bion's three assumptions, and the regressive processes they launch in the workplace.

BASIC GROUP ASSUMPTIONS

Bion's three assumptions are dependency, fight–flight, and pairing. We'll look at each in turn.

Dependency. Individuals in groups often assume—at an unconscious level—that the leader or organization can and should offer protection and guidance similar to that offered in earlier years by parents. Groups relying on what Bion labels the dependency assumption are looking for a strong, charismatic leader to lead the way. The members of such groups are united by common feelings of helplessness, inadequacy, neediness, and fear of the outside world. They perceive the leader as omnipotent and readily give up their autonomy when they perceive help at hand. Remarks typical of groups subject to this process include, "What do you want me/ us to do?" and "I can't make this kind of decision; you'll have to talk to my boss." Such comments reflect the employees' anxiety, insecurity, and professional and emotional immaturity. While unquestioning faith in a leader contributes to goal-directedness and cohesiveness, it also impairs followers' critical judgment and leaves them unwilling to take initiative. Though they're prepared to carry out their leader's directives, they require him or her to take all the initiative and do all the thinking. And once a leader whom followers leaned heavily on is gone, bureaucratic inertia may take hold. People may be frozen in the past, wondering what their leader—if he or she were still around—would have done.

Fight-flight. Another common unconscious assumption is that the organizational world is a dangerous place and organizational participants must resort to fight or flight as defense mechanisms. In groups subject to the fight–flight assumption, an outlook of avoidance or attack predominates. When the fight–flight mechanism takes hold, people have a tendency to split the world into camps of friends and enemies. Fight reactions manifest themselves in aggression against the self, against peers (in the form of envy, jealousy, competition, elimination, boycotting, sibling rivalry, fighting for a position in the group, and privileged relationships with authority figures), or against authority itself. Flight reactions include avoidance of others, absenteeism, and giving up. Remarks typical of people in a fight-flight situation include, "Let's not give those updated figures to the contracts department; they'll just try to take all the credit," and "This organization would be in good shape if it weren't for the so-and-sos who run the place." That sort of us-versus-them language is common. People subject to the fight-flight assumption never take personal responsibility for problems; instead, they routinely (and vindictively) assign blame elsewhere. Subscribing to a rigid, bipolar view of the world, they seek protection from and conquest of "the enemy," in all its varied manifestations.

When not only a group but also its leaders fall victim to the fight-flight assumption, the trouble multiplies exponentially. Externalizing their own internal problems, such leaders inflame their followers against real and/or imagined enemies, using the in-group/out-group division to motivate people and to channel emerging anxiety outward. The shared search for and fight against enemies results in a strong (but rigid) conviction among group members of the correctness and righteousness of their cause, and it energizes them to pursue that cause. It also reinforces the group's identity [4]–[5]. Leaders who encourage fight-flight mechanisms by radiating certainty and conviction create meaning for followers who feel lost—but it's a false meaning, even though the sense of unity it inspires is highly reassuring. Highly dangerous too: followers, confident that their leader's way is the only true way, eliminate doubters and applaud converts, thereby increasing their dependence on their leader.

Pairing. Bion's third unconscious assumption is that pairing up with an individual or group perceived as powerful will help a person cope with anxiety, alienation, and loneliness. Wanting to feel secure but also to be creative, people experiencing the pairing assumption fantasize that the most effective creation will take place in groups of two. Unfortunately, pairing also implies splitting up. The inevitable diversity within groups may result in intra- and inter-group conflict, which in turn may prompt individuals or groups to split up the larger group and build a smaller system—one in which a person can belong and feel secure. This assumption also manifests itself in ganging up against the perceived aggressor or authority figure. In the pairing mode, often seen in high-tech companies, grandiose, unrealistic ideas about innovation may become more important than practicality and profitability. Remarks typical within an organization subject to the pairing assumption include, "Leave it to the two of us; we can solve this problem," and "If only the CEO and COO had a better relationship, our company would be in really good shape."

Social defenses. The basic assumptions discussed above all reveal underlying anxiety about the world and one's place in it. When these assumptions prevail in the workplace, they offer strong proof that the organization's leadership isn't dealing adequately with the emerging anxiety of working in a social setting [1]; [6]–[10]. When the level of anxiety rises in an organization, and its leadership is unable to provide a sufficiently secure holding environment, executives typically rely on existing structures (such as rules, regulations, procedures, organization charts, job descriptions, and organization-specific ways of solving problems) to "contain" that anxiety. When those structures offer insufficient containment—that is, when there are no opportunities to discuss and work through emerging concerns—people in organizations engage in regressive defenses such as splitting, projection, displacement, and denial.

When such defenses become contagious and are adopted organization-wide, we call them social defenses. They can be viewed as new structures, new systems of relationships within the social structure, constructed to help people deal with anxiety, often at the cost of executing the primary task of the organization. The purpose of social defenses (which are like individual defenses, but woven into the fabric of an organization) is to transform and neutralize strong tensions and feelings such as anxiety, shame, guilt, envy, jealousy, rage, sexual frustration, and low self-esteem. As anyone who has stood around a water cooler kibitzing about office politics knows, most organizations are full of things that need to be defended against—threats of layoffs and takeovers, power plays by this underling or that supervisor, and so on—resulting in a veritable miasma of depressive and paranoid anxiety [8]. To combat these "dangers," social defenses work to assure the organizational participants that the workplace is really safe and accepting.

Now, a certain amount of defending, whether individual or social, is a good thing. But when social defenses no longer target a specific, temporary danger but become the organization's dominant mode of operation—the permanent, accepted way of dealing with the angst and unpredictability of life in organizations—they become dysfunctional for the organization as a whole. Though they may still serve a purpose (albeit not constructively), they have become bureaucratic obstacles, embedded in the organizational structure. Once firmly entrenched, they have cultural implications for the whole organization.

For example, the insidious influence of social defenses may contribute to passive-aggressive behavior patterns. In other words, people may routinely express anger and resentment over organizational issues indirectly rather than directly—that is, through negative attitudes and behaviors that are at odds with overtly stated motives. While the organizational culture may have a veneer of cooperation, people block every new idea presented. People who suggest new ideas feel as if they're walking in syrup: there are plenty of sweet promises of cooperation, but nothing gets done; no one follows through. One seemingly rational reason after another is given why it's so difficult for the suggested new project to get off the ground.

Another cultural problem that social defenses foster is rampant indecisiveness. When key executives in an organization are so hungry for certainty in an inherently uncertain world that they can't face the consequences of making mistakes, decision paralysis turns into the prevailing modus operandi. In a culture of indecision, as in a passive-aggressive culture, nothing of substance ever seems to get done. Indecision saps the organization's "social operating mechanisms"—the meetings, reviews, and other situations through which people in the corporation do business—of open, constructive dialogue. Instead of talking honestly about straight facts, decision-makers send underlings off to do information-gathering and analysis and then still more information-gathering and yet more analysis. But all that research doesn't do them any good: there's always a certain amount of ambiguity associated with all the various options and contingencies. It's common for organizations permeated by indecisiveness to hire one consulting firm after the other in an effort to break the impasse in decision-making. Yet the lengthy reports that the consultants produce only add to the indecisiveness. After much expenditure of energy (and a considerable waste of resources), the decision-makers are back exactly at their starting point, and nothing has been done.

Social defenses can also contribute to what can be described as a "culture of process." In organizations with that sort of culture, ritualistic activities that don't contribute to the future success of the organization take precedence over substance. These ritualistic activities—administrative procedures, task forces, and such things—are invoked to deal with the helplessness that people in these organizations feel in the face of uncertainties, ambivalence, and real or imagined dangers. The benefit of such activities is that they predetermine people's actions, restricting thoughts and behaviors before they get out of control. They keep people emotionally uninvolved and thus help them feel safe and in control. While such a way of operating does in fact serve its original purpose—to reduce anxiety—it also replaces compassion, empathy, awareness, and meaning with formality, control, and impersonality. Anxiety comes down because people think that strict performance of the acts in the ritual will ward off some perceived danger, but as these acts gradually obscure personal and organizational realities, people become detached from their inner experience. The bottom-line result? A culture of process guarantees that very little of substance ever gets done.

THE ORGANIZATIONAL IDEAL

Looking further into group and organizational pathology, we discover that many executives experience the need to create idealistic, powerful images of the organizations in which they work. In other words, they create an idealized organization in the mind [11]–[13]. This organizational ideal can be viewed as a wish, something to be desired, a fantasy of the organization that an organizational participant cherishes deep inside him- or herself. Such a construction makes that participant feel stronger, more adequate, and more capable. It becomes part of that person's implicit internalized value set of the organization and his or her social identity. Like all images in the mind, this one can be conscious, preconscious, or unconscious.

Such ideal concepts of the desired organization can be beneficial for the organization, in that they encourage the organizational participant to strive for this desired state. That striving, particularly when the idealization is shared by many people, is a powerful force in creating a highly effective organization. Furthermore, the organizational ideal has other important psychological functions. It takes on a containment role, helping executives deal with the feelings of anxiety that inevitably result in organizations. As the organizational participants identify with the organization—as they perceive the organization as an extremely powerful, perfect entity—their level of anxiety about the dangers in the environment decreases. What could go wrong in this powerful, all-knowing organization? What heights could be reached in this organization where nothing is impossible?

This sort of idealization has its roots in memories of the childhood experience of being loved and protected by powerful caretakers. As we saw in the discussion of narcissism in Chapter 2, as children grow up they incorporate and internalize aspects of the persons they love, admire, or even fear. Furthermore, they have fantasies about what their parents imagine the "ideal child" to be. They also imagine the "ideal self" (the desired state one would like to attain) and the "ideal relation" (the optimal relation one desires). Narcissistic satisfaction is achieved through efforts to reduce the degree to which the present, the real self, and the ideal self differ. The "organizational ideal" is really a variant of what psychoanalysts describe as the ego ideal. But the organizational ideal, like the ego ideal, is really a fantasy that's rarely attained.

The development of the organizational ideal follows a course similar to that of the ego ideal. The organizational ideal is based on a set of identifications based on heroic stories of the organization's achievements that start with one person and then are shared. These stories capture the imagination of the organization's participants and are internalized. These ideal images of the organization, maintained through storytelling, symbols, and ritualistic activities, together are part of the organization's mythology. This idealization process is a never-ending, perceptually fluid activity.

And, because a bold and stimulating organizational ideal creates pride in the organization, organizational leadership encourages (often unconsciously) the dissemination and acceptance of powerful idealized images. At every occasion, public or otherwise, employees are given opportunities to assimilate imagined and desired attributes, values, and attitudes into this organizational ideal. They're expected to identify with what the organization stands for, with its leadership, and with each other. This process of mutual identification contributes to a sense of community [14].

Another way of understanding the influence of the organizational ideal is to recognize it as a transferential process (see Chapter 2, among others). We need to realize that transferential phenomena are not limited to people but also occur between people and organizations [15]–[17]. In effect, leaders who encourage an organizational ideal strengthen their employees' psychological bonding to the organization. In organizational transference, positive qualities originally ascribed to a specific person or persons are transferred to the institution. In other words, executives project human qualities upon the organization; they act as if these properties are part of the organization. Thus the organization as a whole becomes invested with deeply emotional, psychological meaning.

Although the presence of an exalted organizational ideal has its advantages, as I noted earlier—it may drive people to engage in extraordinary efforts—members of an organization under the banner of solidarity can identify themselves so strongly with the organization and its leadership that it impairs their personal judgment. Insecure, dependent organizational participants who want the organization to help them solidify their own identity are precisely those who have the greatest need to believe in an organizational ideal. As the leaders of the organization impart their exalted version of the organizational ideal to their subordinates, they're catering to the dependency needs of their subordinates. That's only one step away from groupthink.

In many organizations, leaders engage in subtle (and sometimes not so subtle) coercive practices that give their people little choice but to subscribe to the prevailing "ideology," as represented by the idealized organizational imagery. When that occurs, people are drawn into a collusive, regressive psychological relationship with the organization and its leaders that revives earlier narcissistic dependency needs. The result is what we call identity deformation—in other words, the subjugation of the self (and one's belief system) to "the party line." People who have the courage to challenge the prevailing organizational ideal are made to feel that they're not living up to expectations, that they're responsible for any problems the organization has. The pressures to conform are such that not participating in the organizational ideal becomes a very unattractive option.

Under such circumstances, a totally unrealistic, glorified organizational ideal may emerge—an ideal which suggests that the organization is incapable of error. It will block any effort to implement change. When leaders successfully push this collective fantasy to the extent that it becomes delusional, reality-testing is lost and failure is imminent. When such a fantasy becomes the prevailing currency, people and companies stop learning from experience—after all, there's no need to learn from mistakes when mistakes are impossible—and lose the ability to be self-critical. With organizational participants locked by their own hand inside a narcissistic capsule, companies enter a downward, helical spiral.

Many organizational disasters have resulted from the inability to let go of an organizational ideal that's far removed from reality. NASA's Challenger disaster is one of the more prominent examples. On January 28, 1986, seven astronauts were killed when the Challenger, the space shuttle they were piloting, exploded just over a minute into the flight. A commission reviewing the accident produced evidence showing that NASA officials had ordered the launch to go ahead despite repeated safety warnings. And you know the rest: the solid rocket booster O-rings failed to seal properly, allowing hot combustion gases to leak from the side of the booster and burn through the external fuel tank. The commission attributed the failure of the O-ring to several factors, including faulty design of the solid rocket boosters, insufficient low-temperature testing of the O-ring material and of the joints that the O-ring sealed, and lack of proper communication between different levels of NASA management.

One interpretation of the disaster—the clinical interpretation that I favor—is that the engineers at NASA identified themselves so strongly with the organization and its leadership that their critical judgment was impaired. NASA had created such a glorified organizational ideal for itself that it viewed itself as infallible, incapable of error but capable of all else. It was the perfect organization. Due to prevailing psychological pressures, this collective fantasy had become so strong within NASA that it stifled reality-testing. Employees lost the courage of their convictions, becoming reluctant to challenge questionable decisions. In such a climate, it was unimaginable that any part of the space shuttle would malfunction. In hindsight, the defective O-rings can be viewed as symbolizing the burned wings of Icarus who, enraptured by his illusions of grandeur, tried to fly to the sun, only to tumble back to earth when his wings melted.

Unfortunately, NASA seems to have learned little from the Challenger accident—demonstrating the insidious survival power of an unrealistic organizational ideal. Seventeen years later, on February 1, 2003, foam falling off the external fuel tank during flight precipitated an explosion that destroyed the space shuttle Columbia and took the lives of its seven astronauts. The events leading up to the destruction of the Columbia indicated the same intense pressures on NASA staff and a similar pattern of disregarded warnings and ignored safety standards culminating in tragedy.

In spite of a concerted effort on the part of certain NASA leaders to change the mindset of the people working on the space program, recent incidents have demonstrated that NASA's organizational ideal is still not in touch with reality. In spite of years of reviews of what caused the Challenger's and the Columbia's explosions, a new disaster was just around the corner when a chunk of insulating foam broke away from the space shuttle Discovery after its launching on July 26, 2005. (This was NASA's first launch since the Columbia disaster.) Immediately after the incident occurred, the shuttle program managers—visibly shaken—announced their decision to ground the space shuttle fleet. Questionable judgment was to blame for this incident as well. NASA's contention that it had constructed the safest fuel tank in shuttle history was shattered two minutes into the flight. According to experts, the malfunctioning in this final case could have led to another disaster if it had happened one minute earlier. Fortunately, in this instance, the shuttle made it safely home [18].

We can conclude from all these incidents, which reveal a mindset of grandiosity, that NASA is still far from being a true learning organization. The narcissistic capsule of assumed perfection that NASA has nurtured over the years needs to be truly broken. That won't be easy, given the unconscious, subtle nature of the fantasy life of the executives working there. Their organizational ideal has taken on a life of its own, sacrificing safe and effective execution of space programs along the way.

Another example of an organizational ideal that turned dysfunctional can be found in a commercial electronics firm whose employees believed they made the most creative designs in the world, for their field. Undeniably, the designers at this "boutique" firm were extremely creative in making designs different from the ordinary. But though they'd been very successful in the past, gradually their designs had become so avant-garde that they didn't sell well in the marketplace and the balance sheet began to show red.

Despite this downward shift, the senior executives in the organization, holding firm to their organizational ideal, continued to act as if there were nothing to worry about. They ignored the external forces of the marketplace and kept on designing as they always had. Though on a few occasions large technology companies had bailed them out by giving them a cash injection, the company's denial of market reality eventually became obvious to outsiders. Some of the larger investors decided to get rid of the CEO—the original source of the corrupted organizational ideal—and replace him with a numbers man. The incoming CEO announced at his first meeting with senior management that, given the sales figures, he had decided to close one of their major factories, a plant that provided employment for a large part of the region. In explaining the move he said, "Money seems to be a dirty word in this organization. The only thing that counts here is design. That way of looking at the marketplace cannot continue!"

NEUROTIC ORGANIZATIONS

The basic group assumptions, social defenses, and toxic organizational ideals that we've been talking about don't simply materialize out of thin air; these processes have a history. The repetition of phenomena such as these in a given workplace suggests the existence of shared scripts in the inner theater of the key power-holders. Organizations tend to reflect the personalities of their leaders [19]–[20], because leaders externalize and act out their inner theater on the public stage of the organization. Their inner dramas develop into corporate cultures, structures, and specific patterns of decision-making. Because leaders "institutionalize" the themes of their inner theater, their influence may continue long after they themselves have gone, determining how the next generation in power runs things.

Exemplary leaders help their companies to become highly effective organizations, while dysfunctional leaders contribute to a dysfunctional organizational culture and organizational "neurosis." In assessing organizational pathology and observing "neurotic" companies, I've found five dominant organizational constellations—each with its own organizational culture, strategic style, and underlying guiding theme—that tend to recur repeatedly (and often in "hybrid" form). If I may simplify via archetypical methodology, these can be summarized as the dramatic/cyclothymic organization, the suspicious organization, the compulsive organization, the detached organization, and the depressive organization.

ORGANIZATIONAL ARCHETYPES

Let's look at the salient aspects of each type of organization.

Dramatic/cyclothymic organizations. The senior executives in dramatic/cyclothymic organizations have an intense drive to receive positive attention from outsiders. They like to impress others with "flow"-type experiences, favor superficiality in all things (e.g., they wear a "happy" mask), demonstrate great swings of emotions, often act on the basis of hunches and gut feelings, and tend to react (or overreact) to minor events. In dramatic/ cyclothymic organizations, senior executives typically have a sense of being in control of their destiny; they don't feel that they're at the mercy of events. Because such leaders tend to follow their own intuitions and dreams, the decision-making in their organizations is marked by boldness, risk-taking, and flamboyance.

Richard Branson's Virgin Group, a very successful company by any account, is an example of a dramatic/cyclothymic organization. The CEO in this organization seeks attention, craves excitement, and opts for drama. Its culture supports the emotional needs of both the leader and the people who work for him. Its strategy is somewhere between bold and impulsive, and its guiding theme can be described as "We want to get attention from and impress the people who count in the world."

Suspicious organizations. Suspicious organizations are characterized by a general atmosphere of distrust and paranoia (especially among the leadership), hypersensitivity to hidden meanings and motivations as well as to relationships and organizational issues, hyper-alertness for problems, and a constant, vigilant lookout for the "enemy." People in these types of organizations are always looking over their shoulder to see who's trying to get them, and searching for ways to confirm their suspicions of others. Because they're looking so hard, they usually find someone or something that they think justifies their paranoia.

The focus on external threats in suspicious organizations leads to a centralization of power and to a conservative, reactive business strategy in which initiative is stifled and inappropriate and rigid responses become commonplace. The former empire of the late Robert Maxwell and the FBI under its director J. Edgar Hoover are good examples of suspicious organizations. Many emerging Russian organizations have similar characteristics [21].

Compulsive organizations. Compulsive organizations are preoccupied with trivialities and characterized by a highly rigid and well-defined set of rules, along with elaborate information systems and ritualized, exhaustive evaluation procedures. These organizations, thorough and exact to a fault, are slow and nonadaptive. Their strategy is tightly calculated and focused, driven by reliance on a narrow, well-established theme (e.g., cost-cutting or quality) to the exclusion of all other factors. Compulsive organizations generally have a hierarchy in which individual executives' status derives directly from their specific position in the hierarchy. Relationships are defined in terms of control and submission. Such organizations have an almost total lack of spontaneity, because a constant sense of anxiety underlies all activities (e.g., "Will we do it right?" "Will they do it right?" "Can we let them do it?" "How will it threaten us?").

IBM under the leadership of John Akers had many of the characteristics of the compulsive organization. In that case, it took Louis Gerstner, with his absolute determination to dispel the rigidity and expand the focus, to break the ritualistic, inward-looking spell—but only when the company had already bled hundreds of millions of dollars [22].

Detached organizations. A cold, unemotional atmosphere characterizes detached organizations; non-involvement with others in and outside the organization is the norm. This organizational climate derives from a leadership that steers clear of hands-on involvement, believing that it's safer to remain distant and isolated than to grow close and collaborative. These organizations, indifferent to praise and criticism alike, are characterized by a lack of excitement and enthusiasm. With top leaders standing back, there's often a leadership vacuum that leads to destructive gamesmanship among mid- and lower-level executives and allows inconsistent and vacillating strategies to flourish. Intolerant of the dependency needs of others, leaders at all levels establish individual fiefdoms and set up barriers that prevent the free flow of information. The empire of the hermit leader Howard Hughes (an empire made up of casinos, Hughes Tool, Pan Am, and other organizations) possessed many of these detached characteristics [23].

Depressive organizations. Inactivity, lack of confidence, extreme conservatism, and insularity are the chief features of depressive organizations. These organizations have a profoundly low sense of pride, often due to skeletons in the closet. With the past dominating their thinking, these organizations are characterized by a strong sense of indecision, an unwillingness to take risks (even small ones), a focus on diminishing or outmoded markets, an undeveloped sense of competition, and apathetic and inactive leadership. These organizations often become extremely bureaucratic and hierarchical, inhibiting meaningful change.

Many companies who do work for governments are depressive organizations, or hybrids that blend depressive and compulsive traits. The Disney empire in the years after the death of its founder was likewise depressive: the successors were at a loss as to how to proceed, and thus simply stagnated for a time. Reader's Digest after the death of its founder suffered a similar fate [20].

STRENGTHS OF EACH STYLE

Each of the neurotic styles described above generally starts out, in diluted form, as a virtue, contributing to an organization's success;

only later, when there's "too much of a good thing," does it become a weakness. Let's look at the strengths of each style.

Organizations characterized by the dramatic/cyclothymic style create entrepreneurial initiatives. They're able to develop a momentum that carries them through critical organizational plateaus and times of organizational revitalization. However, when decisions become too centralized in the hands of the entrepreneur—at the cost of the creative potential of other layers in the organization— the dramatic style becomes a handicap.

Suspicious-style organizations have a good knowledge of threats and opportunities outside the organization and are able to use this knowledge to reduce risks of failure. When taken to excess, however, the suspicious outlook can turn an otherwise healthy organization into a police state.

Compulsive-style organizations are often efficiently operated businesses with finely tuned internal organizational controls and a focused overall strategy. However, if too much analysis leads to paralysis, the thoroughness that was a virtue early in the organization's life cycle becomes a detriment when circumstances call for speed.

Detached-style organizations enjoy the influence of people from various levels in the development of their overall strategy; they're typically willing to consider a broad variety of points of view. But their oscillation, their lack of consistency, and the non-hands-on quality of their leadership can be their downfall.

Organizations marked by the depressive style are noted for their consistency of internal processes. If the maintenance of these internal processes becomes completely detached from the market-place, however, the organization is doomed.

The above set of organizational archetypes provides a framework that can be brought to bear when the need for change is apparent. In an organization that's struggling, an analysis of the prevailing neurotic organizational style can help executives figure out why the organization continues to perpetuate various behaviors and why people resist attempts to change. It helps answer questions such as "Why does X keep happening?" and "Why does something that works someplace else not work here?" Identifying the prevailing neurotic style can also help executives (and others) understand otherwise incomprehensible behavior and actions on the part of their colleagues. For new executives entering a troubled organization, an understanding of the prevailing neurotic style can help to shape their expectations about what needs to be done and what can be done. Finally, for executives at any stage in their career, the neurotic archetypes serve as a warning: the exposed position of and heightened pressure on leaders can encourage extreme manifestations of any emotional instability they have.

PLACING LEADERS ON THE COUCH

Leaders must be able to design effective systems and structures, but those skills alone are no guarantee of success. High performance requires that leaders also be able to create an organizational culture where the people doing the work are committed to excellence. To do so they must understand group processes, social defenses, the organizational ideal, and organizational neurosis.

In this chapter I've highlighted organizational situations where reality-testing has been lost. All such situations are an indictment of leadership. Leaders have the responsibility to prevent pathological group behavior, inappropriate social defenses, and toxic organizational cultures. Because of that responsibility, leaders need to be prepared to symbolically "lie on the couch"—that is, permit an audit of their attitudes and activities to assess the mental health of their organization. And if those are found wanting, leaders need to not only accept organizational change but spearhead it.

Because organizational neurosis is rooted in personal neurosis, organizational change is predicated on personal change. Thus leaders have to learn to challenge their habits and limitations, and act from real choice. Such a confrontation with the self is the only way to not repeat the past. As has been said a number of times in this book, leaders who hope to change need to learn what drives their inner world; they need to recognize the salient themes in their inner theater. To change responses and behaviors in their external world, they need first to change what's happening in their internal world. When they see how hard it is to change themselves, they'll be more aware of the challenges that lie ahead in changing others. The good news is that, as leaders change, others will change as well. To quote Mahatma Gandhi, "We must become the change we want to see."

REFERENCES

1. Foulkes, S. H. (1975). *Group Analytic Psychotherapy: Mehods and Principles*. London, Gordon & Breach.
2. Janis, I. L. (1971). "Groupthink." *Psychology Today* Nov: 43–46.
3. Bion, W. R. (1959). *Experiences in Groups*. London, Tavistock.
4. Lasswell, H. (1960). *Psychopathology and Politics*. New York, Viking Press.
5. Volcan, V. (1988). *The Need to have Enemies and Allies*. Northvale, NJ, Jason Aronson.
6. Anzieux, D. (1984). *The Group and the Unconscious*. London, Routledge.
7. Jaques, E. (1974). *Social Systems as Defense Against Persecutory and Depressive Anxiety. Analysis of Groups*. Eds G. S. Gibbard, J. J. Hartmann and R. D. Mann. San Francisco, Jossey-Bass.
8. Klein, M. (1988). *Love, Guilt and Reparation*. London: Virago Press.
9. Kreeger, L., Ed (1975). *The Large Group: Dynamics and Therapy*. London, Karnac.
10. Menzies, I. E. (1960). "A Case Study of the Functioning of Social Systems as a Defense against Anxiety: A Report on a Study of the Nursing System in a General Hospital." *Human Relations* 13: 95–121.

11. Armstrong, D. (2005). *Organization in the Mind*. London, Karnac.
12. Hirschhorn, L. (1990). *The Workplace Within: Psychodynamics of Organizational Life*. Boston, MIT Press.
13. Schwartz, H. (1990). *Narcissistic Process and Corporate Decay: The Theory of the Organization Ideal*. New York: New York University Press.
14. Freud, S. (1921). "Group Psychology and the Analysis of the Ego," *The Standard Edition of the Complete Psychological Works of Sigmund Freud. Vol. 7*. J. Strachey (editor and translator). London: The Hogarth Press and the Institute of Psychoanalysis.
15. Levinson, H. (1965). "Reciprocation: The Relationship between Man and Organization." *Administrative Science Quarterly* 9: 370–390.
16. Levinson, H. (1972). *Organizational Diagnosis*. Cambridge, Mass., Harvard University Press.
17. Levinson, H. (2002). *Organizational Assessment*. Washington, DC, American Psychological Association.
18. Schwartz, J., A. C. Revkin and M. Wald (2005). *International Herald Tribune*: 2.
19. Kets de Vries, M. F. R. and D. Miller (1984). *The Neurotic Organization*. San Francisco, Jossey-Bass.
20. Kets de Vries, M. F. R. and D. Miller (1988). *Unstable at the Top*. New York, New American Library.
21. Kets de Vries, M. F. R., S. Shekshnia, K. Korotov and E. Florent-Treacy (2004). *The New Russian Business Leaders*. Cheltenham, UK, Edward Elgar.
22. Gerstner, L. (2002). *Who Says Elephants Can't Dance?* New York, Harper Business.
23. Hack, R. (2001). *Hughes*. Beverly Hills, New Millenium Press.

CHAPTER 13

UNRAVELING THE MYSTERY OF ORGANIZATIONS

You know that a conjurer gets no credit when once he has explained his trick; and if I show you too much of my method of working, you will come to the conclusion that I am a very ordinary individual after all.

—Sherlock Holmes, A Study in Scarlet

These are much deeper waters than I had thought.

—Sherlock Holmes, The Reigate Puzzle

Nothing clears up a case so much as stating it to another person.

—Sherlock Holmes, Silver Blaze

The obstacle is the path.

—Zen proverb

The riddles presented in Zen and the mysteries Sherlock Holmes was asked to solve have much in common. In both situations the observer is asked to enter a domain that's beyond the obvious. For example, in a Zen story a merchant loaded with bales of cotton decided to take a rest from the heat of the day within a shelter dominated by a large stone Buddha. When he woke up, he discovered that all his goods had disappeared. Despondently, he reported the matter to the police. The judge assigned to the case decided that the stone Buddha must be responsible. Ordering the Buddha's arrest, he said, "He's supposed to look after people but failed in his holy duty."

The police brought the stone Buddha to court. A noisy crowd gathered, curious to hear what kind of sentence the judge would give the statue. Angry with the boisterous crowd, the judge announced that he was holding the whole bunch of them in contempt of court and imposed both a fine and an imprisonment. Although the crowd hastened to apologize, the judge still imposed the fine: he sentenced each of them to bring a bale of cotton to the court. If they failed to do so, a prison sentence would follow.

The next day the merchant and the judge watched as person after person arrived bearing a bale of cotton. The merchant recognized one of the bales as his, so the police were able to arrest the thief. The merchant recovered all his goods, and the judge returned the remaining cotton bales to the people.

CLINICAL ORGANIZATIONAL INTERVENTIONS

In Part Two of this book I described ways to go about changing the mindset of executives. But changing the mindset of one executive (or a group of them) isn't the same as bringing systematic change in an organization, as the previous chapter's exploration of the psychodynamics of groups showed. Fostering individual and system-wide change through organizational interventions is something most organizations will face repeatedly—and they usually need help to do it. Enter a general consultant or a specially trained change agent. Unfortunately, as was suggested in earlier chapters, far too many people—change-agents and consultants—and the executives who hire them—are inclined to focus on the symptoms of an organizational problem and ignore the underlying causes. More often than not, they deal only with surface behavior. Such consultants can be very talented at numbers-crunching—they're like brains on a stick when it comes to cold facts—but not very good at paying attention to the elusive signals that reveal the heartbeat of an organization. Too often, their slogan is, What can't be directly seen doesn't really exist. Thus they resort to over-simplified quick fixes in trying to institute change [1]–[2].

When change agents want to change particular behavior patterns in an individual (or cluster of individuals), their usual impulse is to put a simplistic behavioral modification program into place. Such a program may have a positive effect, to be sure—but that effect won't last very long. Making that sort of an intervention is like trying to change the weather by turning up the heating system inside one's house. It may keep the inhabitants warmer for a time, but it won't change the temperature outside.

FOCAL AREAS OF INTERVENTION

As any executive knows, the cost of poor leadership, ineffectual management teams, mistaken hiring decisions, corporate culture clashes after a merger or acquisition, and inadequate succession planning can be steep (though not precisely calculable). Likewise, the cost of a large-scale traditional management consultancy effort is high—and that cost is wasted when such an effort is directed at problems that are in essence deeply psychologically rooted but are treated as procedural. When organizational problems are centered on interpersonal communication, group processes, social defenses, uneven leadership, and organization-wide neurosis, money is better spent on the three-dimensional approach to organizational assessment and intervention that clinically informed consultants or change agents employ.

Consultants well versed in the clinical paradigm understand the levers that drive individual and organizational change, and they know just how complex the change process (and the individuals changing) can be. Furthermore, they know how to help people give up their resistances, express their emotions in a situation-appropriate manner, and cultivate a perception of self and others that's in accord with reality [3]–[4]. They also recognize that if system-wide change is going to happen, they need to highlight the "pain" in the system, link past to present through a new vision, help the key players buy into the change effort, and reconfigure systems, structures, cultural elements, and behavior patterns. They know how to help an organization's leadership create a shared mindset, build attitudes that contribute to changed behavior, train for a new set of competencies, create small "wins" leading to improved performance, and set up appropriate reward systems for people who support the intended changes.

Typical areas where the clinically informed consultant can make a contribution include:

- identifying and changing dysfunctional leadership styles
- creating effective executive role constellations
- resolving interpersonal conflict, intergroup conflict, and various forms of collusive relationships (e.g., folie à deux)
- disentangling social defenses
- making sense of organizational cultures
- assessing organizational pathology
- bringing neurotic organizations back to health
- making knowledge management systems work
- creating high-performance teams and high-performance organizations
- planning for more orderly leadership succession

- helping in career planning
- untangling knotty family business problems
- helping create a better work-life balance for leaders and subordinates

Clinically informed consultants use as one crucial source of data the ways in which members of the organization interact with them. What differentiates these consultants from their more traditional counterparts is their skill at using transferential and countertransferential manifestations as a basic experiential and diagnostic tool. The ever-present "triangle of relationships"—in this case, a triangle comprised of the person being interviewed, some significant past "other" from that person's life, and the change agent/consultant—provides a conceptual framework for assessing patterns of response and then pointing out the similarity of past relationships to what's going on in the present. Anyone hoping to make sense of interpersonal encounters at anything but an intuitive level needs to understand these earlier described transferential processes, which are a major part of the clinical consultant's change toolbox.

Clinically informed consultants also recognize the importance of projective identification, a concept introduced in Chapter 6. A psychological defense against unwanted feelings or fantasies, projective identification is a mode of communication as well as a type of human relationship [5]. We can see this process in action when covert dynamics among individuals or groups of individuals get played out in parallel form by other individuals or groups with which they interact. For example, if executives in a department deny or reject (and thus alter) an uncomfortable experience by imagining that it belongs to another group of executives, that latter group—the recipients of the projection—are inducted into the situation by subtle pressure from the first group to think, feel, and act in congruence with the received projection.

Paying attention to transference, countertransference, and projective identification, clinically informed consultants process their observations, looking for thematic unity [6]. They then employ pattern-matching, looking for structural parallels within multi-layered relationships and between current events and earlier incidents (knowing that any aspect of the organizational "text" can have more than one meaning and can be viewed from a number of different perspectives). Creating meaning at multiple levels helps the consultants determine the individual and organizational roots and consequences of actions and decisions. When the link between present relationships and the distant past is made meaningful to people at all levels of the organization, the process of large-scale change is more likely to be successful.

Given their orientation, clinically informed consultants and change agents also recognize the presence of complex resistances (ranging from denial, to lack of access, to firing the messenger). Since the aim of a clinical intervention isn't just symptom suppression—not merely a "flight into health"—but durable, sustainable change, clinical consultants must always be attentive to hidden agendas. They appreciate that manifest, stated problems often cover up issues that are far more complex. They know that there's usually a very good reason why their particular expertise was asked for (even though that reason may not have been, and perhaps can't be, articulated by the client), and they attempt, for the sake of a successful intervention, to identify that reason quickly. In addition to identifying and addressing the organization's core psychological concerns, clinically informed consultants strive to instill in the organization's leadership an interest in and understanding of their own behavior. Ideally, those leaders can internalize the ability to learn and work in the psychological realm, allowing them to address future issues without the help of a consultant.

To illustrate the advantages of a convergence between traditional interventions and the clinical approach in the process of organizational change, I offer below two consulting assignments that benefited from that convergence. Though in each case the intervention seemed to be only a limited success by both the consultant's and the organization's standards, it would have been an even more difficult task with only the traditional organizational practitioner's tool kit.

THE PRICKLY CEO

The first illustration of an intervention whereby a clinically informed consultant added value took place in a telecommunications company. Although the request for consultation came directly from the CEO, a man in his fifties named Richard, it later transpired that he had been strongly encouraged to visit the consultant by the non-executive chairman of his board. After the initial interview, conducted in the CEO's office, the consultant suggested doing a leadership "audit," meaning an assessment of the capabilities and concerns of the top executive team, to be (eventually) followed by a top executive team development workshop to improve the performance of the organization.

From the discussions that the consultant had with executives at various layers in the organization, as well as with non-executive members of the board, it appeared that although the majority of the interviewees appreciated Richard's talent at foreseeing developments in the marketplace, his behavior aroused a great deal of irritation. A number of executives accused him of having too short a fuse and expressed concern over his outbursts of irritation; they felt that he was far too prepared for a fight, even when circumstances called for conciliation. Furthermore, some of the interviewees who had worked closely with him noted that he often resorted to the "mushroom treatment" in organizational matters, surprising them with projects that he had been nurturing in the dark. Very few of his senior people felt that they were kept adequately in the loop as far as the information flow was concerned. Most felt that they weren't given the information and resources to make informed decisions. Some noted that the CEO's uncommunicative style now permeated the organization, with information-hoarding by different players being a preferred mode of operation.

There were objections, too, that the company seemed to be operating in a "fight-or-flight" mode, fomenting suspicion of people and projects; that certain executives were forming fiefdoms; and that trust was an increasingly scarce commodity. Some executives also noted that the company's competitive position had been deteriorating. Moreover, several of their more capable colleagues had left for greener pastures, leaving the company with no obvious successor. One of the non-executive directors insinuated to the consultant that he and a number of the other directors were thinking of contacting a headhunter to explore the possibility of replacing Richard.

At a relaxed moment over dinner one night, as the consultant probed the CEO about his background, Richard explained that he came from a divorced family. His parents had split when he was six years old. Breaking his usual reserve, Richard volunteered some reflections on how he'd reacted to the divorce. (On reflection, the consultant attributed the executive's unusual openness to the latter's awareness of the urgency of the situation.) Richard reported that after the divorce, his mother had quickly remarried, and from that marriage had come one much younger half-brother and one half-sister. Encouraged by the consultant, Richard explained that he'd had a terrible relationship with his stepfather, who sometimes resorted to physical violence to discipline the youngster. Richard still, decades later, resented the fact that his mother, apparently insecure in her relationship with her new husband, had always taken her husband's side in any dispute between the man and the boy. That strained parental relationship resulted in a psychological legacy of humiliation and anger.

It became clear from the conversation that Richard's lack of trust and prickly temper originated in a family constellation that had been unpredictable and hostile. From the time he was a young child, his circumstances had been harsh and lonely, engendering mistrust and necessitating constant vigilance. He also learned early that he had to rely on himself. He discovered that he was better off keeping private any worries that he had. Sharing "secrets" with his mother was a risky business: she couldn't be trusted to keep them to herself. Having learned early the need to be on guard, he retained his constant state of alertness into adulthood. He felt that he needed to be ready for a fight at any time, based on the template created by his relationship with his stepfather. That core conflictual relationship theme shaped the script of his inner theater and dictated his interactions with the world.

While vigilance and aggression (the display of elements of the paranoid and abrasive disposition—see Chapter 5) may have been effective ways of coping with difficult circumstances as a child, they were dysfunctional in Richard's role as CEO. Now that the real threat—the threat of the unpredictable stepfather that he carried with him from childhood—could no longer be addressed, Richard substituted various external threats instead, taking preemptive action whenever he could in order to gain a modicum of control. Turning the passive into the active became a favorite modus operandi. Given his inner script, it wasn't surprising that Richard was secretive with colleagues and was constantly waging war against perceived enemies (his latest fight being with two of his non-executive directors).

With the information gleaned from his many interviews, the consultant was now in a better position to explore with Richard some of the connections between his past and his present behavior. The consultant watched for moments when he could "strike when the iron was cold"—that is, when Richard could listen to unpleasant information without going into defensive maneuvers. After a number of discussions with the consultant, Richard began to recognize his own responsibility for the mess he had created and no longer blamed all his problems on others. (The stimulus provided by office scuttlebutt that his job was on the line helped greatly to focus his mind.) That realization made him take the initiative to reach out to the people he had previously considered his "enemies."

Richard made a valiant effort to be a better communicator as well, though he realized, especially after the revelations of the consultation that his personality was never going to allow him to be the "welcome wagon" of the world. He now saw the wisdom of building on his strengths and finding others to compensate for his weaknesses. Realizing that there were too many people in the organization who (by design or indoctrination) were likewise poor communicators, Richard hired a new VP of Human Resources. That single step went a long way toward making the company more transparent. Richard's efforts to change, with the support and encouragement of the consultant, created a significant improvement as well, allowing him to mend his relationship with various members of the board. Able to appreciate his talent as a strategist and turnaround artist once he had become less prickly and more open, the board discontinued its search for a replacement CEO. With greater emotional stability in the organization, the consultant decided that a top executive team development workshop (as described in Chapter 11) would be next on the agenda, helping the executives to build trust, commitment, and accountability, and helping them become more effective at constructive conflict resolution.

The example of Richard shows how a person can harm both himself and his organization, not through malice or lack of talent, but through ignorance of his own inner theater and slavery to psychological patterns of which he is unaware. By addressing these issues—by making conscious what had been unconscious and then working to address leadership behavior patterns that were determined to be dysfunctional—the consultant and CEO together were able to disable prevailing individual resistances and social defenses to heal a form of organizational neurosis.

THROUGH THE LOOKING GLASS: THE STRATEC COLLUSION

The preceding Case of the Prickly CEO presents more than just a coach-client or consultant-client relationship. Because the consultation took place within an organizational context, the consultant needed to take a systemic approach. The following case, The Stratec Collusion, illustrates an even more obviously systemic psychodynamic intervention.

This intervention started when most of the partners of one of the local offices of Stratec, a global consulting firm, concluded that the partner group was no longer functioning effectively. There were ample indications that this was the case. Partner meetings were poorly attended. There were always a few partners who came late and a few who didn't come at all, claiming that they should be excused because they had to deal with important clients. The general consensus was that no meaningful decisions were made during these partner meetings anymore. There was no focus to the sessions; there was no priority-setting; there was no follow-up. One partner had been heard to complain that the meetings resembled sessions of a debating society, while another groused that there was a lot of talk but little action. Many partners had also expressed their concern about a lack of leadership. Though the partner group had a nominal head—the managing partner—nobody seemed to be really in charge. Clearly, the office was no longer functioning at optimal capacity.

And it wasn't only the partners who were complaining. The malaise of the partner group had spread throughout the office, and now the consultants and other junior staff members were also commenting about a decline in morale in the workplace. What once had been an exciting, stimulating place to work had become just another ordinary consulting firm. Some of the consultants feared that this would cause problems in the long run, because it would make the search for talent more difficult. There were already signs of trouble in the short term. For example, transfer of knowledge—in the past a major source of competitive advantage in the group—was no longer handled effectively, in large part because backstabbing was so pervasive. No longer was Stratec a place where people shared (and learned from) client successes and defeats; no longer was there a free flow of information for the benefit of clients and partners alike. Even the partners had so little contact that they barely knew what the others were doing.

Because of growing business opportunities in the region where this office was located, the number of partners at Stratec had grown rapidly over the last decade. What had once been a small group of individuals who understood each other almost intuitively, collaborated intimately, and spent long hours together building up the office into its present form had changed into a loosely connected group of many individuals. Some of the partners mentioned that the collegial atmosphere that had been Stratec's hallmark in the early days had all but disappeared. Rather than working to maintain good relationships in the office, the partners now focused almost exclusively on their clients. As a result, claimed some old-timers, the office had become a way station on the career path.

The anonymous atmosphere at the office was exacerbated by the fact that some of the partners weren't "homegrown"—that is, they hadn't gone through the usual career trajectory of the firm (moving over time, and in many stages, from associate consultant to partner). Instead, they had been hired from the outside at full partner level. These "lateral hires" had been brought in to help the firm gain a speedier entry into specific market segments. Some consultants had made the observation, however, that the firm had never been very good at integrating lateral hires.

Reflecting on their current situation, many partners were of the opinion that the economies of scale were increasingly negated by diseconomies of size. According to them, the partners were no longer a team, out to conquer the world, but a bunch of individuals who happened to share the same offices. The leadership style of the partners had changed from management by walking around to management by voice and e-mail, and it smacked more of politics than of loyalty or cooperation.

This growing malaise was reflected in the bottom line. The findings of a recent company-wide study had shown that the revenue per partner at this particular office was considerably lower than at most other offices of Stratec. This finding was disturbing to many of the partners, in light of their great track record: they had always been leaders in revenue generation. Now, though, with consulting projects staffed by regularly changing teams, collaboration was apparently not as effective as it had been when the office was smaller.

There were outside pressures as well: a number of competing companies had entered what had been Stratec's traditional niche in the consulting market in this office's region, putting great pressure on the partner group to be more effective. After enjoying a period in which they could operate on autopilot regarding marketing their services, they now had to work hard to bring in new customers.

Some of the senior partners had asked themselves whether a number of the new partners—insiders and lateral hires alike— might be responsible for the present malaise. In hindsight, they felt that the bar for entry to the partnership level had been set too low during the boom times, and they wondered how much these new partners were really contributing to the bottom line.

Criticism went both ways, though: many of the newer partners felt that some of the senior partners were "fat cats," complacent in their tenured seniority. These older partners were, as they themselves admitted, no longer as involved in rainmaking and office matters as they used to be. While a number of the newer partners acknowledged that some of their more senior colleagues had contributed greatly to the success of the office and now had the right to take it a little easy, others strongly disagreed. They believed that during these difficult times everyone should make his or her best effort. This was not a time to rest on one's laurels.

Those partners who advocated this point of view also disagreed with the Human Resource management view that a lesser effort at work would be adequately sanctioned through the compensation system. True enough, the annual bonus would be smaller for a person who wasn't working at full capacity, but (according to the complainants) that would be an inadequate sanction against people who were already quite wealthy. In the meantime, these older partners were taking away valuable resources. The younger, more aggressive partners felt (but rarely said) that all partners should be fully involved in the activities of the office or should take the consequences and resign.

And yet some of the more junior partners wondered whether they could hack it without the seniors. Were they capable of being rainmakers in these difficult times? Did they possess the solid networking skills of the more senior partners? Would they be able to drum up new business when the seniors were no longer there to assist? Moreover, as full-fledged partners, would they be able to ask the seniors to help them acquire such skills, or would admitting their feelings of inadequacy be too painful?

At one of the monthly partner meetings the discontent bubbled up into a consensus that the present state of affairs simply couldn't continue. The group voted to hire Alice Borden, a well-known consultant who specialized in human resource management. The assignment given to her was to address the question of how to become more effective as a partner group.

To facilitate her intervention, Alice decided to take along a colleague, Adam. She liked being able to test her perceptions of a consulting situation with someone else. As her first task, Alice requested interviews with all the members of the partner group (and some of the more junior consultants), to get a better grasp of the situation at the office. Her hope was that by doing these interviews she and Adam would not only get a better understanding of the salient issues, but they also could explain to the partners the use of a set of survey instrumentation—including 360-degree feedback tools that would give insight into various personality, leadership, interpersonal, group, culture, and strategic issues—that they would like to employ as the basis for a group discussion during a special off-site meeting. Alice had described to the two partners who had given her the original invitation how she had used these survey instruments effectively in the past to create high-performance teams. The two partners had given her the official go-ahead, expressing their view that the use of such survey material would be a good idea.

During the interviews, however, Alice and Adam became aware of an enormous amount of resistance on the part of various partners to having to deal with the 360-degree and other survey instrumentation. A number of them noted that some of the questions in the 360-degree feedback instrument were overly personal, and they expressed reservations about how the responses would be used in a group setting. Their comments were rather puzzling to Alice and Adam, who had used similar material in many different organizations (and cultures) without any problems. Given that all the partners, without exception, had strongly stated that something needed to be done to help them work more effectively as a group, Alice and Adam suspected that something was going on beneath the surface. After all, the feedback and survey instruments were intended only as an icebreaker to highlight some of the problems in the partner group. Why, then, when they talked about the use of these instruments, did some of the partners get a pained look on their faces and question the use of this kind of material? Personally, these partners said, they had no problems with the material and would be happy to complete the questionnaires; but, they continued, they wondered how some of the others would feel, using such instrumentation in a group setting. When pressed about what they saw as the problem, they explained that some of the senior partners had had bad experiences with using personal material before.

The "clinical" supervision. At their wits' end, Alice and Adam decided to discuss their problem with a colleague who had a clinical background. When they explained what they had experienced, he noted that they had been looking at the problem at only one level. He remarked that, true enough, if their assessment of the situation was correct, there seemed to be consensus about what needed to be done to have the partner group work more effectively. At what he called the manifest level, many of the partners seemed to agree that the office wasn't working well, that productivity wasn't what it used to be, that the place had become too anonymous, that there was a problem concerning trust. According to their assessment, many of the partners acknowledged that the office had lost its sense of direction (a paradoxical finding for a strategic consulting firm!) and that transfer of best consulting practices was taking place clumsily if at all.

At that manifest level, most members of the partnership seemed to agree that something needed to be done about corporate governance. Some kind of structure needed to be put into place to facilitate the decision-making process. Many had indicated that, after a period of strong, focused leadership, inspired leadership was now lacking. The managing partner, a capable administrator, was described by most of his colleagues as lacking charisma. The other partners feared that he lacked the personal magnetism to pull this group of "wild ducks" into formation. Several of them noted the irony in the fact that the new managing partner had taken his position on their own recommendation—a recommendation given by the majority of the present partners at the office to the management board of the consulting firm worldwide.

Having reviewed with Alice and Adam these manifest concerns, their clinical colleague suggested that they excavate for latent concerns as well. Clearly there were significant, but unexpressed, issues that contributed to the present malaise. Alice and Adam would need to determine why many of the partners were so reluctant to take the steps that seemed so obvious—steps that, in their own consulting work, the partners would surely recommend to their clients. The colleague suggested to Alice and Adam that their sense of frustration could be interpreted as a manifestation of social reality, but also of unconscious ideation. He even mentioned—in what psychologists call a "countertransferential" (or projective identification) interpretation—they should try to interpret their present state of frustration: they could view it as a great gift, because it could be seen as symptomatic of the level of frustration among the partners.

Their colleague also introduced to them the concept of "secondary gains," which as we saw earlier says that manifest malfunctioning (in this case, the present malaise at the office) can offer elusive psychological advantages. As an example of a secondary gain, he pointed out that the dysfunctional nature of the partner meetings (though painful for all in attendance) guaranteed that some of the firm's most critical issues, such as the declining revenue per partner, would not be addressed. Instead, time was always wasted on more trivial matters.

He also reminded Alice and Adam that during their interviews, many people had hinted that not all of the partners were still pulling their weight, that some of the older partners wanted time to smell the roses and were bringing down revenues as a result. This seemed to contradict the corporate myth expressed by quite a few of the senior partners that, despite bottom-line concerns, the office worked together as a happy community.

And yet, their clinical colleague emphasized, Alice and Adam hadn't been able to get anyone to do anything more than hint at this contradiction. Apparently the Stratec partners felt that charging a few older colleagues with no longer contributing sufficiently to the firm was too anxiety-inducing to attempt; they weren't willing to publicly break the illusion that they were a collaborative and cooperative community. Furthermore, some partners apparently were afraid that by entering into a dialogue about that sort of issue they would open a Pandora's box so full of complaints that the office would implode and the most important rainmakers would take their talents elsewhere—probably a valid fear. Given the cost, conflict avoidance seemed preferable, in spite of the backstabbing that was its consequence. That's why the suggestion by Alice and Adam to use survey and multi-rater feedback to start a discussion was so scary for many of them. There hadn't been sufficient assurances of "safety."

Moreover, if Alice and Adam attempted to make the individual contributions of lagging partners more transparent through a 360-degree and survey feedback process, the result could be a decision to introduce greater accountability for all, and in all arenas. Their colleague suggested that a number of the partners would view greater accountability as a threat to their present autonomy. In the eyes of those partners, though things were bad, the creation of a corporate governance structure that demanded greater clarity about their own contribution—that asked what each person was doing and established controls on activity—would be far worse. He suggested that if these partners were honest with themselves, many of them would have to admit that they really liked their present freedom; they enjoyed not having to explain how they spent their time; they liked working at home and putting in odd hours without having to defend these practices.

Alice and Adam's colleague saw in the partners' concern about public sharing of information what he called a "social defense." Social defenses, he explained, are ways of dealing with the anxiety that's part and parcel of life in organizations (see Chapter 12). When there's no "containment" of such anxiety—that is, when there are no opportunities to discuss and deal with heartfelt concerns—people in organizations are inclined to engage in defensive routines such as "splitting" (dividing the world into black-and-white, us-versus-them categories), projective identification (assigning to other people the "negative" feelings one has but cannot acknowledge), and denial (not accepting responsibility for certain matters). He explained that these mechanisms, which are universal modes of communication (but which can seriously impair organizational functioning by shifting attention away from work), are psychological defenses against unwanted feelings or fantasies. They serve to transform and neutralize strong tensions and feelings such as anxiety, shame, guilt, envy, jealousy, rage, sexual frustration, and low self-esteem. Very often an organization's bureaucratic features, with all the rules and regulations, checks and counter-checks, are part of a social defense structure whereby form trumps substance: so much time is spent on trivial matters that the real work that should be done gets short shrift.

Although these social defenses can be seen as adaptive at one level—in this case, for example, they could be seen as an effort to maintain the illusion of being a "happy family" and thus helped avoid potentially disruptive conflict—at another level they contribute to a distortion of inner and outer reality, derailing effective organizational functioning. At Stratec, social defenses allowed the partners to withdraw partially from the responsibility that came with their ownership position, resulting in stagnant meetings and ineffective communication. Social defenses also contributed to weak leadership at the office: the partners had given themselves an "alibi" by selecting a leader; however, it was no accident that the man chosen wasn't very effective.

As suggested earlier, the present impasse had been triggered by diseconomies of size. With the recent growth of the office, the partners weren't as close as they had been. This predictable con-sequence could have been dealt with, but the partners chose to put little effort into maintaining a sense of community. Instead, they pursued more personal agendas, and as a result they forfeited the trust that been built up over the years among junior personnel. In the absence of trust, a political climate flourished in the office: subgroups developed and backstabbing became the communication tool of choice. Constructive conflict resolution went out the window as well, since its key ingredient is trust. Whenever the newly politicized Stratec faced a difficult decision, the partners opted for denial over resolution. In abandoning constructive conflict resolution, they also gave up commitment and accountability, factors essential to a healthy bottom line.

The key to resolution of the present impasse, Alice and Adam's colleague told them, lay in greater transparency. Stratec could reinvigorate itself only if the partners were prepared to deal with their problems head on, to discuss the undiscussables, to stop the infighting and air out the increasingly politicized atmosphere at the office. Only by speaking honestly and listening undefensively could they distinguish reality from fantasy and combat the paranoid thinking and scapegoating that threatened to sink the firm.

It would take courage to instigate and continue an honest discussion of the kind of leadership needed to gear up the office during these difficult times. The partners would have to ask themselves some tough questions: Would a more junior managing partner do better in the leadership role? Would the more senior partners, who had played that role in the past, permit a relative newcomer to function at full potential? Were there—and should there be—different career trajectories for junior and senior partners? And should some senior partners be eased out?

Being willing to deal with the latent problems that festered at a subconscious level would also imply that the partners would have to bite the bullet and accept a more comprehensive form of corporate governance, even if that change would mean restricting the freedom they had enjoyed until now. With the growth of the office rendering the old intuitive governance of the partner group ineffective, mutually agreed-upon control systems needed to be introduced to enhance decision-making, with a select number of colleagues (including a couple of the more promising junior members) empowered to make meaningful decisions on behalf of the group.

To overcome the latent problems, the partners also needed to address the level of transparency of accountability acceptable to all, increasing it to ensure fair process. As a group, they needed to spell out the role expectations for each partner, and they needed to discuss frankly whether all partners were pulling equal (or at least adequate) weight. If they concluded that certain partners were pulling down the bottom line, the stronger majority would need to pressure the laggards to leave the company.

None of these necessary steps could happen, though, as Alice and Adam's colleague pointed out to them, until the partners realized that it was their own prevailing social defenses that had served to prevent such a discussion from taking place. They needed to acknowledge that their defensiveness had contributed to a floundering of the work process. They needed to recognize that, paradoxically, their rational manifest "solutions" to their fears and concerns had contributed to a great deal of irrationality at the latent level. In order to make Stratec a high-performance organization again—an organization ready and able to take on the future—they would have to address these more subtle latent processes as well.

A postscript. Alice and Adam decided to take the bull by the horns and go ahead with their planned event—a three-day workshop—despite the resistance the partners had shown to their survey instrumentation. When Alice called the managing partner to firm up the details, however, he told her that their contribution to the event would have to be curtailed to just a half-day. A number of the senior partners had decided, he said, that the days the group would spend together would be more effectively used to discuss strategies for obtaining new clients. Given the confidential nature of such a discussion, Alice and Adam weren't invited to be part of the remaining two and a half days.

Alice and Adam were frustrated by the curtailment of their contribution. It bothered them even more, though, that the partner responsible for human resources (a relatively junior partner) wanted to know in advance every detail of the brief presentation they planned to make. In a conference call that included the managing partner, he demanded that they describe in great detail their planned presentation. More than once both men cautioned them not to be too direct in giving certain types of feedback, in order not to irritate some of the senior partners. Both consultants deeply resented being micromanaged, but against their better judgment they decided not to object. They weren't ready to analyse their feelings of anger and irritation about being micromanaged—feelings that they could have used as additional data in making sense of the dialogue.

Alice and Adam's resentment turned to dread as the day of the meeting dawned. They summoned their courage and stood in front of the group of partners, where first they gave a general presentation about high-performance teams and organizations and then pointed out a number of salient issues they had observed in the office. During the first part of their presentation, the atmosphere was icy, to say the least; the partners listened to the presentation stone-facedly, and without making any comments. During the second part of the presentation, however, matters started to change. After considerable prompting from Alice, a lively discussion developed, with a number of the partners expressing a willingness to address the more elusive, latent issues in some other forum so that a better system of corporate governance could be put into place and they could all work more effectively.

All too soon, Alice and Adam's time was up. Without having had a chance to help the partners arrive at any action recommendations, they were thanked for their contribution and dismissed; the partners would have to tackle the latent issues further themselves, and formulate their own recommendations. Leaving the hotel where the meeting had been held, they both had a bitter taste in their mouth. They felt as if they had been made the sacrificial scapegoats. In retrospect, they wondered how they might have dealt with the situation differently.

When Alice and Adam discussed what had happened with their more clinically trained colleague, he pointed out that by not really acknowledging early in the process the underlying, "irrational" dynamics of the office, they had contributed to the apparent failure of their intervention. Furthermore, they hadn't offered a strong enough rationale to persuade the majority of the partners of the benefits of discussing among themselves the outcomes of the survey and multiparty feedback. Most important, they hadn't created a holding environment that felt safe enough for the participants to open up frankly. Alice and Adam had been so hung up on doing surveys and gathering multiparty feedback, the clinical consultant said, that they hadn't realized just how worried the partners were about sharing personal information in public. They hadn't given enough assurances that their intervention technique would be beneficial.

A number of weeks later, one of the senior partners, in town on business, called Alice and asked if he could meet with her. Over coffee, he told her that a number of the partners had been rather disappointed with their intervention. Given her reputation, he said, they had expected more of her. As they talked, though, Alice sensed from his conversation that the atmosphere at the office had improved. It sounded as if the partners were now more willing to interact with each other. Moreover, the non-charismatic managing partner appeared to have become more assertive. For example, he had created a task force that had already put a governance structure into place. According to the visiting partner, morale at the office was much better than it had been in a long time, and relationships were more collegial. Once again the partners were exchanging ideas about projects in progress, for example.

Maybe, thought Alice, her efforts to bring out latent issues had been somewhat effective after all. By taking on the role of change agent, she had been the catalyst for change—though taking on the role of scapegoat certainly wasn't what she'd had in mind when she accepted the assignment. In hindsight, however, she realized that she may have triggered the scapegoating herself: her lack of insight about secondary gains, countertransferential processes, social defenses, and resistance had been contributing factors. She saw now that by failing to read the partners' anxiety correctly, and by failing to pick up on transferential processes and other subtle clues, she and Adam had jeopardized their intervention. Alice consoled herself with the knowledge that she understood better how she had contributed to the failure of Stratec's change effort.

CONSULTING WITH THE THIRD EAR

As both these examples illustrate, many people are unaware of irrational processes when dealing with issues of leadership and change; in fact, they're typically unaware that such processes even exist. For proof of irrational processes, however, we need look no further than self-destructive behavior: that people choose to engage in self-destructive activities defies any rational logic. If we choose to play Sherlock Holmes in our organizations, listening with the third ear of intuition, our investigation will reveal a great deal of hidden rationale.

It's that hidden rationale that the clinically oriented consultant driving a change effort in a struggling organization looks for. The process involves the same challenges that face his or her counterpart engaged in dynamic psychotherapy, psychoanalysis, or leadership coaching with an individual—but on a bigger, more systemic scale. Clinically oriented consultants working to improve an organization work at two levels: with individuals, and with the overall organizational system. As is the case with individuals, psychological awareness within an organization is the first step toward psychological health. It's important, then, that people at all levels of the hierarchy become aware of the unconscious currents underlying observable work behavior.

It's the fact that unconscious currents are by definition outside of ordinary awareness that makes bringing them to consciousness typically the task of an outside consultant, someone who is less likely to be caught up in the existing organizational system. Simply pointing out salient issues and collusive processes is rarely enough, however; typically, the consultant has to make such issues more explicit, perhaps by asking clarifying questions. The process is a four-part one comprised of clarification, confrontation, insight, and working through [7]. The client is presented with specific problem areas. Inconsistencies in activities are highlighted and clarified. The client is confronted with specific contradictions, making for different levels of insight. Collusions are unraveled. He or she then works through a discovery process with the help of key members of the organization, analysing problems more closely, bringing them into sharper focus, and finding acceptable solutions.

One crucial source of data for clinically informed consultants is the way that the various members of the organization interact with them. (This is a process to which Alice and Adam, in our earlier case example, should have paid more attention.) That interaction, and the transferential role from the past that a client assigns the consultant—perhaps father figure or nag, all-knowing authority figure, or snot-nosed youngster—often tells the consultant more than what the client actually says. When the situation permits it, transference interpretations can be shared with clients. However, given the usual short timeframe in consultancy assignments (as opposed to more traditional therapy or coaching situations), consultants must exercise great caution in doing so. Whether they share the information or not, consultants should definitely take note of transference and keep it in mind while designing and implementing their intervention. More often than not, the challenge to the consultant is not to say out loud what he or she is observing!

At its heart, the business of the dynamically informed consultant is change, and change takes time. It involves overcoming resistances, giving up things one has cherished in the past, mastering loss, and changing one's inner representational world of fantasies, beliefs, and attitudes. This process of giving up the old and mulling over variations on the new—a mourning process, really—is an essential element of change. And the clinically informed organizational consultant is involved all the way, from breaking the status quo, to getting people to give up secondary gains and try new solutions, to dealing with the ambivalence of taking or not taking action, to rolling with the resistances.

Though clinically informed management consultants can steer organizations through change efforts of all kinds, their training equips them to be especially helpful in diagnosing dysfunctional organizational cultures, working through the trauma of mergers and acquisitions, identifying ineffective leadership styles, building more effective management teams, unraveling collusive superior-subordinate relationships, providing insight into family business stalemates, and dealing with loss, disappointment, and career and life-cycle issues. Most importantly, however, they can be extremely helpful in creating more effective, humane, and economically viable organizations. Any area of business life that has central psychological underpinnings is a likely candidate for organizational "analysis."

Often clinically informed consultants find themselves in the role of leadership or strategic coaches, trying to help a client better understand the implications of certain actions and behavior patterns. As mentioned earlier, psychotherapeutic training helps them know not only what to say but also what not to say. It's important to make timely observations, of course; but it's also important to keep quiet sometimes, even when certain insights are obvious. As has been mentioned repeatedly before, in psychotherapy the rule is to "strike when the iron is cold." When the "iron" is too hot, the client may not be ready to hear what the consultant offers. Thus timing is essential. If the consultant handles his or her task well, clients find themselves more emotionally intelligent—more psychologically sophisticated, we might say—after the intervention than before.

Clinically informed consultants can be particularly helpful in family business situations, given their knowledge of organizations, family systems, and psychodynamics [8]. They're often called in to resolve escalating battles between entrepreneurial parents (generally fathers) and their children, usually centered on the theme of succession. The challenge requires that they unravel the prevailing family myths, deal with defensive reactions, and negotiate solutions acceptable to all parties. Often they encounter family members who would rather perpetuate the crisis than arrive at an unwelcome (though realistic) resolution. In that case, their first job is to get family members out of that defensive stance. Their thorough clinical understanding of human dynamics helps them avoid being drawn into defenses and collusions themselves, allowing them to focus on using available data to help solve the client's problems.

CONNECTING WITH A CLINICALLY INFORMED CONSULTANT

Organizational consultation by a clinically informed consultant usually starts with a contact made by one of the organization's executives, often the CEO, who describes a dilemma he or she is facing. As any consultant with experience has learned the hard way, the original, stated problem is very often not the real problem, but only a signifier of other, deeper problems. The challenge for the consultant is to integrate the manifest problem with the issues that are concealed by it. Though most organizations exert pressure to come up with instant answers, the consultant must take adequate time to reflect on the problem. That reflection is enhanced if the consultant shares the assignment with a colleague and can thus discuss observations and analyse transference and counter-transference reactions.

After the initial contact, the consultant typically continues discussions about the problem with other key members of the organization to obtain a wide spectrum of perspectives. Complete access to everyone within an organization is essential to the success of such a consultation. Any thwarting of access (whether done subtly or directly) is grist for interpretation. Because in clinically informed consultation there's little difference between the diagnostic stage and the intervention stage, such interpretation is both diagnostic and "therapeutic." The mere fact of data-gathering implies that the intervention has begun. The organizational participants' fantasies have been set into motion.

Typically, suggestions for change start at the surface, reaching a deeper level only when a measure of trust has developed between the consultant and the client. A solid working alliance among the various parties is essential if the consultant hopes to clarify issues, confront the principal players effectively about emerging problems, identify resistances, and make interpretations. Thus interventions typically progress from suggestions to key people about structural changes to observations about various means of communication to the pros and cons of a particular leadership style.

STAYING IN FOR THE LONG HAUL

Many business leaders have become more emotionally astute in recent years. Having seen organizational fads come and go, they now realize that most organizational problems are deeply ingrained and as such aren't susceptible to quick-fix formulas. These experienced leaders have become wary of organizational snake-oil salespeople and their simplistic (but costly) interventions. The "downsizing, rightsizing, capsizing" formulas of many organizational consultants have made these leaders aware of the price of faulty organizational intervention. Many of them have paid their dues many times over, in the form of dysfunctional leadership, ineffective culture integration programs, poorly planned leadership development, and inadequate succession planning.

Clinically informed consultation brings a dose of realism to organizational intervention, though it shouldn't be seen as a cure-all and certainly doesn't herald the coming of a new messiah. Still, it makes sense that in-depth approaches to organizational consultation have a greater chance than superficial solutions to address the deeply entrenched causes of organizational problems. Organizational life is like a mirror: what we see out there, we first have to discover inside.

Clinically trained consultants, unlike many traditional consultants, don't simply make a diagnosis and provide a set of recommendations, leaving it to the client to implement the suggestions. Rather, such consultants help the client make their recommendations a reality. They're not in the consultation for the short run. The aim of the psychoanalytically informed consultation isn't a temporary "high," but lasting change. The consultant wants to move beyond reductionistic formulas to sustainable transformation. Such an orientation often makes for enduring client-consultant relationships. Though the aim of every consultation is greater self-efficacy for the client (rather than an ongoing situation of dependency), the consultant's services may be asked for repeatedly on an as-needed basis over a period of years. The aim of the consultant, however, is to help clients engage in self-analytic activities so that they can learn how to engage in interventions on their own. The ultimate goal of the consultant is to create healthy, effective organizations.

EMULATING SHERLOCK HOLMES

One point I would like to reemphasize in differentiating clinically oriented interventions from more traditional ones is that clinically informed consultants use personal interaction with the client as a crucial source of data. The challenge is to pick up on subtle signals that the client gives off, so as to correctly read the transference and then to use countertransference effectively. To show the importance of this step, a Zen story is illustrative.

A Zen master, while crossing a river, lost a cherished silver cup given to him by his pupils. Hoping to retrieve it, he first sent his eyes to look for the cup, but they weren't successful. Still full of hope, he sent his ears, but they weren't successful either. Disappointed, but not yet without hope, he sent his nose. Still no luck. Then, in a desperate effort, he sent all of his senses to find the cup. Unfortunately, once again there were no results. In a final effort, he sent his "not-search" to find the cup. To his great delight, his "not-search" did find it.

Comparable to a Zen master's "not-search" approach, Wilfred Bion used to say that a psychoanalyst "should impose upon himself the positive discipline of eschewing memory and desire" [9], p. 31. Listening to the client, the psychoanalyst should use free-floating attention and listen extremely carefully. The psychoanalyst should be open to experience, having no preconceived notions of why the client behaves in certain ways. The same advice applies to the consultant or leadership coach. In interacting with their clients, they evoke and provoke; they engage in a highly complicated process of human communication. But most importantly, they have to be open to experience. Paying attention to transference and countertransference reactions, taking in and responding to their own deep feelings, they create a meaningful basis to help clients acquire insight into their problems.

In order for such a sophisticated dance between executives and consultants to be effective, both parties need to be able to look in the mirror without flinching, although the mirror can be like a trompe l'oeil, a visual deception. They need to have the courage to face reality. All too often, however, when people don't like what they see reflected back at them, their natural reaction is to smash the glass. But leaders seeking to put a misdirected organizational ship back on course need to be willing to ask the tough questions: Have they been acting in the best interest of their people or only in their own best interest? Have they been seeing their organization as a community of people or only as a profit-making institution? How might they have acted more appropriately? What could they have done differently? Too many senior executives take a short-term perspective, refusing to see the human side of the workplace. They mandate restructurings and reorganizations designed for short-term gains without accepting responsibility for the personal consequences such practices have for employees. In other words, they break the trust given to them by loyal followers. Without knowing or intending it, they end up managing for economic decline.

Traditional consultants who have the courage to include the clinical approach in their repertoire—who, like Sherlock Holmes, are willing to tackle the submerged psychological dynamics that characterize *any* organization (and that threaten, wherever they hide, to derail effectiveness)—are in for a pleasant surprise. They come to realize that life in organizations isn't to be wept over or laughed at, but to be understood and then improved. The deep understanding that the clinical perspective offers lays the building blocks for effective intervention.

Thus the advocates of traditional consulting approaches and of the clinical orientation to organizational intervention would do well to join forces. It's not uncommon for consultants who subscribe to the myth of the rational executive—and it is a myth, I assure you—to contribute to (rather than help diagnose and cure) organizational neurosis. They wouldn't fall into that trap if they incorporated the clinical perspective. Sherlock Holmes once said, quite fatalistically: "Everything comes in circles. . . . It's all been done before, and will be again." The challenge for the clinically informed consultant is to break the many vicious cycles that plague the workplace, helping to create organizations where people feel and do their best!

REFERENCES

1. Kilburg, R. R. (2004). "When Shadows Fall: Using Psychodynamic Approaches in Executive Coaching." *Consulting Psychology Journal: Practice and Research* 56(4): 246–268.
2. Levinson, H. (2002). *Organizational Assessment*. Washington, DC, American Psychological Association.
3. Kets de Vries, M. F. R. (2002). *Can CEOs Change? Yes But Only If They Want To*. INSEAD Working Papers Series. Fontainebleau.
4. McCullough Vaillant, L. (1997). *Changing Character*. New York, Basic Books.
5. Ogden, T. H. (1982). *Projective Identification and Psychotherapeutic Technique*. New York, Jason Aronson.
6. Kets de Vries, M. and D. Miller (1987). "Interpreting Organizational Texts." *Journal of Management Studies* 24(3): 233–347.
7. Kets de Vries, M. F. R. and D. Miller (1984). *The Neurotic Organization*. San Francisco, Jossey-Bass.
8. Kets de Vries, M. F. R. (1996). Family Business: *Human Dilemmas in the Family Firm*. London, Thompson.
9. Bion, W. R. (1970). *Attention and Interpretation*. London, Tavistock.

CHAPTER 14

CONCLUSION: CREATING "AUTHENTIZOTIC" ORGANIZATIONS

To try to be authentic these days, to ask questions of the people in power—it's difficult. This administration has evolved new techniques to handle people like me. Their strategy, in a word, is simple: ignore them.

—Ron Suskind

It takes a very long time to become young.

—Pablo Picasso

In the book of life's questions, the answers are not in the back.

—Charles Schultz

Chop wood, carry water.

—Zen proverb

There's a Zen story about a king whose deepest wish was to be remembered as a wise ruler by his people. Given this desire, he kept pondering what made a ruler wise. What were the key issues wise rulers dealt with? How did wise rulers reach their decisions? How did wise rulers spend their time?

The king decided to present his conundrum to his subjects. He had an announcement made throughout the kingdom that whoever was able to answer this question to the king's satisfaction would be well rewarded. Many of the king's subjects responded to the call. One suggested that wise rulers needed to set up precise time schedules, consecrating every hour, day, month, and year for certain tasks, and then follow that schedule to the minute. Another thought that prioritization was the key. Still another insisted that, since no single person could ever hope to have all the knowledge and foresight necessary to make good decisions, wise rulers were those who chose advisers well and heeded their advice. Another one of the king's subjects suggested that a wise ruler would appoint administrators to handle ongoing activities and use his or her own time improving relationships with the kings in neighboring countries. Someone else suggested that a wise ruler would consult religious leaders, soothsayers, or magicians.

The king was gratified by the outpouring of responses, but he wasn't satisfied. In his heart of hearts, he didn't like any of the answers. No reward was given.

As he thought more about his conundrum, the king remembered that he'd once heard of a hermit who lived high in the mountains. This hermit was supposed to be a truly wise and enlightened man. The king wondered if the hermit would be able to tell him what a wise ruler did. It seemed worth a try. The king discovered, however, that seeing the hermit posed a problem. The hermit never left the mountains. Furthermore, he welcomed only the poor, refusing to have anything to do with people of wealth, power, or status.

The king decided to visit him anyway, but in disguise, wearing simple peasant clothes. With some of his attendants he undertook the arduous journey to the mountains. When the king arrived at the foot of the peak where the hermit lived, he ordered his attendants to wait for him. Reaching the hermit's hut after a long, solitary climb, the king found the hermit busy, tending a small vegetable garden. When the hermit saw the stranger, he nodded his head politely in greeting but didn't stop working.

The king approached him and said, "I've come from afar to ask your help. I'd like to know what it takes to be a wise ruler. What do rulers have to do to become wise? The hermit, continuing to dig, listened attentively but didn't offer a response. The king noted, given the hermit's advanced age that gardening didn't come easily to him. The king repeated his question, but the hermit only smiled and kept working. Eventually, the king said, "You must be tired. Let me give you a hand." The hermit, still silent, gratefully gave the king his shovel. A few hours passed as the king planted rows of seeds alongside a patch of healthy vegetable plants. When all the seeds were in the ground, he addressed the hermit again, asking what it took to be a wise ruler. Again, the hermit didn't respond. Instead, giving the king a pail, he pointed to a stream in the distance.

The king took the pail in hand and walked to the stream to get water for the garden. While bending over fill the pail, the king suddenly felt two hands grabbing him from behind, trying to push him under. Only through an inhuman effort did he manage to free himself and prevent drowning. While disentangling himself, the king successfully threw the attacker in the water. As the attacker was floating away, the king recognized him as one of his retainers. The king was completely taken aback, because he had always thought of this retainer as a truly trustworthy person. He realized now how wrong he had been in his judgment. He wondered if the retainer's strange deed was an act of revenge: the man had been furious some months earlier when the king hadn't chosen him to lead his ruling council.

In a state of shock about his very narrow escape, the king returned to the hut of the hermit and told him what had happened.

After recounting his near murder, he once more asked the hermit if the old man could give him an answer to his question.

The hermit looked at the king and said, "But your question has already been answered." "In what way," the king asked, baffled. The hermit responded, "If you hadn't taken pity on me in my old age and given me a helping hand in the garden, I'm not sure if I would have made it through the coming winter. By showing compassion for my predicament, you helped me in my most important pursuit: planning for my next harvest. The moral that can be learned from your act of compassion is that where there's no vision, a ruler's subjects will perish. You had the foresight to take care of what's most essential to me to survive the year."

"Before you arrived, I was at my wit's end about how to finish my vegetable garden before the winter. I didn't know whether I would have enough energy to complete the task. By giving me a helping hand and making a truly empathic gesture, you increased my spirit. You motivated me to keep up my efforts. In addition— and quite ironically—if you hadn't helped me to get water for the vegetables, your retainer wouldn't have attacked you and you wouldn't have known his real motivations. For many years he could have plotted against you, making your life miserable. Thus by helping me, you really helped yourself. When you help others, you create a virtuous cycle."

The king was silent for some time, reflecting on what the hermit had said. But apparently the hermit wasn't finished yet. The old man stood a little straighter and motioned for the king to have a seat on a nearby log. Clearing his throat, he spoke as if from a lectern: "From this brief encounter you should take a few lessons with you. As I mentioned, every ruler needs to have foresight about the future. Because we grow great by our dreams, all wise rulers are dreamers. But wise rulers don't dream alone; they take others with them. They realize that every single life can become great if a person works toward a goal into which that person puts his or her whole heart and soul. Ordinary people believe only in the possible, while extraordinary people—and that includes all wise rulers—visualize not what's possible or probable, but rather what's impossible, and then they begin to see it as possible."

The hermit pulled a handkerchief from his sleeve and wiped his brow. He bent and shook the pail as if hoping there might be a few remaining drops of water to quench his thirst. Then, standing straight again, he continued: "Furthermore, as I mentioned, wise rulers don't act by themselves. Wise rulers surround themselves with a group of trusted, capable people who support them in making their vision a reality. Knowing that they can attain their dreams only with the help of others, wise rulers select their team carefully, making sure that everyone stands behind them. The last thing a ruler needs is to have wounded princes sabotage his decisions. With a solid team in place, wise leaders listen attentively to what everyone who works for them has to say, and build on each team member's strengths."

"Furthermore, wise rulers help their people learn and develop. They encourage their people; they cheer them on. Nothing great was ever achieved without enthusiasm. In fact, enthusiasm is the greatest asset in the world. It beats money, power, and influence. Wise rulers inspire their people to engage in efforts beyond expectations; they motivate for excellence. Foregoing management by guilt, they give each team member constructive feedback. They invite feedback from others in return, which helps to keep their feet firmly planted on the ground. They create an atmosphere of constructive conflict resolution, where no one is afraid to ask questions or give opinions."

"As you have demonstrated yourself by showing compassion to me, every ruler needs to have empathy. To rule effectively, rulers need not only to have enough self-knowledge to figure out what they're all about, but they also need to be capable of putting themselves in their subjects' shoes. A test that wise rulers should submit themselves to on a regular basis is asking themselves whether they'd like to have themselves as king."

The hermit looked thoughtful and put up first one finger, then another and another and another, as if enumerating points in his head. Then he began again. "Returning to the question of empathy," he said, "wise rulers have to come across as authentic: they need to show that they care deeply about their people and about the mission they're undertaking."

The king sat for a while, considering the hermit's sage advice, and then thanked his host for sharing his wisdom. He returned home determined to be the wise ruler the hermit had described.

TRANSCENDING THE LEADERSHIP CRISIS

Unfortunately, wise rulers—men and women who follow the hermit's advice—are exceedingly rare, in politics as in business. Most leaders aren't in the league the hermit described. Many have no focus, don't know how to select or build a team, lack coaching skills, are poor listeners, don't know how to inspire their people, put their interests ahead of their people's—the list goes on and on. Leaders with character faults such as these breed skepticism, cynicism, distrust, and perfunctory performance.

Some societal observers talk of a leadership crisis, and perhaps they're right. Too many leaders manage for the short run, incapable of making the tough decisions that are needed for long-term survival. Too many leaders say one thing and do another, violating the trust of their people. Too many leaders abuse the word empowerment, leaving it an empty slogan. Too many leaders say, "People are our greatest asset"—and then let half the workforce go. It's no wonder there's been an increase in employee alienation, dissatisfaction, exclusion, apathy, and disempowerment.

The irony is that many dysfunctional leaders mean well; they truly do. But they're psychologically illiterate, as unaware of their strengths as they are of their weaknesses. They don't know how they act or how they're perceived, much less why. They're unable to integrate the shadow side of their behavior into conscious awareness, because they don't know they have a shadow side. It's quite ironic that although many leaders see value in learning new skills, they rarely see value in taking a closer look at the ingrained character patterns that they bring to the use of those skills. And yet it's those very patterns that dictate behavior and decisions!

Unfortunately, as long as dysfunctional behavior patterns are unconscious, leaders aren't able to align stated practices with what they really practice. Walking the talk isn't possible if they don't see their limp. As long as they're unaware of the script in their inner theater, they'll continue to send mixed and confusing messages to others. This is a fixable problem, and yet because unearthing the mental and emotional patterns that dictate behavior can be both uncomfortable and disorienting, many leaders opt not to even try. Too often, people in positions of leadership prefer not to take that painful journey into the self. They find it much easier not to look. They prefer not to take personal responsibility for organizational setbacks, because it's so much simpler to blame others (or the economy) for their own lack of performance, poor communication, ineffective problem-solving, and inappropriate behavior. That lack of personal involvement may be successful in the short run, but eventually it will ruin their credibility. The people who work for a leader who isn't willing to take ownership of his or her emotions and actions end up feeling manipulated and misled, and they respond with a lack of commitment to the organization. A leader's dysfunctional behavior patterns not only show up as a rot at the top, but they also spread rot throughout the organization.

TRUE SELF VERSUS FALSE SELF

Like the wise king in the story above, many leaders (political, business or otherwise) struggle with the kind of persona they should present to the outside world. They wonder how to present themselves; how they should act for maximum effectiveness. They ask themselves, What are the dos and don'ts of being successful as a leader? What should I show of myself? Can I show my true self, the real essence of who I am, or would that get in the way of good management?

In Shakespeare's play Hamlet we find Polonius's wise advice to Laertes:

> "This above all: To thine own self be true,
> And it must follow, as the night the day,
> Thou canst not then be false to any man." (Hamlet, 1.iii, p. 78)

This is easier said than done, of course. Leaders who have a strong sense of who they are—and they're the minority, for sure—are true to themselves without hesitation, but leaders who lack this sense of self send out confusing signals. What's worse, such leaders may not be aware (or may be only subliminally aware) that their presentation of self in the public domain is less than sincere. As William Shakespeare once said, "Life is but a stage and we are but actors upon it." Perhaps taking that line as normative, some leaders present a false image of themselves at all times, but uncomfortably—as if reading from a script written for someone else. They're always on stage, but speaking the wrong lines and playing the wrong part.

Many leaders have become so conditioned to playing a part, to putting on a mask, that they've forgotten any other way to be. They don't act or react according to their own beliefs, but according what they think others think those beliefs should be. Polls and opinion leaders tell them what to do. And as the years go by, the part begins to feel familiar, the mask so often used that it hardens into an iron mask that can't be removed. Even for people used to this sort of "theater," always having to play a role—never being able to be oneself—is a burden that grows heavier with the years.

Eventually people forget what their true self is about. Having played a role, or several different roles (depending on the audience), for so long, they become confused about what they stand for. On a true-false self spectrum, the person takes on increasingly a false self persona.

When leaders always take on roles, when they live under the shadow of an imposed identity, they can't become well-rounded human beings. Furthermore, it becomes difficult to build genuine connections with other people. That restriction on self and on relationships spells trouble: mental health specialists maintain that the experience and presentation of an authentic sense of self is central to our ability to function as effective, healthy human beings [1]. Only by trying to show what we really stand for, only by allowing congruence between our inner and outer theater, can we feel truly alive and genuinely passionate about what we're doing. In the business arena, only then can we truly have a transforming impact on the people that we lead. Without a clear sense of self, one can't relate in an authentic and effective way to others.

On the other hand, people who are authentic, who are more able to function according to their true self, tend to be more centered, balanced, compassionate, forgiving, sensitive, peaceful, secure, and self-confident. They have a more optimistic outlook on life, report a higher level of self-esteem, and feel a greater sense of life satisfaction. And because they feel more alive, they're more likely to pursue whatever they're doing with zest and enjoyment, and to be committed to causes they believe in. In addition, they're realistic about life's possibilities and thus less likely to engage in self-delusion. In terms of relationships, authentic people tend to be socially engaged, given their capacity to express their emotions in a sincere manner. That quality makes them receptive to others, and vice versa.

Authenticity implies accepting oneself, warts and all. It means acting according to one's values, preferences, and needs as opposed to acting merely to please others. Authentic people demonstrate behavior that reflects self-determination, autonomy, and choice, as opposed to behavior that's been imposed on them by others. Valuing openness and truthfulness in their close relationships, they summon the courage to be vulnerable through self-disclosure, so as to develop genuine intimacy and trust, whether among friends or in the workplace [2].

So if presenting more of one's true self makes a person happier, why do so many people—so many leaders, in particular—wear a mask? From a developmental perspective, a major contributing factor is that many of these people (as children) were never permitted to express their real feelings and pursue their own needs. Very little psychological space was given to them when they were growing up. Their stories typically reveal that they were forced to become extensions of whoever was taking care of them. By that I mean that the needs of others became more important than their own. In an environment that they perceived as dangerous, they used pleasing others as a survival tactic. If they were daring enough to express a wish or feeling, it only led to difficulties: anger, perhaps, or abandonment. Unable to express themselves honestly, they failed to establish a wholesome, secure sense of self. For the purpose of emotional survival, they had no choice but to conform and to present a false self, a persona more acceptable to the external world. Normal, adaptive socialization processes were overridden by the child's survival urge. Thus they would assume a more extreme position on the true-false self axis.

This false self, then, is a form of "protective reaction" against feelings of rejection, pain, and abandonment. It's a way of avoiding psychological injury. If it continues over time, the developing child has no foundation for a secure sense of identity; instead, the ground is laid for a stunted, disfigured, impoverished sense of self. As time goes by, the true self becomes too weak to stand up to the overbearing false self; it retreats, coming out only in disguise. The false self has in effect become the person. This sort of development creates individuals who are out of tune with themselves, out of touch with what they really are. And because they don't feel good in their skin, they continue to seek the protection of role-playing and gamesmanship—but unconsciously: the false self has become such an inseparable part of their way of dealing with the external world that they don't even recognize it as a protective shell. Once formed and functioning, the false self stifles any further development of the true self. The false self has become a proxy for the true self, able to absorb any pain that the caretakers (or later important figures) inflict on it.

Though the true self is all but forgotten, it lives in tension with the false self. Because of this tension, inauthentic people lack spontaneity, curiosity, and creativity, and they're dependent on the reactions of others. Because of their insecurity, they count on gamesmanship to get ahead, and they prefer short-term expediency over long-term effectiveness. Lacking a strong sense of self, they end up thinking, feeling, and behaving in ways that are contrary to their well-suppressed inner feelings. That breeds more tension, and a strong sense of unreality.

In relating with others, inauthentic people depict emotions, but something seems to be missing. They behave as if they had intense emotional experiences; they behave as if they had a strong emotional life. In reality, though—as the people they deal with soon realize—their emotional experiences are extremely shallow. Thus inauthentic people are incapable of engaging in truly intimate relationships. Although they give the appearance of normality, demonstrating ordinary human emotions, that normality is a pretense; chameleon-like, they adopt whatever emotion or quality the situation seems to call for. Although they pretend to feel or to care, deep inside they feel or care very little. Although they pretend to be interested in others, it's mostly show. The inability to invest emotionally in anything leads to feelings of self-estrangement: inauthentic people feel disconnected from their environment, empty at the core [3].

This inability to connect makes work, life, and play activities unbalanced for inauthentic people. Not as noticeable early in their career, this problem tends to come to the fore as people age; increasingly they begin to feel unintegrated and depersonalized. As they become more unfocused, empty, and insecure, they may come to realize that something is wrong in their dealings with others; they may find it harder to deny their responsibility in this matter. Eventually, it may dawn on them that it's they themselves, not others, who are the problem.

Unfortunately, the business setting is a stage where the false self seems to flourish. Presenting a false self may even be a professional advantage, because it facilitates conforming to organizational norms, doing what's expected. Chameleon-like behavior—the ability to pick up signals from the outside and adjust one's actions accordingly (exactly as one was trained to do in childhood)—serves the ambitious businessperson well. Given the superficiality of relationships in many organizations, the inability to present a true sense of self makes it easy for both novice office workers and executives to change their role according to the requirements of the situation. They're perfectly willing to demonstrate "true" commitment to whatever the organization stands for—it's only a game.

This gamesmanship comes with a price, however. Being out of touch with one's inner world—being dominated by a false self—produces feelings of distress and alienation. The more successful the inauthentic individual gets to be, the more unreal he or she typically feels. Although they're successful in doing what's expected of them, they feel increasingly estranged from their inner world. There's more and more of a disconnect. As their own feelings of doubt and anxiety grow, their inauthenticity begins to be picked up by their audience. The people to whom they direct their gamesmanship, sensing that something is off, begin to feel manipulated. Those in the "audience" begin to recognize that what they're seeing is all smoke and mirrors. They realize that they're victims of true impression management.

AUTHENTICITY: BEYOND THE GULAG ORGANIZATION

Why all this talk of false selves and true selves? Because a sense of true self, of feeling good in one's skin, an experience of authenticity, is absolutely essential to effective, sustainable leadership. Leaders who want to get the best out of their people need to possess this quality; no ifs, ands or buts. But combining authenticity and leadership results in a very different leadership style from the 20th-century model.

Leadership in the New World of Work

Leaders in the 21st century need to realize that the command, control, compartmentalization organization is a thing of the past. In our postindustrial society, where knowledge workers are the majority, getting the best out of people requires leadership that fosters interaction, information, and innovation. To be successful, organizations need leaders who are able to present themselves as they are, who have confidence in combination with humility, and who are viewed by others as having integrity and being worthy of trust. To be such a leader, people must be aware of (and trust in) their motives, feelings, and desires; recognize their strengths and weaknesses; understand their personality characteristics and emotional states; and know how their unconscious feelings (and the upbringing that caused those feelings) affect their behavior. They must limit "stagecraft" and gamesmanship in interacting with others, responding to people with sincerity and sensitivity because they truly care about others. They must take responsibility for their actions, living the principles they espouse. And they must be willing to face reality as it is, not as they wish it were, rejecting selective perception.

Effective leadership in the 21st century will depend heavily on networking structures, which imply a focus on relationships. That's why authentic leadership will be crucial to business success in the coming century. Authentic leadership already offers a competitive advantage, because such leadership contributes to an honest assessment of why a particular business exists and what the priorities of the organization will be. Authentic leaders possess a greater dose of emotional intelligence. Because authentic leaders are more in tune with their inner theater (and thus are better able to pay attention to the inner theater of others), they are more equipped to "read" and articulate what lies unspoken in the hearts and minds of their employees. That sense of understanding creates in employees a sense of involvement and commitment. Thus authentic leaders—executives more in touch with their true selves—by speaking to the collective imagination of their people, create a group identity.

Authentic leaders pay great attention to the work environment. They realize that congruence between the needs of the employees and the needs of the organization is essential to organizational effectiveness. They recognize that if the organization's leadership is able to create such congruence, their people will enjoy a feeling of self-determination; they will feel in control of their destiny. Knowing that they're powerful only to the extent that they empower other people, they want their staff to have a voice in what they do and where they go. By helping people believe in themselves, and by acknowledging and addressing people's needs and wishes, authentic leaders are able to pull extraordinary effort and creativity out of their staff.

Although authentic leaders realize that competitive wages are important, they also know that their employees are looking for more than money, because they themselves share the same outlook. Although well paid for their services, they don't fall victim to the greed factor (as a number of prominent US CEOs have recently done). Rather, they truly want people to believe that they're making a difference, both to the organization and, in some small sense, to the world. Thus authentic leaders build organizations where the contributions of all employees are valued and recognized. That's what empowerment is all about.

In addition, authentic leaders go to great lengths to contribute to their people's sense of competence, helping them gain a feeling of personal growth and development. Because they know that people are stimulated by learning new things, they take responsibility for developing their people. They realize that if their employees are expected to make an extraordinary effort in a rapidly changing world, they need to gain new knowledge and develop new competencies. They also need to share this knowledge with others. Thus shared learning is a key pattern in organizations headed by leaders who are authentic.

Authentic leaders are cultural architects, creating a framework for the kind of values that make an organization a great place to work. They introduce a set of meta-values into their organizations—values that transcend the more traditional, generic listing of values found in most organizations. These values incorporate and use the motivational need systems discussed in Chapter 1.

The first of these meta-values is a sense of community. When employees feel a sense of belonging in the workplace, trust and mutual respect flourish, people are prepared to help others, the work group becomes cohesive, and goal-directedness thrives. An organization's sense of community can be enhanced in various ways. These include building an organizational architecture that favors small units, pushing decision-making down, ensuring fair process, aspiring toward transparency, and practicing distributed, shared leadership. This last element is a tenet of faith for authentic leaders, who are committed to developing leadership capabilities at every level of the organization. Distributed leadership is a strange beast: it's made possible by a sense of community, but it also encourages a sense of community. In organizations where everyone takes a part in leadership, authentic leaders take vicarious pleasure in coaching their younger executives and watching their accomplishments. This experience of generativity—of caring for others—is a source of creativity and contributes to feelings of continuity in the mentor, who can see his or her efforts continuing through the work of successors.

Authentic leaders realize that taking people on an exciting, adventurous journey gratifies humankind's essential motivational need for exploration and assertion. Exploration, enjoyment, entrepreneurship, creativity, and innovation are all closely linked. Thus the second meta-value is a sense of enjoyment. In truly effective companies, employees enjoy their work. Indeed, they "have fun"—words not often associated with the workplace. And yet playfulness fosters mental health. Furthermore, authentic leaders realize that happy employees make for happy customers. Employees will find it hard to smile at a customer when they are not happy themselves. They recognize that in far too many companies a sense of enjoyment is either ignored or, worse, discouraged. They know that if employees feel that they're working in a gulag, they won't want to make the extra effort for their clientele. Furthermore, they know that in gulag organizations, imagination is stifled and innovation squelched.

Finally, authentic leaders pay attention to the third meta-value: a sense of meaning. They know that people will work for money but will die for a cause. As has been said, the best use for life is to spend it on something that will outlast it. Authentic leaders know that that statement applies to life in organizations too. They realize that when what an organization does is presented in the context of transcending one's personal needs—presented as improving people's quality of life, say, or helping people, or contributing something to society—the impact on workers is extremely powerful.

With that understanding, authentic leaders are able to create a sense of meaning that gets the best out of their people, drawing forth imagination and creativity. In such organizations people experience a sense of "flow"—that is, a feeling of total involvement and concentration in whatever they're doing [4]. Authentic leaders know that people are at their best, at their happiest, when they're fully engaged in work that they enjoy on a journey toward a goal that they themselves established.

Authentizotic Organizations

Organizations and leadership that cultivate and honor the above meta-values are what I like to call "authentizotic," a label that melds the Greek words authenteekos (authentic) and zoteekos (vital to life). In its broadest sense, that first part of the label, authentic, describes something that conforms to fact and is therefore worthy of trust and reliance. As with the executive who is authentic, an authentic workplace is one that has a compelling connective quality for its employees in its vision, mission, culture, and structure. The organization's leadership has communicated clearly and convincingly not only the how of work but also the why, revealing meaning in each person's task. The organization's leadership walks the talk; they set the example.

The zoteekos (vital to life) element of the authentizotic organization refers to those aspects of the workplace that give people the sense of flow mentioned earlier and help build a sense of personal wholeness, making people feel complete and alive. People feel that they're appreciated, that their contributions are recognized. Zoteekos allows for self-assertion in the workplace and produces a sense of effectiveness and competency, of autonomy, of initiative, creativity, entrepreneurship, and industry; it also responds to the human need for exploration.

The challenge for twenty-first-century leadership is to develop authentic leaders and employees, and to create authentizotic organizations. The acquisition of greater authenticity will take time, but it's time well spent. The work of understanding one's own inner theater and that of one's colleagues will be a challenge, but it's well worth the effort. The time and energy spent on improving emotional intelligence results not just in personal gratification (though such work is personally rewarding), but also in value for the organization and its people.

Authentizotic organizations, recognizing the value of such work, help their people accomplish it. They encourage their leaders to invite professional help in uncovering their psychological drivers and making the personal shifts necessary for greater authenticity in leadership; and they offer interventions such as those described in Part Two of this book. They recognize the need for transitional space as their people embark on radical change and new beginnings.

Authentizotic organizations acknowledge that happiness isn't an outside job; it's an inside job. They recognize that people want not only a job, but also a life, because the quality of life determines the quality of relationships. Thus authentizotic organizations are easily recognized: their employees maintain a healthy balance between personal and organizational life, they take time for self-examination, and they exercise their imagination daily. They're not only just doing but also being. As the psychoanalyst Erich Fromm once said, "Man's main task in life is to give birth to himself, to become what he potentially is. The most important product of his effort is his own personality." Authentizotic organizations recognize that all people would like to know before they die what they're running from, and to, and why.

Authentizotic organizations encourage their people to think, and then—saints preserve us!—encourage them to take revolutionary action. They help people learn to trust the men and women they work for, enjoy what they're doing, and feel passion for and pride in their work. They minimize secrecy and encourage information-sharing, see diversity of all kinds as a competitive advantage, are open to change, and strive to be the building blocks in creating better societies.

The positive ambiance created by authentic leaders in authentizotic organizations creates "virtuous cycles" for both leaders and followers: in helping others, people help themselves. And those virtuous cycles cultivate both authenticity and passion, which are at the heart of effectiveness in the business world. As noted earlier, people who experience passion are acting in accordance with their true self. The French philosopher Diderot once said, "Only passions, great passions, can elevate the soul to great things." Authentic leaders take that credo to heart: they believe that if they create authentizotic organizations, the work that they and their people do will succeed in tomorrow's marketplace, and that their organizations will ride with grace the new global economy's surging waves of change.

REFERENCES

1. Winnicott, D. W. (1975). *Through Paediatrics to Psycho-Analysis*. New York, Basic Books.
2. Trilling, L. (1982). *Sincerity and Authenticity*. Cambridge, Mass. Harvard University Press.
3. Deutsch, H. (1942). "Some Forms of Emotional Disturbance and their Relationship to Schizophrenia," *Psychoanalytic Quarterly* 11: 301–321.
4. Csikszentmihalyi, M. (1990). *Flow: The Psychology of Optimal Experience*. New York: Harper and Row.

INDEX

Index compiled by Terry Halliday